ART OF
THE
WORLD

# ART OF THE WORLD

## THE HISTORICAL, SOCIOLOGICAL

## AND RELIGIOUS BACKGROUNDS

'NON-EUROPEAN CULTURES'

# INDIA

## FIVE THOUSAND YEARS OF INDIAN ART

### BY HERMANN GOETZ

McGRAW-HILL BOOK COMPANY, INC.

NEW YORK · TORONTO · LONDON

© 1959. HOLLE & CO VERLAG BADEN-BADEN
COLOR PLATES PRINTED IN GERMANY
TEXT PRINTED IN HOLLAND
LIBRARY OF CONGRESS CATALOG CARD NUMBER 59—13434

*Dedicated to my wife,*

*collaborator in the researches of a lifetime*

*and companion in all my explorations*

When Holle Verlag asked me to write a history of Indian art, I
accepted their invitation with pleasure. After spending a lifetime in
the study of this branch of knowledge — as librarian, curator, university professor and director of one of the leading museums in the
country — and after living among Indians for a quarter of a century
and visiting the monuments of India on the spot, one feels impelled to
gather all one's experience and discoveries into a single comprehensive work.

Although Hindu religion and Hindu philosophy mean much to me,
I cannot agree to the romantic theory of a solely mystical India and
an exclusively religious Indian art. I feel that Indian art is too rich
and too varied to allow of this simplification, which has in any case
been abandoned by all serious Indian scholars. Instead I have tried to
show how the forms of art have developed out of their natural historical origins, and to track the spread of these forms in the various centuries and regions. I have been at pains to do justice to present and
past, to Buddhist and Hindu as well as Islamic art and to understand
all their assumptions. I have dealt with Islamic and Buddhist art in
rather less detail and I have treated the art of Greater India only in its
relation to India proper, because Islamic and Buddhist art as well as
the art of South-East Asia and Indonesia will be surveyed in two
future volumes in the series "Art of the World". Bearing in mind the
limited space at my disposal I have been unable to give full reasons
for my views, but I hope that I have given my readers enough evidence
for them to test my assertions.

In my transliteration of proper names I have followed the spelling
used in most English books on Indian history and art. For many place-
names I have adopted the modern official spelling (Mathurā, Tiruchirāpalli, Madurai, etc.). As for the names of old dynasties, personages,
or places the orthography in the inscriptions varies so erratically that
my usual spelling follows international usage rather than historical fact.

I would like to extend special thanks to Mr. V. L. Devkar, M.Sc., my
successor as director of the Baroda Museum, and Dr. J. M. Mehta,
vice-chancellor of Maharaja Sayaji Rao University, Baroda, as well as
to the Director-General of Archaeology in New Delhi for the generous
help they gave in allowing me to use the libraries in their charge. It was
exceptionally difficult to procure material for colour photographs,
and I would like to thank warmly the museums and libraries for
allowing objects from their collections to be photographed and repro-

duced. I am grateful to Fräulein Magdalene Duckwitz, the D.A.I. collection and Messrs. C. L. Gairola, R. Herzog, A. L. Syed, N. Ramakrishna and Harbans Singh for lending their colour positives. Finally I want to acknowledge the untiring help of my wife, whose devoted cooperation has made the completion of this text possible.
I hope that this book will contribute to a better understanding of India and a better knowledge of its rich and rewarding culture, which has commanded our lifelong devotion.

*Baroda, 28th September 1958.*

HERMANN GOETZ

# LIST OF ILLUSTRATIONS

## ACKNOWLEDGMENTS

We would like to thank the following individuals, museums and collections for permission to reproduce
works of art in this volume and for their help in checking negatives:

Baroda Museum,
    Baroda 49, 79, 98, 103, 137, 159, 160, 208, 228, 232
Bibliothèque Nationale, Paris          204, 211, 224
British Museum, London                         58, 67
S. D. Chavda, Bombay                              239
Chester Beatty Library, Dublin         203, 213, 222
Indian Museum, South Kensington, London    226
Museum of Fine Arts, Boston  3, 138, 207, 219, 230

Musée Guimet, Paris          61, 64, 75, 178, 217
Museum van Aziatische Kunst, Amsterdam     175
National Museum, New Delhi                     83
Patna Museum                                   47
Rietberg Museum, Zürich                       177
Rāksmuseum voor Volkenkunde, Leiden    76, 181
Staatliche Museen, Berlin                     215

## PHOTOGRAPHERS

The coloured photographs on the pages indicated were kindly put at our disposal by the following:

W. Bruggmann, Winterthur                          177
DAI-Bildarchiv (K. H. Buschmann),
    Stuttgart                               54, 96, 118
M. Duckwitz, New Delhi                            111
Dr. C. K. Gairola, New Delhi                      101
R. Herzog, Wiesbaden                         120, 156
Harbans Singh, New Delhi   Front of the slip-case

J. A. Lavand, Paris          61, 64, 75, 178, 217
N. Ramakrishna, Mayuram                   171, 172
Rex Roberts Studios, Dublin       202, 212, 222
M. Sarabhai, Ahmedabad                          242
J. Skeel, Orpington                     58, 67, 234
A. L. Syed,
    Palanpur   127, 128, 151, 168, 174, 182, 194, 221

# CONTENTS

# I. INTRODUCTION

India is a subcontinent of Asia, approximately the size of Europe without Russia, and its civilization can be traced back over at least five thousand years. During these millennia art has flourished in all those vast territories. Innumerable monuments are still known to us, and yet they represent only a diminutive fraction of what once existed. Most of the famous cities of the past have disappeared, and only huge mounds indicate the sites where they once stood; the towns of today stand on strata over strata of earlier settlements of which only foundations, potsherds and occasional finds are left; there is hardly a village which does not preserve the name of a once rich town, or where mounds do not invite excavation; there are many hundreds of little known hill forts; and every year important ruins are discovered. Yet the monuments still standing are more numerous than all that survives in Europe.

But are we entitled to interpret these monuments as integral aspects of one and the same tradition? Even the monuments known to the average tourist reveal a diversity which seems to defy any attempt at interrelation. What have the quiet Persian forms, the delicate abstract ornaments, the dreamy atmosphere of the Tāj Mahal at Agra in common with the South Indian temples, hectic piles of superimposed shrines carrying a multitude of statues of terrific gods and sensuous goddesses and reliefs of extravagant mystic visions? What have these latter again to do with the simplicity, joy of life and realism of early Buddhist art, and again with the town ruins of the proto-historic "Indus Civilization", resembling much more closely the remains of ancient Sumerian civilization in the Near East, than anything created later on in India?

The problem is no less elusive than that of European art. For what is the common denominator in Aegean, Greek, Etruscan, Roman, Byzantine, Gothic, Renaissance and modern European art? Knossos and Rembrandt, the Lady of Elche and Delacroix, Hosios Lukas and Félicien Rops, the Utrecht Psalter and Beardsley, Michelangelo and Gauguin seem to be worlds apart. And yet, seen from China or Baghdad, they are children of one common tradition. However, it is easier to define the gulf which separates them from the Far Eastern or the

*WHAT IS INDIAN ART?*

*The variety of monuments*

13

Islamic milieu, than to find out what they have in common. Popular slogans like Western individualism and realism versus Eastern mass mentality and mysticism prove to be nonsense when subjected to closer scrutiny. Rather, it is a common geographical background which induces them to make use of the same stock of traditional forms and symbols, the same climate which inspires them to similar ways of self-expression, however different their reactions may otherwise have been as children of early or modern, young or decaying nations and civilizations.

The same is true for India. Europe forms the western peninsula of the huge Europeo-Asiatic land mass; India, however, is its southern subcontinent. Europe has been separated from Asia by the Mediterranean and the Black Sea as well as by the steppes and forests of Asia Minor and Russia; India has been isolated from other parts of Asia by the forbidding mountain ranges of Afghanistan, Tibet and Yunnan, by the Arabian Sea and the Gulf of Bengal. This isolation has caused a certain inbreeding of ideas and symbols in the Occidental world; it has engendered a similarly characteristic evolution of common ideas and symbols in India and Eastern Asia. Periodical irruptions of Asiatic conquerors and ideas and the struggle of individual peoples for power and cultural ideals have kept the European tradition from stagnation; invasions from or through Western and Central Asia and similar internal struggles have provided for a not less conspicuous diversity of Indian culture and art. We are, therefore, entitled to claim a unity of Indian tradition, different from that of other high civilizations. But we have likewise to acknowledge a diversity which makes it utterly impossible to bring all aspects of Indian art to one denominator. The "Ideals of Indian Art" proclaimed by pioneer scholars like E. B. Havell or A. K. Coomaraswamy, and repeated by quite a number of less original writers, are those of Mediaeval Hindu art, and to some degree of the Buddhist art preceding it, elaborating a certain amount of even older concepts, but certainly not applicable to later times. An honest picture of Indian art has to keep in mind the different character of the successive phases of Indian civilization which produced that art.

*Unity of Indian tradition*

CLIMATE THE NATURAL FOUNDATIONS OF INDIAN CIVILIZATION AND ART: India is a tropical country where the weather alternates between torrid heat, a steaming humidity and a few pleasant months reminding one of spring and early summer in Europe. Man's relation to nature, therefore, is much more intimate than in cooler climates. Even when he has to take shelter from the sun or the rains, he has to live in open, well ventilated rooms with ants, birds, lizards, toads, snakes, even monkeys as his uninvited company, and flowers and trees always within his sight. Water is the most needed element, bringing life to man, beasts and plants, auspicious, sacred! Water vessels, ablutions and libations play a key role in religious ceremonies. Water flowers like the various species of lotus are the most sacred and common emblems. The shores of lakes, natural as well as artificial, and the banks of rivers are the favourite places for temples, religious bathing "ghāts" (flights of steps) and houses. The great rivers are benign deities. But this outlook on nature is limited. Only rarely is the air clear. Most of the year it vibrates in the scorching heat, or is a steaming mist in which even nearby things look unreal, and distant ones become invisible. In the dry heat the air is full of dust and evil stenches; when the rains break, it is soaked with the heavy smell of flowers. What a contrast with the crystal-clear air of the Greek isles, or the sweet summers and cold snows of Europe! Only where high mountains — and they are not many — rise above this hot haze into a purer atmosphere does the vista widen. World of saints, genii and gods! But even above these there towers the Himalaya, its ice peaks gleaming along the northern horizon, like a phantasmagoria, distinctly clear amongst the masses of floating clouds, but without apparent connection with the lower ranges accessible to man; the grandest vision man can have, the top of the world, the axis of the universe, seat of the highest deities.

Man has to adjust himself to this oppressive atmosphere. Except for a few winter months he can wear only a minimum of clothing, indeed more ornaments than clothes. The heat enervates him, sets him dreaming, lets the most improbable events appear possible. But the coolness of the winter and of the monsoon awakens a more intense sensitivity and enthusiasm for the beauties of life, and arouses an energy when nothing seems beyond reach. Man is the slave as well as the lord of the universe. Both reactions, however, arouse an intensive sexuality, without the inhibitions of our occidental world, frank, but also delicate; and this exuberant sexuality is in its turn restrained by the fear of being completely absorbed by it, by the desire to preserve one's own personality and free will, if necessary at the price of denying sexuality completely.

In these conditions all the contrasts of Indian civilization are rooted, its acceptance and rejection of nature, and of all the pleasures of life

*Contrasts*

15

and love, its gross humour and solemn serenity, its abasement before the divine and its dreams of supermen, its realism and mysticism, its sensuality and asceticism. And these are reflected in Indian art, in its tension between naturalism and idealism, sensuousness and abstraction, humorous realism and sublime mysticism.

*Climatic zones* But this climate is not uniform. For India adjoins Central Asia as well as the monsoon area of South-East Asia. In the north the Himalaya forms a climatic barrier. But from the west the deserts and steppes of Western and South-Western Asia penetrate beyond the Indus into the Panjab, Rajasthan west of the Aravalli mountains (Thar Desert) and Saurashtra, ending in two tongues of comparatively dry, but cultivable land through the upper Ganges plain and over the high plateaus of the Deccan. The east and south, and most of Central India are covered by the wet swamps of the Ganges and Brahmaputra valleys, the river deltas and fertile coastal plains of the Deccan, or by the thick, rain-swept forests of the Assam Hills, of eastern Central India and along the eastern and western slopes of the Deccan plateau, ending in the south in the Nilgiris and Travancore mountains.

These two climatic zones also represent two types of civilization. The forests which once, when the country was less denuded than it is today, extended up to the Panjab and, along the mountains, up to Afghanistan, were the home of small and rather primitive tribes, bound to the soil and the village, economically self-contained, obsessed by gloomy visions of fertility and death, deities of the earth, orgiastic rites and human sacrifices, ruled by magicians, priests and princes of reputedly divine origin. In the deserts and steppes, the nomads reared their herds, occasionally growing also some additional grain; they raided their neighbours' villages and cattlepens in endless feuds, conquered the countries of the agricultural jungle tribes, organized trade caravans to far distant countries, believed in the dignity and power of man — at least of their own race —, and venerated heavenly deities, ideal projections of conquerors and kings. But the monsoon sweeps every year over the whole of India, starting in the south and east with endless heavy downpours and inundations, ending in the north-west in sultry weather occasionally broken by ineffectual thunderstorms. In the winter and spring the dry heat spreads over most of the interior, leaving merely the coastal belts unaffected. Thus both types of civilization had their seasonal opportunity and were intertwined, though in varying patterns; the jungle agriculturists becoming the subject

16

serf class; their divine kings, or robber tribes of the jungle, or nomads from the north-west becoming the rulers of a sort of "colonial" society. It has been the synthesis of these two styles of life which has shaped Indian civilization and thus also Indian art.

The desert and the monsoon zone, however, are welded together by natural barriers; in the north-west the mountains of Baluchistan and Afghanistan, in the north the Hindukush and Himalaya, in the north-east the mountain forests of Upper Assam, Burma and Yunnan, in the south-west the Arab Sea and in the south-east the Gulf of Bengal. These barriers have isolated India so much that she could evolve a characteristic civilization of her own, but not sufficiently as to exclude an influx of foreign peoples, cultures and ideas. The Indus Valley and the Panjab are accessible from Iran, Afghanistan and Central Asia, though over difficult routes passing through deserts and over high passes. Assam can be reached from Upper Burma, though through no less difficult jungle. The Indus delta was already in contact with Iraq and Arabia in pre-Christian times. The coasts of the Deccan peninsula, and especially its southern tip, were opened to shipping by the monsoon which during half of the year allowed ships to cross the ocean direct from west to east, and during the other half from east to west. Thus India came in contact with Central and South-western Asia, Iraq, Arabia, Egypt, (and through them with the Mediterranean), Upper Burma, Indonesia and China.

The main movement of peoples in Asia, however, has been from Central Asia to the maritime countries, because the Central Asian steppes and deserts periodically forced their inhabitants to emigrate. One tribe pushed the other onward until huge hordes accumulated, invading and subjecting the agricultural countries surrounding the steppe belt. There the older populations, so far as they were not enslaved, retreated towards the more easily defensible peninsulas and the humid coasts which the Central Asian conquerors, accustomed to a dry climate, did not like. This was the case also in India. The main trend of political and cultural developments there has been a migration occasionally from the north-east, but generally from the north-west towards the interior and then towards the south. But this movement was hemmed in by a second line of barriers, the Thar desert and the Central Indian jungles beyond the Indus Valley and the Panjab, the swamps of the Ganges and Brahmaputra behind the Assamese mountains; and the Vindhya-Mahadeo-Maikal ranges protecting the northern frontier of the Deccan and the steep cliffs of the "Ghats" its sea coasts. Every invasion or cultural irruption was there hemmed in long enough to be more or less absorbed, to be sufficiently Indianized before it expanded into the interior of the country.

THE PEOPLE The result of all these developments has been a very mixed population and a not less mixed civilization. Though "European" types predominate in the North-west, Mongoloids in the North-east, dark "Mediterraneans" in the South, though the North speaks "Indo-Aryan" languages related to Europe, the South "Dravidian" languages possibly connected with ancient Sumerian, Khurrite etc. in South-western Asia, though the upper classes tend to be fairer than the lower ones, it would be rather risky to draw too simple conclusions from such observations. For though the conquerors generally came from Western and Central Asia, though they became the ruling classes, though they seem to have imposed their languages on the country, they often enough had to yield to the religious ideas of the masses and the standards of "orthodoxy" determined by them, and were pushed down the social ladder, if they were either conquered themselves by other newcomers or were not accepted by the orthodox. But temporarily certain types predominated with certain accents on religious, social and aesthetic ideals, and to these correspond certain successive types of Indian civilization and art, of very different character, though linked by a common stock of motifs and symbols.

PHASES OF
INDIAN CULTURE We shall try roughly to define these phases in the following outline, leaving the historical details to the subsequent chapters.

1. THE INDUS OR HARAPPA CIVILIZATION in the Indus Valley, the Panjab, and Bujarāt from the 3rd millennium B.C. to c. 1400 B.C.: It was a city civilization where an apparently "Khurrite" (i.e. Armenoid) upper class with cultural connections to Sumer and the Ancient Eastern highlands ruled over a primitive Indian proletariat still at the Stone-Age level. After its destruction by the Aryans, its remnants spread eastwards, becoming an important contributor to later Hindu culture in Northern India and probably also to Dravidian civilization in South India.

2. THE "ARYAN"-INDIAN CIVILIZATION (Vedic, Buddhist and Jain) c. 1200 B.C. to A.D. 300, transformed in the Gupta Empire (c. 330—530) and its successor states (c. 530—770) into Mediaeval Hindu civilization. During these one and a half millennia it passed from the semi-nomadism of the barbarian Aryans, relatives of the Iranians and of

the Mitanni (c. 1400 B.C.) in upper Iraq, through the feudalism of the early Gangetic kingdoms (reflected in the Mahābhārata and the Purānas) to the republics and petty kingdoms of the Buddha's time and to centralized grand powers (Nandas, Mauryas, Śātavāhanas, Guptas) ruled by despotic kings through a centralized bureaucracy and a professional army. For centuries foreign conquerors (Greeks, Parthians, Scythians, Kushānas, White Huns) ruled over vast areas of Northern India, without, however, seriously affecting the social structure. The "colonial" system of the four "estates" (*varna*), i.e. knights, priests, landlords and indigenous serfs, dissolved into a society of many classes which was dominated by the rich merchants of the cities. The "hero" heavenly deities of the barbarian Aryans were emasculated by the sacrificial magic of the priests and mixed with the indigenous deities, sacrifices becoming a state function; while the people turned to various new religions and philosophies, the aristocracy to the monotheism of Vishnu-Krishna, the middle classes to Buddhism and Jainism, the villagers to the ancient fertility cult of Śiva, identified with the Vedic storm god Rudra. Buddhism and Jainism, supported by the wealthy merchants and also respected by a number of kings, and having a following also in the lower urban classes because of their democratic character, dominated the arts. In the Gupta Empire this civilization reached its zenith. Its characteristic was the dominance of man in this world as the enjoyer of power, wealth and love, and in religion as sacrificer, magician, yogi and saint. Art, therefore, was predominantly secular and open to new inspirations. Religious art, which is best preserved, treated the saints as supermen, and the gods as beings akin to men, though on a higher level of existence. In the struggle against the invading Huns, Śūlikas, Gūrjaras and other barbarian tribes the flourishing Gupta towns were destroyed, the wealthy mercantile class impoverished, and the leadership passed into the hands of the military class and the new dynasties descended from successful generals. A similar revolution, the rise of hitherto obscure tribes, shook the South, and there also the capitalistic middle class, though not ruined, became subservient to a strong military monarchy. With the decline of this middle class Buddhism and Jainism lost their influence, and with them the art which had dominated India for more than thousand years.

*The Guptas*

3. MEDIAEVAL HINDU CIVILIZATION, c. 770—1200: The new military class established its domination by means of what was believed to be a

counter-reformation. The new rulers were of very mixed origin, genuine members of the old aristocracy, former princes and feudal lords employed in army and administrative posts for generations, officers risen from the ranks, and foreign troops (Scythians, Huns, Gūrjaras, Deccan tribes) now claiming descent from the feudal houses mentioned in the great national epics, the Mahābhārata and Rāmāyana, and thus ultimately from the gods. They needed the support of the wandering nomadic tribes and of the peasantry from which the soldiers were recruited, and had to patronize their primitive cults. And they had to league themselves with the priests who had influence over those masses, but who, as traditional advisers, astrologers and chaplains, also occupied court positions. The result was a syncretistic monotheism claiming to be a revival of the ancient Vedic religion after the end of the evil "Kali Age" when foreign barbarians and heretics (i.e. Buddhists and Jains) had dominated the earth. As a matter of fact it was more. The innumerable local deities were identified with Vishnu and Rudra-Siva, their legends co-ordinated in the *Purānas* (Old Traditions) and integrated with a philosophy evolved from certain deistic trends in the *Upanishads*, the last commentaries to the ancient sacrificial textbooks. The process had begun already in the time of the Buddha, under the Mauraya, Sunga and Sātavāhana dynasties, to result in the development of two major and three minor systems, Vishnuism and Saivism, and Sāktism, Brahmā and sun worship, fundamentally identical in their general outlook, differing only on the importance of the various gods, and in details of ritual and methods of salvation. When society developed into a rigid hierarchy of

*Caste hierarchy*  innumerable castes where each lower one had to pay deference to its superiors, religion also abased man before the gods. Instead of knowledge (*jnāna*) and self-control (*yoga*) the leading motive of religion became devotion (*bhakti*) to a deity revealing itself in many, benign as well as terrible, aspects, and served by a hierarchy of minor deities. The temples became mystic machines (microcosms of the world) full of magic powers, where the idol (the local presence of the deity) was served, like an earthly ruler, by a host of priests, monks and dancing girls. Everything, social status, profession, law, literature, art, was supposed to be based on sacred tradition, and was laid down in numerous hand-books. Classical Sanskrit, an artificial language elaborated from the living Sanskrit of pre-Christian times, became the all-Indian medium of communication of the upper classes. India was thoroughly divided. The state had become the monopoly of princes unscrupulously contending for supremacy, and of nobles transferring their allegiance to the highest bidder; intellectual culture was the privilege of a small class of conceited priests, scholars, monks and courtiers. The people, utterly exploited, had become politically indifferent, merely engrossed in sectarian squabbles. The country was ripe for the collapse of mediaeval Hindu civilization.

4. INDO-ISLAMIC CIVILIZATION, c. A.D. 1200—1803: The Muslim conquerors, mainly Turks, later also Persians and even Arabs and negroes, looked down on India as a heathen country to be held subject and exploited by reckless terror. They controlled the country from a few strategic centres, permitting the Hindu aristocracy to administer their estates as long as it paid tribute, and the brahmins to attend to the Hindu cult, as long as they did it unobtrusively. But slowly the Muslim attitude veered round to a closer collaboration with the indigenous population, especially when the vast Delhi empire had disintegrated into a number of provincial sultanates. Though the supremacy of Islam was sternly maintained, Hindus became government officials, contractors and even soldiers, Hindu ladies entered the royal harems, Hindu music, dance, secular poetry (even in Sanskrit), astrology, etc. were condescendingly encouraged, Hindu motifs penetrated more and more into Islamic art.

Simultaneously the Hindu states recovered in less accessible areas, in the Himalaya, Eastern Bengal, Rajasthan, Central India and the utmost South. A renaissance movement attempted to restore the institutions, religion, art and literature of pre-Islamic days but eventually proved sterile. It was swept away by a mass revival, a popular mysticism, venerating Vishnu, in his incarnations as Krishna and Rama, as the god of all-embracing love; a rich poetry in the folk languages; devotional songs; erotic lyrics; heroic epics; didactic stories; and an original creative art directly inspired by all these new ideas. This new cultural development, grown from actual life experience, accepted the mixed Muslim-Hindu style of life which had developed during the last centuries.

When the Mughals (A.D. 1526—1803—1857) conquered India, another period of "colonial" rule by Turkish foreigners seemed to begin. But the opposition of the Indian Muslims forced the Mughals into an alliance with the North Indian Hindu aristocracy, the Rajputs. The result was the eventual synthesis of contemporaneous Islamic and Hindu culture in most ways of life. Even the resumption of

*The Mughals*

an orthodox Muslim policy by the Mughal emperors in the 17th century could not break this cultural fusion. In the 18th century the empire disintegrated into a loose federation of Hindu and Muslim states, and classical Mughal civilization became, with slight modifications, the heritage of the whole of India.

5. MODERN INDIAN CIVILIZATION, c. A.D. 1803 until today: The British India Company conquered India in the disguise of just one more of the many, practically independent, feudatories of the Mughal emperors, and for some time the British pretended still to acknowledge the Mughal court living on their pensions, and to respect the late Mughal civilization of the time. After 1832—37 they altered their *British penetration* policy, aspiring at a rapid Anglicization and Christianization of the country but arousing increasing Indian opposition which exploded in the great Mutiny of 1857—58. It could be quelled with great difficulty only by the British armies released from the Crimean War. The British government, which now took over the administration, was forced on the one hand to acknowledge the status of the still surviving Indian states, on the other to pledge the development of the country towards modern occidental civilization and democracy. Modern railways, industries, schools, colleges and universities shot up; Indians had to be admitted to higher and higher government posts; Indian upper-class life became increasingly similar to European. After long obstinate resistance the British bureaucracy, dependent mainly on Indian officials and Indian troops, had to yield to Mahatma Gandhi's non-co-operation movement when hard pressed during two world wars. In 1947 India became independent, the princely states disappeared and Pakistan became a separate Muslim state. Since then the modernization of India has progressed by leaps and bounds. But it has meant more than a simple westernization. Since the late 18th century European scholars had begun to discover the treasures of ancient Indian culture, and the national movement re-integrated them into education. In this process, however, they ceased to be an unquestioned living tradition and turned into the humanistic background of a modern way of life which otherwise becomes increasingly similar to that of Europe and America. In which form a synthesis between the traditional Indian background and modern industrial civilization will develop, we can not yet foretell. But it appears most probable that a return to the Indian tradition of the last twelve hundred years is out of question, even if it might temporarily be attempt-

ed by some conservative reaction. Today it is rather the freely developing Indian civilization of the Aryan-Indian (Buddhist to early Hindu) age, especially the city culture of the Gupta Empire which attracts India. Future development will propably adopt diverse concepts of the past, without regard to any special period, as long as they can be associated with modern needs and ideas.

From this survey it will be evident that we have to deal with at least five successive types of Indian art, each growing from a heritage bequeathed by its predecessor, but each steering in a very different direction, subject to different influences, serving different types of society, aspiring at the expression of different ideals. First, in the Indus Valley, the rather sober and realistic, well regulated art of a predominantly mercantile society. Then in the Aryan-Indian period an art full of the joy of life — notwithstanding certain ascetic trends of the time —, an intense observation of nature, first full of an awe of its inscrutable magic forces, then with a familiarity developing into an almost illusionistic realism, ultimately intensified to an intellectual awareness achieving that most perfect synthesis of worldly refinement and grandiose spirituality that was Gupta art. In the Middle Ages a consciously traditional art, under which the Gupta, and the parallel Pallava heritage evolved to their utmost potentialities, first profoundly mystic, later becoming increasingly superficial as cold theological speculation took the place of fervent faith, and again worldly though under the disguise of religious images, and at last ending in a mere competition for the biggest temple with the greatest number of dull mass-produced sculptures. In the Indo-Islamic period on one side, Muslim art, grandiose and ambitious, with an astonishing wealth of exquisite abstract or floral ornaments, fundamentally foreign and yet distinguished from the art of other Muslim countries by its mixture of archaic Iranian and adapted Hindu features; on the other, late Hindu art, starting from an antiquarian renaissance and ending in a semi-Islamic style saturated with indigenous love of nature, eroticism and mysticism. And modern Indian art, switching from a slavish imitation of European to a not less slavish imitation of ancient Indian models, now in search of a synthesis starting from basic principles.

As a matter of fact we are confronted with even more types because sometimes there was a split in the evolutionary processes. Thus a semi-Hellenistic frontier style, trying to evolve a Buddhist imagery from Graeco-Roman models, developed in the Western Panjab and Afghanistan in the first five centuries of the Christian era; similarly a

PHASES OF
INDIAN ART

23

semi-Roman style flourished in Kashmir from the 8th century onwards. Mediaeval Hindu art broke up into rather different styles in Northern India, the Deccan and the South; the first taking the temple tower, the second the cult-hall, the third the temple enclosure as the basis of planning; the first starting from Gupta, the last from South-Indian Buddhist sculpture and painting, the second being a synthesis of both. And Bengal evolved a separate style (a sort of hieratic Gupta Baroque and Rococo) spreading to Nepal, Tibet, Burma and Indonesia. The art of the Islamic Period is divided into two utterly different Muslim styles by the irruption of the Mughals, and this latter likewise divided contemporaneous Hindu art into two different styles. Not to speak of

*Local styles* all the local styles which developed outside India proper, in the Tarim Basin, Nepal, Burma, Malaya, Sumatra, Java, Bali, Siam, Cambodia and Annam (Champā) which are beyond the scope of this book. The diversity of art styles and the wealth of forms evolved, of images visualized, of emotions and ideals expressed, of aesthetic solutions found, are overwhelming. And yet, seen from the angle of any other civilization, all this diversity is reduced to a fundamental unity, to what we can only call Indian art.

## II. BEGINNINGS OF INDIAN ART

PREHISTORY

The antiquity of man in India is believed to go back about half a million years. Small tribes of Negrito pygmies — related to the negroes of Africa — wandered over the then thickly forested country, hunting and collecting whatever they could find to eat, and putting up their camps along river beds or in natural caves. Only one datable skull has hitherto been traced; but they survive even today in the Andaman Islands east of India; and some jungle tribes in South India such as the Kādars and Pulaiyāns, and in Malaya (Semangs) still show some Negrito characteristics. They used crude stone implements (palaeoliths), axes, adzes and hammers, later also blades and burins manufactured from quartzite pebbles chipped off along one edge. In the Narmada Valley cave paintings have also been discovered similar to those found in France and Spain. Later, Proto-Australians immigrated, surviving in the Chenchus, Malayans, Kādars, Kurumbas, Yeruvas and other jungle tribes of Central and Southern India. Still later came the proto-Mediterraneans, who had some last negroid characteristics. Their type is common among the Dravidians of South India. They introduced agriculture and used microliths, i.e. small flakes of flint and jasper once mounted in wooden or bone handles, as arrows, knives, swords, etc. About 4000 B.C. the art of grinding and polishing stone into instruments of various shapes, pottery, weaving and other arts were known, and quite a fair standard of village life had developed. Then Austro-Asiatic tribes pushed in from the east, leaving a certain mongoloid strain in the later Hindu population of Assam, Bengal, Bihar and Uttar Pradesh, surviving in the Central Indian jungles up to the present day (Gonds, Santāls, Bhils, etc.). Next, "Armenoid" and "Alpine" peoples came from Central Asia via Iran, in the course of time infiltrating also into Maharashtra and at last to Southern India (Tamilnad).

NORTH-WEST FRONTIER

Excavations at Amri in Sind, Kulli, Nandanā, Rana Ghundāi, Quetta, etc. in Baluchistan have revealed the immigration, in the later 4th millennium B.C., of further tribes whose culture was closely related to that at Uruk in lower, Jemdet Nasr in central and Tell-Halaf in upper Mesopotamia (Iraq). They were peasants who cultivated barley and wheat, bred cattle, used bronze implements, engraved (with plait-work designs) or painted their pottery, nicely turned on the wheel, and venerated a nude fertility goddess. The pots, vases, beakers, stands, dishes, braziers, etc. of the Kulli type are painted in black, occasionally also in red with horizontal friezes of bulls, lions, ibexes, birds, trees, etc. between bands of waving lines and circles, roughly reminiscent of similar motifs on Greek geometrical vases, but more correctly of similar early pottery ware from South-Western Iran. In those of the Rana Ghundāi type the animal figures have deteriorated in favour of a partition by broad bands, radial lines, rectangular and irregular panels, triangles, etc. Nal pottery uses rather naturalistic animal figures, including fishes, and tangent or intersecting circles, chessboard designs, etc. Amri and Nandana ware combines the qualities of the Kulli with that of the Nal designs. The clay figurines, likewise painted, represent also animals, but especially women, either nude, or wearing a shirt, a shawl over their hair, and a lot of chains and jewelry over their breasts. Many are mere busts, and especially the nude ones may be idols of the great mother goddess once so generally venerated in South-western Asia. The technique is crude, a piece of clay drawn out and shaped with a few finger pressures, headcloth, eyes, ornaments being separately formed from some small slips of clay afterwards pressed on the figurine.

"INDUS" OR "HARAPPĀ" CULTURE

About the end of the first half of the 3rd millennium B.C. a city civilization was born in the Indus Valley. The transition from village life was so sudden that an inspiration from outside, from ancient Sumerian civilization, seems most probable. We know that the great merchants of Sumer undertook sea voyages over the Persian Gulf to Bahrain and Oman, and they may well have also reached the Indus Valley. The general type of that new civilization in the Indus Valley is in fact most similar to that of ancient Sumer. Indian seals, beads and other finds discovered at Tell Asmar, Tell Billa, Susa, Khafaje, Ur, Kish, Lagash, Adab, Tepe Gawra and Mari prove that this contact with the Ancient East continued, probably through trade in cotton, incense, ivory, slaves, etc. between c. 2500 B.C. to 1500 B.C. And yet that contact cannot have been more than an inspiration. For whatever aspect of this earliest high civilization of India we study in detail, it is different from similar phenomena in Mesopotamia. The natural conditions of the Indus Valley, a long, navigable river irrigating a belt of fertile land — then much broader than today — protected by deserts on both sides, were most favourable to the growth of intensive trade, as well as of a common administrative and defence system. Almost seventy settlements have hitherto been discovered ranging from Sutkāgen-Dor in Makrān to Rūpar where the Sutlej leaves the foothills of the Himalaya and Lothāl in Gujarat. Many seem to have been rather small commercial and industrial centres (best known are the ruins of Chanhu-Daro). Some, like Sutkāgen-Dor, Rūpar, Lakkabaval, Amra, Somnāth, Lothal were distant trade outposts; others were frontier fortresses, for instance Dābarkot, at the exit of the Quetta route from the mountains of Northern Baluchistan, or Ali Murād, in the western desert of Lower Sind.

But the most important cities were Mohenjo-Dāro ('City of the Dead') not far from Lārkāna in Central Sind, and Harappā near Montgomery (Central Panjab). Both are so immensely larger than all the other settlements, and their buildings so much more impressive that we cannot avoid the conclusion that they had been the capitals of the state which had created the Indus (or Harappā) civilization. Mohenjo-Dāro once covered an area of a square kilometre; Harappā had approximately the same size, though stretched out in a semicircle along a bend of the river Rāvi. Both cities were crossed at regular intervals by several, almost straight, avenues in north-south and east-west directions. The blocks of houses so formed were again subdivided by smaller, not quite so regular streets from which one had access to the individual houses. At the western end of both cities there were huge citadels enclosing temples and other religious buildings, assembly halls, granaries, barracks, etc. The granaries were near the river and were equipped with quays, loading ramps, work rooms, labourers' barracks, etc. The cities themselves seem originally not to have been fortified.

Most buildings were erected in baked bricks, though sundried mud bricks were also used for interior walls or as filling of platforms, ramps, bastions, etc. Probably the walls were covered with mud plaster. The streets were provided with an almost modern system of corbel-vaulted drains, the houses with tube wells. The houses themselves were laid out around courts and were generally two, sometimes more, storeys high. In their plan and structure there appear, however, many variations, though we can merely guess their individual purpose. There were palaces, rich and poor houses, workshops, bazars, hostels, barracks for police or slaves.

The temples unfortunately represent a problem not yet solved definitely. Several buildings, generally with exceptionally thick — and therefore originally high — walls have been claimed as such. One of

*Temples*

27

these (VR-area at Mohenjo-Dāro) is approached from the south by two symmetrically disposed stairs leading to a monumental double gate; in the small court a ring of bricks seems once to have enclosed a sacred tree or the statuette of a sitting bearded man, the fragments of which were found within the precincts. In the citadel of Mohenjo-Dāro another religious building has been discovered, the centre of which is a tank to which, at both ends, steps lead down from a surrounding passage; adjacent, there are a pilastered hall and several sets of rooms or cellas. As in India baths have always played an important role in religious ceremonies, the whole building looks like a sort of monastery or priests' house; another building nearby has been interpreted as a "college"; in another one, small secluded cells have been discovered which might have served for meditation. And nearby there are also the retaining walls of two huge platforms, the purpose of which is unknown but which might have been the substructures of "high temples", such as had been common in the ancient Orient.

The fortifications of the citadel at Mohenjo-Dāro have disappeared, except for the remnants of a few towers. On the other hand, the ramparts of the Harappā citadel are still in a reasonably good condition. They form a parallelogram some 460 yards from north to south, and 215 yards from east to west, and consist of a tapering wall of mud-bricks 45 feet wide at the basis and of approximately the same height, strengthened by a revetment of baked bricks 4 feet broad, and a flood rampart a further 45 feet wide. Behind, there is a platform of mud bricks, 20—25 feet high, on top of which vestiges of six successive settlements can be traced. The fortification wall had projecting rectangular towers at regular intervals; the most important towers were at the north-western and south-eastern corners. On the western side a succession of ramps led from a re-entrant up to the citadel; another gate seems to have been on the north side, near the river.

Curiously enough, hardly anything of architectural decoration has been discovered. All the buildings are of a monotonous simplicity; only in a single case bricks seem to have been laid with the intention of creating a decorative pattern. But we have to reckon with the possibility that colour may once have made the buildings more appealing.

*Sculpture* Likewise the number of real sculptures and bronzes is very small, the overwhelming majority of such works consisting of faience and terracotta figurines, and finally steatite seals. Only thirteen statuettes or fragments of such, of steatite, limestone or alabaster, have been found, even the biggest of them no more than 16½ inches high. Eleven of them represent elderly bearded men clad in a loose cotton garment (in the best known example covered with great clover-leaves), possibly priest kings once ruling over the Indus Valley. In their general type — the compact bodies, the simple costume, the excessively large heads, the inlaid eyes and ornaments — these statuettes remind on of early Sumerian work; and yet their long, narrow heads with the often conspicuously protruding "Jewish" (i.e. Armenoid) nose have nothing in common with the broad Sumerian skulls on their short, thick necks. A puzzling problem is offered by two torsos from Harappā whose heads and arms, once fastened with pegs, have been lost. One (of red stone) looks almost like a miniature copy of a classic "Greek athlete", whereas the other (of grey lime stone) is in a dancing posture. Whom they represent, we cannot say. However, it is remarkable that the type of the "Greek" figurine later became common as the Kāyotsarga pose of deified saints (Tīrthankaras) of the Jain sect which, though known only since the 6th century B.C., boasts of a history claiming to go back thousands of years further into the past, and the

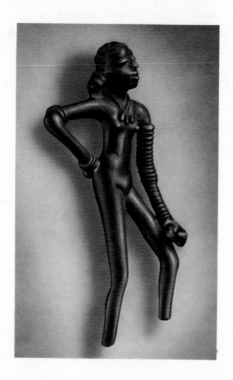

Dancing girl, copper statuette from Mohenjo-Dāro, about 4″ high. Probably 3rd millennium B.C. *National Museum, New Delhi.*

art of which has preserved other symbols of Mohenjo-Dāro times as well. The other figurine, on the other hand, is exactly in the posture of god Śiva as Lord of Dance (Natarājā) in Mediaeval Hindu art. Thus, both may be interpreted as cult idols.

The two small bronzes from Mohenjo-Dāro represent nude dancing girls. One is rather crude, but the other is a very lively statuette of a very young Austro-Asiatic slave girl, her hair in a thick roll falling from above the left ear to her right shoulder, her right arm pressed on her hip, her left one, loaded with some dozens of heavy bangles, hanging down to hold a bowl, the (lost) feet stamping the ground with a slight swinging of the hips. The faiences consist mainly of animals, monkeys, squirrels, etc.

The terracottas seem to have been house idols, votives or toys. Very common are female figures, generally very crudely modelled, decked with numerous girdles, chains, necklaces, earrings, and an impressive headdress fanning out at the top; sometimes they look pregnant, sometimes they hold a baby to their breast, sometimes they wear also a loin cloth, sometimes the headdress ends on both sides in shell-like cups or panniers which had once been used as oil-lamps. How far these figures were images of the Great Mother Goddess, how far votives in hope for fertility, how far predecessors of the Dīpalakshmī's (female statuettes holding an oil lamp) of later Hindu art, we have no means of knowing. Next, there come male figurines with an immense nose, goggle-eyes and a sensuous mouth (formed in a mould) which look like caricatures of the "priest"-statuettes. Three-quarters of the terracottas, however, represent cattle, humped and short-horn bulls, buffaloes (but never cows), also dogs, sheep, elephants, rhinocerosses, pigs, monkeys, turtles, birds (sometimes as whistles!), in one case a horse, and finally model carts. Here too some may be votives, e.g. the doves, in the Ancient East symbols of the great Mother Goddess. But the majority are obviously children's toys.

*Steatite Seals* Certainly the most interesting pieces of sculpture are the steatite seals, normally $3/4$ to $1\frac{1}{4}$ inches square, with a perforated boss at the back. Very occasionally circular and cylinder seals also occur which are probably due to foreign influence. All these seals show, on top, brief pictographic inscriptions and, under these, various animals, sometimes also obvious deities and ritual scenes. The script reveals some distant relationship with early Sumerian and proto-Elamite signs, but has developed independently. Quite a number of attempts have been made to decipher it, reading it as Sanskrit, a West-Indogermanic

Holy (?) bull in front of a ritual manger, inscription
above. Seal from Mohenjo-Dāro, c. 2500-2300 B.C.
*Original size.*

language akin to Hittite and Latin, or as an early form of Dravidian
(of which a branch, Brahūi, is still spoken in Baluchistan, though
otherwise it is restricted today to Southern India). But none of those
interpretations has hitherto found acceptance. Most of the figures, cut
in intaglio technique, represent an ox-like beast with one protruding
long horn ("unicorn") — which, however, may stand for two horns,
the second hidden by the first one — in front of which an unexplained
object stands, variously interpreted as a "standard", a brazier for incense or a "sacred manger". Similarly we find short-horned bulls,
buffaloes, zebus, rhinocerosses, tigers, elephants, antelopes, crocodiles,
etc., though not so commonly. From the whole context it is evident
that these figures are religious symbols, possibly deities. The bull has
been equated with Nandi, the emblem of the Hindu god Śiva, the
tiger with that of the goddess Durgā, a view supported by the fact that
phallic and ring stones (i.e. the *linga* and *yoni* of Śiva and Devī) have
been traced in the Indus civilization. But these equations are not
certain. A flying eagle with a snake on another seal reminds one of the
Hindu sun-bird Garuda, enemy of the Nāgas. A pipal tree (ficus
religiosa) between two women is another symbol which later became
common in Buddhist and Hindu art. On a few other seals a horned
yogin is depicted, with erected member, covered with bangles and surrounded by wild animals; this has with more probability been identified as an old form of Śiva, viz. Paśupati, "the Lord (i.e. protector) of
the cattle"; the erected member is the characteristic of another very
old form of the god, Lakuliśa; the horns, on the other hand, are a very
common symbol of divinity in Egypt, the ancient Near East, and even
of the European devil (insofar as he is the heir of pre-Christian gods);
in India they turn up as the emblem of Śiva-ite attendant figures in
early Pallava art. Another seal shows the same (?) god, horned, his
matted hair falling down his back, revealing himself between the

branches of a tree, before which a priest kneels accompanied by a bull (or goat) with a human face (as in ancient Babylonia), while in the foreground seven votaries with pointed headdresses and plaited hair seem to execute a ritual dance. Other scenes, however, are reminiscent of the Sumerian hero Gilgamesh holding two lions, and of his companion the bull-man (Minotaur) Eabani (Enkidu). It is worth observing that whereas the animals are depicted with remarkable skill, the human figures are very stiff and conventional. Nearly related to these steatite seals are copper tablets, possibly amulets, inscribed on one side with similar pictographs, on the other bearing animal figures.

*Painted pottery* Painting we know merely from the decoration of pots, a mass-produced folk art which surely cannot be treated on the same level as the aristocratic style of the statuettes and steatite seals. Nevertheless, even this folk art sheds some light on the general character of Indus Valley painting. The pictures, drawn in swift, slapdash, black lines show a mixture of geometrical motifs, criss-cross lines, scales, chessboard patterns, rows of dotted circles, or intersecting circles, etc. with almost naturalistic representations of leaves, trees, birds (sometimes peacocks), occasionally also deer, goats, jackals. In contrast, the rare human figures (woman with child, fisherman with his nets) are executed in a stiff and highly simplified manner reminding one of the scenes on early Greek geometrical vases. Though originally related to the painted pottery of Baluchistan (Rana Ghundāi and Kulli), the sprawling, luscious painting style of the then green Indus plains stands in a marked contrast to the dry and rigid, but also more powerful compositions of the barren Baluchistan mountains.

*Applied art* We are better informed on the many aspects of industrial art. Here two entirely different levels are evident: The upper class used bronze objects of every imaginable type, statuettes (dancing girls, buffalo, birds), vases, jugs, cosmetic jars (e.g. from Chanhu-Dāro), mirrors, razor-blades, axes, spearheads, knives, saws, angle-hooks, pins, staff-heads, generally plain, but of pleasing shape, sometimes also decorated with figures; silver ornaments; lead; various pectoral ornaments, pin-heads, etc. of steatite, shell and faience or inlaid with the latter; exquisite beads and necklaces of gold and semi-precious stones (especially cornelian) some of which had been imported; steatite boxes; ivory combs, weights, dices, etc. The ordinary people still used flint knives, amulets, bangles, bead-chains, etc. made of clay, and a great variety of pots, some of which (egg-shaped) are still used by Hindu yogis.

In the second Millennium B.C. the Indus civilization began to disintegrate. The reasons are not known; but it seems that the authority of the ruling class had been shaken. Whereas hitherto generation after generation had rebuilt their houses following the same town plan (there are 7 strata to show this), now people huddled together in overcrowded warrens, no longer cared and pushed their shabbily built houses into and across the former streets. There are indications that the open towns were now fortified. As at the same time the ruins of minor towns like Chanhu-Daro were occupied by much more primitive peoples (the so-called Jhukar Culture), it seems that the civilized population of the Indus Valley retired into the now fortified cities much as the population of the Roman Empire did in the 3rd and 4th century A.D. At last, about 1400 B.C. the Indus Civilization collapsed. In Mohenjo-Dāro skeletons of fleeing people, massacred and never buried afterwards, have been excavated at two spots; they were still in the same position in which they had fallen, their last possessions in their hands, under the swords of the invaders. And then on the ruins there are vestiges of merely temporary buildings and cemeteries of very barbarian tribes (the so-called Jhangar Culture).

*Decline and fall*

However, this was not yet the end. The remnants of the Indus people seem to have retired to the Ghaggar Valley in the Thar Desert, to Saurāshtra and Gujarat. But at last they were conquered and absorbed into the new society evolving after the Aryan conquest. They seem, however, to have been responsible for many of the changes which Aryan civilization underwent in the Gangetic plains, the intrusion of *yoga* by the side of *yajna* (sacrifice), the transformation of the sacrifice into a magic machine, the cult of Śiva Paśupati and of the Devī, and quite a number of art symbols and conventions (e.g. yogi, Nandipada, holy tree, Dīpalakshmī, vāhanas of Hindu gods), etc.

## PREHISTORY OF SOUTHERN INDIA

The prehistory of Southern India — which lasted until about the 3rd century B.C. — is much more complex. It seems fairly probable that the same type of Mediterranean people who created the Indus Civilization, advanced through Mahārāshtra to the Tamil country; that it is responsible for the prevalence of brachycephals there; and that it imposed its language, the Dravidian, on the South. But there are no direct links with the Indus Civilization; instead, many observations speak for a direct contact with Iran, Iraq, Arabia, Syria and Egypt. The South-Indian cult of Śiva and Pārvatī links up with the cult of the moon god and the "Lady of the Mountain" at Ur, their ceremonial nuptials, their palace-temple, the temple slaves, the hierodules (*deva-*

*dāsīs*). South Indian painted pottery often resembles that of Tepe Hissar in Iran. Egyptian alabaster vases were discovered in Malabar. Terracotta sarcophagi, with or without legs, have their counterparts in Syria. The most common form of burial was the cromlech or stone circle, containing either a cist or an urn, or both; funeral accessories are large egg-shaped pots on ring-stands, polished blacktopped pots and lapislazuli beads. The cists, built of thick stone slabs, often have a hole on the northern or eastern side. This type, which seems to have migrated north rather late (c. 200 B.C.) from the uttermost South, appears to have come from overseas, the coast of the Arabian Sea, Egypt, Syria, Cyprus, even Brittany. The urn-burials of Ādichanallūr (Tinnevelly district) contain golden diadems and mouthpieces, iron and bronze implements which are again related to Bronze Age finds in Palestine (Gaza, Gerar) and Cyprus. Rock tombs in the Deccan (Purandhar) resemble those of early Jewish times in Palestine. The cairns and barrows of the Nilgiris, on the other hand, have yielded bronze bowls similar to those found at Nimrud (Assyria) and Wan (Armenia). All these finds point to trade relations by sea which are also proved by the Indian names of articles imported into Egypt, Palestine (e.g. Solomon's expedition to Ophir = Sopara near Bombay), Syria and Assyria. The more regrettable it is that all literary evidence is missing and that the history of the famous Śamgam Age (generally dated c. 300 B.C.—A.D. 300) of Tamil literature remains shadowy, and that only in the second half of the first millennium of the Christian era can we first tread on firm historical ground.

*Burial*

# III. EARLY INDIAN ART

The tribes who at last wiped out the Indus civilization, were the Indo-Aryans, a branch of the Indo-European group which in the 3rd—2nd millennium B.C. expanded from the steppes south of the Ural to the east and west, imposing their language in various forms on most of Europe, on the highlands of South Western Asia, on the greater part of India, and for some period also on Central Asia up to the borders of China. The Indo-Aryans had in the 2nd millennium B.C. separated from the Irano-Aryans after a religious schism. They migrated from their common homeland Erānvej (the present Russian Turkestan) via Afghanistan to India, whereas the Iranians settled in Iran (Persia), and another group, the Mitannis, founded a kingdom in Upper Mesopotamia about 1400 B.C. The Indo-Aryans were unruly, warlike semi-nomads, raising cattle and horses, though growing, in addition, some barley; they lived in fortified wooden villages, were organized in clans, tribes and tribal federations, and venerated heavenly deities, as vigorous, boisterous and warlike as their devotees. They were formidable warriors, protected by leather armour, fighting with hardened bronze swords, long bows and arrows. The chieftains and their nobles fought on light war-chariots drawn by swift horses. These gave them a mobility and fighting superiority against which the slow spearmen of the Indus civilization were helpless. Thus the Indo-Aryans moved eastwards, fighting as much between themselves as with the indigenous population which they exterminated or enslaved. They overran the open country, stormed the fortified towns (*pur*) of the Indus Valley, and slowly migrated eastwards, conquering the whole of Northern India c. 1400—1000 B.C.

But during this progress their civilization was considerably changed. As they imposed themselves on the indigenous population of Northern India, they became the ruling classes of a colonial-feudal society, priests (*brahmans*), warriors (*kshatriyas*) and yeomen (*vaisyas*), distinguished from the indigenous serfs (*sūdras*) by their fairer skin (*varna*). The social equality of olden times gave way to a rigid gradation of rights, duties and legal status. Castles and towns developed. The cult changed into a magic by means of which the priests could force the gods to comply with their demands. Sacrifices became in-

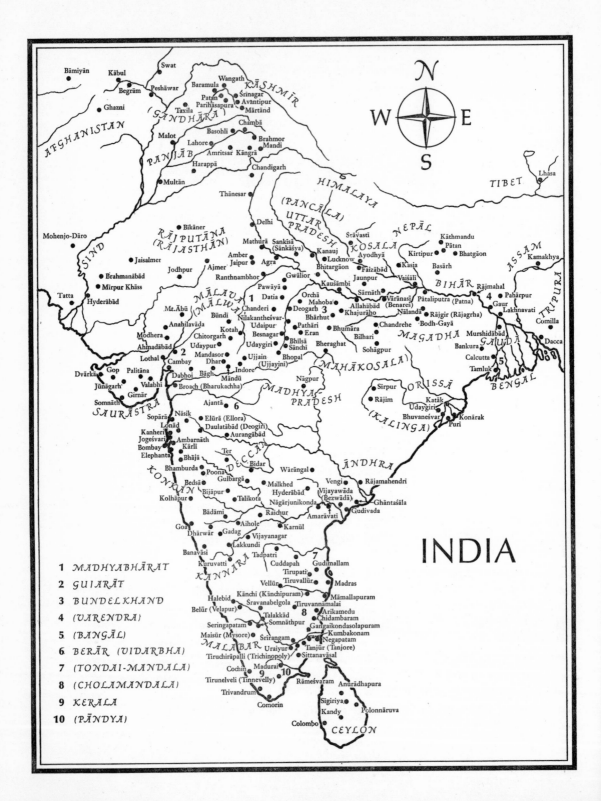

INDIA

1 MADHYABHĀRAT
2 GUJARĀT
3 BUNDELKHAND
4 (VARENDRA)
5 (BANGĀL)
6 BERĀR (VIDARBHA)
7 (TONDAI-MANDALA)
8 (CHOLAMANDALA)
9 KERALA
10 (PĀNDYA)

creasingly expensive so that at last only the kings could afford them. The priests, threatening to ruin any niggardly sacrificer by turning their magic against him, extorted immense fees and claimed a social rank even above the kings. Aryan society broke up. Indigenous tribes, who had made a successful stand, were acknowledged as kshatriyas when their kings succeeded, by liberal gifts, in winning over some influential group of brahmans. But the one-sided emphasis on sacrifice estranged the kshatriyas and vaisyas who turned to indigenous cults, to the yoga cult of the former Indus civilization, or to free speculation, which resulted finally in several new religious systems. The brahmans had to accept the yogis, and at last themselves turned to yoga by the side of *yajna* (sacrifice).

The old gods of whom Indra, lord of heaven, remained especially in popular favour, sank down to a level not far above that of indigenous local genii, *yakshas* (dwarfs), *rākshasas* (giants) and *nāgas* (snakes, water-spirits). Vishnu, identified with the hero Krishna Vāsudeva, became the centre of a new monotheism. Rudra, identified with the Pasupati of Mohenjo-Dāro times, attracted the village people and was feared also by the higher classes. The sacrifice of the brahmans was personified in a special god, Brahma who, however, never became very popular. Speculation on the magic power of the sacrifice (brahman) was amalgamated with the yoga experiences of man's ultimate self (ātman), resulting in a pantheism (Upanishads, Vedānta) which at last turned into a cult centering round Vishnu-Krishna (Bhagavad Gītā) and Śiva-Rudra. In contrast, Sāmkhya, Yoga and Jainism denied God, accepting however the eternal existence of the individual soul, whereas Buddhism reduced the soul to a bundle of impressions and urges causally determined by, but not identical with, similar residua of former souls.

*Monotheism*

But all other aspects of this decisive period of Indian history we can reconstruct only from occasional hints in the vast body of contemporaneous ritualistic, magic and philosophical literature, the Vedas or from the later compendia of traditional lore, the classic epics (Mahābhārata and Rāmāyana) and the collections of Hindu myths (Purānas). The latter describe splendid palaces decorated with statues and murals, and towns with strong fortifications, elegant streets and rich houses. Though the detailed descriptions of these tales, like the Bible, the Iliad, the Odyssey, the Nibelungen or the Arthurian legends, project later conditions into an earlier, much simpler age, we must nevertheless accept the fact that towns, palaces and castles had existed

EARLIEST
INDO-ARYAN ART

at the time when these tales originated. But hardly anything has hitherto been discovered.

The reason for this apparent contradiction is that these constructions were built mainly of mud and wood. In the North Indian plain building stone is available only in a few places (e.g. near Delhi and Āgra), even the foothills of the Himalaya yield only an almost useless conglomerate. On the other hand, clay is the most common material in an alluvial plain, and good timber was to be had in plenty in an age when vast forests, inhabited by primitive tribes, robbers and hermits, still separated town from town, and village from village. Thus it was only natural that an architecture of wood and mud, and a sculpture in wood and clay developed. Ancient Indian literature refers to construction in wood or sun-dried brick whenever it specifies. Megasthenes, the Seleucid ambassador to the court of the Maurya emperor Chandragupta (324—300 B.C.), mentions in his account (preserved mainly in excerpts by Arrian) that the capital Pataliputra was constructed of earthern ramparts and wooden palisades behind broad moats. The earliest Indian stone monuments imitate beam and rafter construction, and their reliefs depict houses and towns completely constructed in wood. Religious sculpture, as far as it may already have developed, in most cases used unbaked clay. For even today it is the custom at festivals to set up similar painted idols and later on to throw them into a river or tank where they again dissolve into mud. And folk customs of this kind are generally very old.

What we know of the architecture of the earliest Indo-Aryans is meagre enough: huts, round and square, occasionally even more than one storey high, and constructed with bamboo beams (*vaṃśa*). The huts and cattle pens of the villages were protected by hedges, palisades or earth walls. The chieftains were buried in earthen mounds heaped over a wooden funeral chamber erected round a central post. When the Aryans had settled in the Gangetic plains, the houses (*harmya*) became richer, comprising a number of rooms, including a place for the sacred fire (*garhapatya*), a women's quarter (*patnīnām sadana*), and stables; the construction was still of bamboo, the walls being erected against beams supported by four posts and finished with reed work and grass, and the roof being thatched in the same way with grass; the furniture consisted of beds, couches, pillows and coverlets. Still later the Grihya-Sūtras mention more spacious houses, with an assembly hall, resting rooms, stores, a nursery and latrine, surrounded by gardens, ponds and wells; and they offer detailed instructions for their construction and for the religious ceremonies connected with them. We learn also of the construction of roads and bridges and the lay-out of public squares and of many luxury articles such as plates, cups and spoons of gold and silver, iron knives, needles, mirrors, bedsteads, rich costumes and jewelry. Images of deities were also known, though not very common, but it is not clear whether they were mere symbols, or had some human resemblance. But hitherto we have had no archaeological evidence except for a few bronze weapons of South-West Asian affinities (a sword from Fort Munro, a trunnion celt from Shalozan, shaft-hole axes from Shāhī Tump and Mohenjo-Dāro, all in the Indus area), and potsherds of a crude grey ware. How far equally crude idols of a nude goddess can be attributed to this period is still uncertain.

After the middle of the 6th century B.C., the time of Mahāvīra and of the Buddha (the founders of Jainism and Buddhism), the many small kingdoms and republics of Northern India were absorbed by a few competing great powers until in the late 4th century the Maurya Empire emerged as the first — and for long also the last — all-Indian state. The leading and eventually successful country in this struggle was Magadha, the present South Bihār. King Bimbisāra (544—493 B.C.) chose as his capital Girivraja in a valley of the mountains south of Patna, and renamed it Rājagriha ('royal residence'), the present Rājgir. It seems to have been a modest town (c. 4½ miles in circumference) enclosed by an earthwork and moat with gates. His successor Ajātaśatru (493—462 B.C.) felt secure enough to build a likewise fortified suburb, New Rājagriha, in the plain just outside the valley. But then Magadha was threatened with an invasion by her most dangerous competitor, King Pradyota of Avanti (Mālwa). Ajātaśatru found himself forced to protect Rājgriha by an additional defence line running for almost thirty miles along the crest of the surrounding hills. These cyclopic walls are still standing. Where the valley opens in the direction of New Rājagriha, a huge platform has been erected, Jarāsandha-kā Baithak (the Throne of Rājā Jarasandha, a mythical king), the character of which has long been misunderstood because of some small caves in its front-side (probably of later date). Similar platforms are also found in the heart of the town. All these constructions, however, are merely the foundations of buildings in timber and mud, probably several storeys high, such as we see depicted on later reliefs; Jarāsandha-kā-Baithak was probably the substructure of a tower from which the broken foreground at the river outlet, which was rather difficult to defend, could be well controlled. Similar cyclopic walls can be traced also on mountains in other parts of India, but they have never been investigated properly, and though some of them may prove to be very old, others are surely mediaeval.

Ajāśatru had already founded a fort at the confluence of the rivers Ganges and Son, in order to keep in check the Lichhavi tribe of North Bihār-Pātaliputra (the present Patna) which was soon to supersede Rājāgriha. For this long tongue of land, protected by high dikes, between two of the most important rivers and surrounded by marshy plains which turned into lakes during the rainy season, was as impregnable as the older capital, but formed at the same time a natural centre of communications and trade. King Udayin there laid out a suburb Kusumapura, which King Munda made his residence, and though the Śiśunaga emperors returned to Rājagriha, after the Nandas it became the capital of India for a thousand years.

It is difficult to say how many of the remains of other Indian cities go back to this time. At present we have reliable evidence only for Vaiśālī in North Bihār and for Ahichhatra, the capital of Panchala (Oudh). The walls of the latter, of baked bricks, still rise to a height of 40 to 50 feet; in the centre of the town there stood a large temple on which the principal streets converged.

At Rājagriha the kings Bimbisāra and Ajātaśatru had already built vast halls, monasteries several storeys high (*Mahāvihāras*) and Buddhist relic shrines (*Dhātu-Chaitya, Stūpa*), one of them enshrining most of the bones and ashes of the Buddha. But none of them still exist. They were rebuilt many times because of their special sacredness. For the Buddha had often stayed at Rājagriha, especially on Gridhrakūta (Vulture's Hill) east of the Old Town; an ancient road still leads up to it, full of memories of the great teacher's life, and studded with memorial shrines. Mahāvīra had also lived at Rājagriha, and at present many Jain temples stand on all the surrounding hills. But the only early Jain monument there is the Sonbhandār Cave.

*Sculpture*  We know that figure sculpture flourished at that time. For the early Buddhist scriptures not only make references to idols of gods and goddesses, but also impose punishments on sexual intercourse with them, a crime which at least points to a very realistic execution of these figures. But the attempts to attribute certain sculptures (statues of Śisunaga emperors, c. 400 B.C., Patna gold plaque of Śiva and Pārvati) to this period, have not found acceptance.

The Jātakas (Buddhist fairy-tales), which reflect conditions in the centuries before and during the career of the Buddha, mention that the artisans were organized in eighteen guilds — wood-workers, smiths, painters, ivory workers, etc.

However, the victories of Alexander the Great created a new world situation which was to have its influence also on India. His invasion of the Panjab 327—26 B.C. proved abortive; but the indirect effects on India were immense. Chandragupta Maurya, probably an illegitimate member of the Nanda Dynasty of Magadha who had been forced to flee from home, collected an army in order to liberate the Panjab from the Macedonians and Greeks; this aim accomplished, he overthrew the last Nanda emperor c. 323 B.C. Now that the mighty Persian Empire had disappeared, Chandragupta aspired to assume the role of the leading Asiatic emperor himself. From the Greeks he had learned much of Hellenistic statecraft. Persian emigrants, political refugees, scholars, unemployed artists, were available in sufficient numbers. After the treaty with Seleukos I Nikator in 304 B.C. a Greek princess entered the imperial harem at Pātaliputra, a Seleucid embassy was established there, and Greek merchants, artisans, artists, dancers, etc. poured into India. A special government department had to be created for their accomodation and supervision.

Chandragupta's empire expanded over the whole of India except her farthest southern tip which was merely raided, and over Afghanistan south of the Hindukush. These immense countries were held together by a centralized bureaucracy, kept in check in its turn by a ruthless secret service. It was an empire driven by a nationalistic ideal and yet without a sufficient national background. The idea of the Chakravartin, the 'world emperor', had been familiar to Indian princes for centuries and played a certain role in their court ceremonies. The upper classes were also conscious of the cultural unity of most of the sub-continent. But few had opportunities to travel so far, and the overwhelming majority of the population knew only the narrow atmosphere of their tribal kingdoms. It was, therefore, inevitable that the Maurya court should borrow certain paraphernalia of its new glory from the outside world, and that such adaptations should be fully integrated into the national ideology. However, one of the principal paraphernalia of power is art; for art has to create the splendour of power and the symbols of divine election by which to impress the masses into submission and loyalty.

Pātaliputra grew into a vast city, 10 miles in length and 2 miles in breadth, surrounded by a wooden wall pierced with loopholes for the discharge of arrows, crowned with 560 towers and provided with

*Chandragupta Maurya*

*Pātaliputra*

41

60 gates. Part of these wooden fortifications have been excavated, south of the present embankment, at Bulandībāgh. It is a double row of palisades, interlinked by horizontal beams and filled with earth; at one place the outlet of a drain was found, constructed of massive posts and planks jointed by iron strips. Strabo reports that the palaces of Pātaliputra compared very favourably with those of the Achaemenian kings at Susa and Ekbatana; the excavations of Waddell and Spooner at the village Kumrāhār in fact brought to light the remnants of a hall, similar to the Hundred Pillar Hall of Darius at Persepolis. Its ceiling had once been supported by a hundred huge, plain but highly polished stone columns. There is no evidence of Iranian bullhead capitals; but they are said once to have been decorated with vines like the Persian columns. So it is not surprising that the court ceremonial in these halls had likewise been influenced by Achaemenian models.

*Aśoka* The decisive development of stone construction, however, set in under Chandragupta's second successor, *Aśoka the Great* (c. 273—236 B.C.). A ruthless general and administrator in his younger years, he became profoundly impressed by the horrors which proved necessary in suppressing a general revolt in Kalinga (Orissa), and was converted to Buddhism. He preached its ethics in twenty-five edicts, engraved on rocks and pillars, over the length and breadth of his empire. He appointed special officers (*dharmamahāmātras*) to look after the moral condition of the people, to suppress many of the primitive religious customs, to discourage the slaughter and sacrifice of animals, and to encourage the foundation of charitable institutions. He sent missionaries overseas, to Ceylon, Burma, Kashmir, Nepal, even to the Hellenistic kingdoms of the Mediterranean. And he founded innumerable ("84000") *stūpas* (relic shrines and monasteries).

*Development of the stūpa* Of course, there were not so many relics of the Buddha or even of his principal disciples. But Aśoka's policy had a different aim, and we have to study this in order to understand the *character and development of the stūpa,* the most important monument of Buddhist art. The stūpa is a massive hemispherical structure, surrounded by a balustrade and crowned by a stone umbrella. So it is just a variety of the funeral tumulus, surrounded by a stone circle, such as had been usual in later prehistoric times, like those erected also by the Vedic Indo-Aryans above the remains of prominent chiefs and kings. Such *tumuli* have been discovered at *Lauriya-Nandangarh* (near Bettiāh in the Champāran district, North Bihār); though they have proved to be not earlier than the Maurya period, some of them seem not to be stūpas and still to preserve certain characteristics of the Vedic burial mound, e.g. the central pillar and even small gold leaves stamped with the image of the earth goddess (Prithvī) referred to in the ancient hymns. But even these are enclosed by a brick platform and a retaining wall, with an interior system of radial and circular walls, and in most mounds the wooden pillar has been replaced by one in brick. Likewise their lightly swelling outline does not yet resemble a hemisphere; but this outline was still characteristic of some of Aśoka's stūpas, e.g. those erected at Lalita-Pāttan and Kīrti-pur in Nepal.

However the *stupa* soon became more than a funeral mound. It became a *magic-mystic instrument* by means of which the enshrined relics — and these might be even old monk's garments, begging bowls, holy scriptures, later even images of the Buddha and his historical or mythical predecessors — would have a maximum of influence on their surroundings. As already mentioned, the Vedic sacrifices had at last become part of the court ceremonial, and the brahmans performing them were court officials, whatever the religious ideas of the rulers and of their courts might have been. Even in purely Buddhist countries like Ceylon, Burma, Siam or Cambodia, such court brahmans were later on retained by the rulers. And these brahmans, of course, played a role at the court of Chandragupta who had set himself up as Indian 'world emperor' (Chakravartin, Samrāt) and who had been guided in his career by a great brahman statesman, Kautilya (Chānakya). However, these sacrifices were performed on specially prepared altars, the shape, indeed every brick of which stood in a symbolic relation to the universe. The most powerful sacrifice, however, had been that of one, or even several human beings (*Mahāpurushayajña*), in which every limb of the sacrificial victim was also spread on the altar in a symbolic-magical relation to the universe. When the ashes of such an outstanding personality as the great world teacher, the Buddha, were deposited in a stūpa by a mighty king like Ajātaśatru or later by Aśoka, it was inevitable that such ideas of sacrificial magic should slip in. The ashes were placed in a central reliquary (*dhātu*) at the bottom of the brick shaft (*yashti*). The latter became the world axis, the central world mountain Meru. The hemisphere (*garbha* or *ānda*, egg, i.e. world-egg; *dhātu + garbha > dagoba > pagoda*) of the stūpa was interpreted as the vault of the firmament, a little enclosure on top (*harmikā*) as the house of the gods ruling over this earth (in Ceylon: *devata kotuva*), the set of seven superimposed umbrellas (*chattravali*) on top symbolized the succession of higher heavens losing themselves in the transcendental absolute. The stūpa proper was surrounded by a railing (*vedikā*), consisting of posts (*thaba*) connected by horizontal beams (*sūchī*) and covered by a coping stone (*ushnīsha*), which symbolized the circulation of the stars, of the hours, of the seasons around the world mountain; and that balustrade was interrupted by gateways (*torana*) in the four directions of the horizon. Between the stūpa and the railing was the *pradakshinapātha,* for circumambulation of the sanctuary, in the same direction as sun and stars move. Later on this symbolism was to be developed even much further, the ashes being distributed over nine chambers corresponding to the eight cardinal points and the zenith, the parts of the stupa being regarded as symbols of the elements, the divine Buddhas (of later theology), etc. In their basic form these concepts must have been current at the latest in the time of Aśoka.

*Collapse of the pantheon*

But with them the magic role of the stūpa was not yet exhausted. By that time the old Indo-Aryan pantheon had utterly disintegrated. While for the court brahmans the gods had become shadowy symbols of the sacrificial magic power (brahman), for the people they had merged with the innumerable *yakshas* and *yakshīs*. These were local tutelary deities like the *baals* and *ashthorets* of the Bible, terrible and friendly, wilfully destroying human and animal life when not propitiated by human sacrifices, but also granting fertility and prosperity. Many were indigenous demons, such as Mānibhadra, Pūrnabhadra, Bhūtamukha, Pañchika, others *rākshasas* (giants) like Hāritī, others *nāgas* (watersnakes), others Vedic gods such as Indra, Vishnu, Brihaspati, others heroes of the past; others later became known as Buddhist or Hindu deities. Boisterous festivals with music, dance, processions and often gross customs were celebrated in their honour. Aśoka tried to suppress these customs and erected a stūpa wherever such a yaksha held sway, in the same way as later on Christian missionaries built churches on the centres of heathen cults. As a result, the yakshas and yakshīs, including the more generally acknowledged gods Indra and Śakra (Brahmā) were by and by reduced to divine devotees of the Buddhist religion and tutelary spirits of the Buddhist shrines. Thus India was covered with stūpas emanating their good magic influence over the whole country.

As Aśoka's successors Daśaratha and Samprati favoured the competing Ājivika and Jain sects, this development had its parallels also in Jainism. There were likewise Jain stūpas, though later they were replaced by temples; and a couple of Yakshas were associated with each of the 24 Jain world teachers, the Jinas or Tirthankaras.

Most of *Aśoka's stūpas* can no longer be traced. Others, at places which became centres of pilgrimage such as Sārnāth, Śrāvastī, Taxila, Vaiśālī, Piprahwa (= Kapilavastu), Sānchī were enlarged so much by later generations that nothing of their original structure is visible. Only those in Nepal (four at Lalita-Pāttana, one at Kīrtipur), though likewise embellished, have retained their original shape. Aśoka also built a temple for the Bodhi-Tree at Bodh-Gayā (in Bihār), under which the Buddha had found enlightenment and discovered the Truth. Though it, too, had to give way to an imposing later temple, at least representations of it have come down to us on the reliefs of the Great Stūpa of Sānchī. It was merely an elaboration of an already common type of sanctuary (*chaitya*), i.e. a balustrade enclosing the holy tree of a yakshī (*vrikshakā* = dryad), hung with streamers and surrounded by flagstaffs with the symbol of the respective deity. Similar sanctuaries, with a throne under the tree, were erected in memory of various saints. Aśoka surrounded the Bodhi Tree and the throne of the Buddha (*vajrāsana* = diamond throne) beneath it with an open colonnade carrying a roofed-in upper gallery accompanied by balconies on which decorative umbrellas were standing. This building, in its turn, stood inside an enclosure fenced off by a lower balustrade.

The *monasteries* (*vihāra*) were situated in gardens (*ārāma*) and consisted of rows of cells for the monks, an assembly hall (*chaityasālā*) and a refectory. But none of the Maurya period have survived. Instead we know a number of Ājīvika hermitages in the Barābar and Nāgārjuni hills, in the neighbourhood of Rājagriha, the first having inscriptions of the twelfth and nineteenth year of Aśoka's reign, the latter one of his successor Daśaratha. Most of them are plain rock chambers with a vaulted ceiling and highly polished walls. The Sudāma and Lomaśa Rishi caves, however, consist of two chambers, an interior round one and a larger anteroom opening on its one long side to the terrace outside; they look as if a circular hut at the end of a courtyard had been imitated inside the rock. The Lomaśa Rishi cave has an exterior entrance shaped like the front of a house of that time; two slightly inclined posts carry a "wooden" vaulted roof, the rafters of which are still visible; the roof, slightly pointed, ends in a finial; an inner arch decorated with a frieze of elephants frames the quadrangular door. The Gopika cave, the largest of all, probably a refectory, ends in two apses.

Lion capital from Aśoka's column at Sārnāth, 240 B.C., made of polished sandstone. On the abacus the 'Wheel of the Law' repeated four times, between a bull, a horse, a lion and an elephant, said to be symbols of the Buddha. 7' high. *National Museum, New Delhi.*

*Aśoka's columns*   The most important monuments of Maurya art, however, are the *columns set up by Aśoka,* several of which bear his famous edict inscriptions. These pillars, set up at Basarh-Bakhīra (pre-Aśoka), Sānka-śya (c. 255 B.C.), Rummindei (250 B.C.), Rāmpurva (244, 243 B.C.), Lauriyā-Nandangarh (242 B.C.), Sārnāth (240 B.C.), Sānchī (235 B.C.) and Salemgarh (about the same time), consist of a plain but highly polished, slightly tapering shaft (about 10 yards high) without base, but with a bell capital carrying an abacus on which a symbolic animal is mounted. During the few decades in which these pillars were set up, their shafts grew taller and taller; their capitals developed from a clumsy cap to an elegant "bell" of lotus petals; their abacus from a broad square slab to a step-like projecting disc decorated first with honeysuckle and rosettes, then with a frieze of *hamsas* (geese), finally with a frieze of four "Wheels of the Law" (*dharmachakra*), symbols of the Buddhist faith) alternating with a horse, bull, elephant and lion (interpreted as symbols of the four cardinal points); their top

46

from a clumsy elephant or bull, to lions and finally to four mightly half-lions or half-bulls facing in four directions and carrying a big "Wheel of the Law". Superficially these pillars remind one of Achaemenid columns, and yet they are different in every detail. For the custom of setting up such pillars at town gates, on public squares and in front of sanctuaries was indigenous. And so it is rather in certain characteristics of their execution that the foreign impact is felt. The honeysuckle frieze of the Rāmpurva capital and the lions of the Sārnāth and Sānchī pillars in particular reveal an un-Indian, colonial Greek hand.

After Asoka's death the imperial workshops produced also *cult statues* in the characteristic highly polished Chunār limestone. Whether the two Tīrthankar statues from Lohanipur (Patna Museum) can be attributed to the reign of Samprati, who favoured the Jains, seems doubtful; they are more probably contemporaneous with the Sonbandhār Jain Cave at Rājgir which, in view of a Śunga sgrafitto, may be as early as the end of the Maurya dynasty. Likewise a series of *Statues*

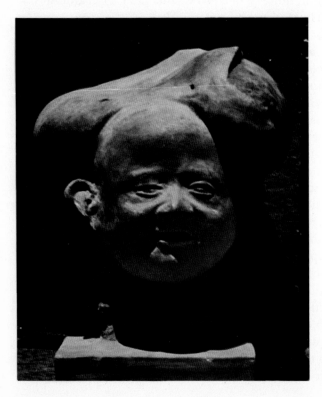

Boy's head. Terracotta from Bulandī Bāgh. Late Maurya or śunga style. 4½" high. *Patna Museum.*

47

statues with all the characteristics of the imperial workshop at Pātaliputra has been discovered; a yaksha at Patna, a yakshī (the famous
Chaurībearer) at Dīdaiganj nearby, other yakshas at Pārkham and
Palwal near Mathurā, and Sopāra (?) near Bombay, the yaksha king
Mānibhadra at Barodā near Mathurā and two at Pāwāya, and finally
the goddess Śrī-Lakshmi at Besnagar (Vidiśā). Their modelling is very
archaic, the bodies are hardly lifted out of the stone block, the dress
touches the pedestal, the feet hardly emerge under the costume, the
arms are pressed to the body, the head is hardly distinguishable from
a broad neck and thick hair. In fact, the commentator Patañjali mentions that the last Mauryas, in order to replenish their treasury, sold
images of non-Vedic gods like Śiva, Skanda and Viśākha. The fact that
such statues were found just near capitals of new states like Padmāvatī
(Pāwāya) and Mathurā, creates the impression that this sale of idols
had in fact been a sort of investiture. And the practice seems to have
been followed also by the weak Śunga and Kānva emperors. For some
of the statues, e.g. the more freely modelled Besnagar Lakshmī and
the Dīdanganj yakshī, must be of considerably later date, almost link-
ing up with the early Mathurā school.

No less problematic are the terracotta figures from Bulandībāgh near
Patna, amazingly alive and individual. Were they influenced by
Alexandrian models, or are they of a later period? Most Maurya terracottas are not so fine; their faces have been made with the help of a
standard mould whereas their other limbs are modelled by hand,
generally with quite fantastic, huge headgear.

*Maurya painting* seems to have reached a rather high standard, if we
may venture conclusions from the drawing of an elephant by the side
of Aśoka's Kalsi rock edict. Maurya pottery is characterized by a
highly polished black surface.

SUNGA ART   The Maurya regime was not popular. Its semi-foreign character, its
despotic methods lending themselves to abuses by the officials against
which redress in distant Pātaliputra proved almost impossible, the
suppression of popular customs and cults led to repeated bloody
revolts. Aśoka abolished the hated secret police, but his attempt to impose through his officials a morality not understood by the masses was
not popular. When his sons and grandsons quarrelled, Kalinga and
the South became at last independent under the Chedi and Śātavāhana dynasties, and the western provinces under branches of the
Maurya house. In 187 B.C. the general Pushyamitra Śunga slew the
last Maurya emperor, Brihadratha, during a parade. But he and his

48

successors had soon to defend themselves against the invasion of the Bactrian Greeks, and the Śunga empire soon dissolved into a loose federation. The next dynasty of the Kānvas (75—30 B.C.) had little power, and Northern India disintegrated into a multitude of local kingdoms, under various branches of the Mitra, Nāga, Kosala and other dynasties who temporarily had to acknowledge Greek and later Scythian overlords. Now the local popular traditions and cults reasserted themselves. The grandeur of Maurya court art disappeared before the natural growth of a homely folk art, naïve, but full of adventurous experiments and having recourse to symbols and motifs of very different origin, many in fact borrowed from South-Western Asia.

The number of monuments also of this time is small, as timber and clay continued to be the most common building materials. But baked bricks were now used more often, and terracotta figurines are numerous. The most important stone structure of this time is the *stūpa of Bārhut* the fragments of which are the pride of the Indian Museum in

Horse-headed Yakshī and a man, probably a representation of the Padakusalamanava-Jātaka. Yakshīs were often portrayed with horseheads. People believed that they seduced young men in order to devour them afterwards. Śunga terracotta. 4½″ high. *Baroda Museum.*

Tree goddess (Yakshī or Vrikshakā) Chulakoka Devatā. From the Bhārhut balustrade. 7′ high. *Indian Museum, Calcutta.*

Calcutta. Bārhut (in the former Nagod State) is situated about a hundred miles southwest of Allahābād, where from the once much-frequented highroad from Vidiśā (Bhīlsa in Bhopāl) to Pātaliputra (Patna) a side-road branches off to Kaúsāmbī and Banāras. When the Greek conqueror Menander (c. 155—140 B.C.) invaded Central India, he marched along this very route and through Bārhut when the stūpa was just completed. According to an inscription on its eastern gateway it was erected under the Śunga emperors, but other inscriptions mention donations by several queens of the Mitra dynasty, rich merchants, artisans and nuns from all parts of India, Pātaliputra, Kaúsāmbī and Mathurā in the North as well as Nāsik, Karhād in the Deccan, Berār, even from the farthest South.

The railing and its gates and pillars — all that survives — are curiously massive, as if the masons had been afraid that the imitations of a wood construction in the less elastic stone might not prove stable. And no less heavy and clumsy are the sculptures, the figures of tutelary yakshas, yakshīs, nāgas, vrikshakās (dryads) on the posts, the Buddhist scenes and fairy tales decorating the roundels (*chakra*) and half-roundels as well as the connecting beams, and finally the creepers, flowers, fruits and animals embellishing the coping stones. The pillars are bundles of badly imitated Aśoka columns. The statues hardly emerge from the stone block, many are of a hieratic rigidity, though others attempt a certain movement, one leg bent, the arms detached, resting on the hip or holding the branch of a tree. The reliefs are flat, the scenes composed as if they were seen from above, overlapping of figures being avoided as far as was possible.

The figures themselves are short, often out of proportion, clad in grotesque, boorish costumes.

And notwithstanding all these weaknesses, this art is a delight. One feels that the artists did their best, that they worked carefully and had something to say. The figures have a natural dignity and they are charged with an unconscious energy. The scenes are vivid, full of a naive joie de vivre, a keen observation of the world, an eagerness to narrate the homely fairy-tales which the Buddhist monks had turned into edifying biographies of the Buddha's former lives, as a monkey, an elephant, a merchant, a prince, etc. The Buddha, however, is never represented; he had discouraged such idolization. Instead we see his lotus feet, the Tree of Enlightenment, the Wheel of the Law, his stūpa adored by hosts of gods, demons, men and animals. And likewise no detail is omitted, not the people in the streets, the women in the houses, dances and music, the animals of the forest, demons and gods. We see the wooden architecture of the time, the city gates of timber and bricks, with their towering galleries, the wooden houses of several storeys, with their vaulted roofs and vaulted dormer-windows, temples surmounted by a dome and gates of honour crowned by whole sets of arches, columns carrying the figures of gods, idols, etc. The individual figures are also well observed. We see them from the most amazing angles, *en face,* from the side, from the back, foreshortened from above, flying through the air. And the animals are on a level with man, with real characters, well observed, familiar.

The toranas represent a progress both in construction and decoration. They are much more elegant, the figures of their reliefs slimmer, their composition more complicated. The same can be said of the *stūpas of Sānchī* (founded by Aśoka), which the Śunga kings of nearby Vidiśa (Bhīlsa) vastly enlarged, placed on terraces and surrounded with new railings. The great stūpa has a diameter of 106 feet, its substructure one of 120 feet. Of the two smaller stūpas in which the ashes of several of the Buddha's most intimate disciples have been deposited, no. 2 has no terrace, but a nice archaic balustrade, no. 3 only a balustrade along the edge of the substructure and a detached torana in front of the stairs to the terrace. However, only the sculptures of stūpa 2 belong to this period, figures of yakshas and yakshīs in bold relief like those at Bhārhut, and decorative panels, still flat and clumsy, but less boorish and of richer composition. But most reliefs, especially all the toranas, were added only after the overthrow of the Śungas of Vidiśa by the Śātavāhana kings of the Deccan.

*The stūpas of Sānchi*

51

The next stage is represented by the round assembly hall at Bairāt (Virātapura) near Jaipur, and the slim Garuda column which Heliodorus, ambassador of the Indo-Greek king, Antialkidas, to the kings of Vidisa, had set up to 'Vasudeva (i.e. Vishnu-Krishna) the God of Gods' at Besnagar near Bhilsa.

The Śunga style reached its consummation in the great balustrade enclosing, in a vast quadrangle, the Bodhi Tree and the *Chankrama* (i.e. the first walk of the Buddha after his enlightenment) at Bodh-Gayā in Bihār. It was erected under the last Kānva kings in the early 1st century B.C. The once heavy pillars and coping stones have now narrowed, decorated with well-modelled lotus-medallions enclosing male or female heads, or heraldic animals; the half-roundels on top of the columns bear Jātaka scenes represented by a few well conceived, though still somewhat thickset figures and accessories. The columns at the gates have rich scenes, in a likewise simplified architectural setting, some solemn, some depicting the sun god, Śrī the goddess of fertility and wealth, others of a charming gaiety, even frivolity; or they bear the images of gods (Indra) or of Yakshas and Yakshīs.

Even later are a few Jain votive reliefs (Āyagapata = Āryakapatta) found at Mathurā (north of Agra), in the time of the first Scythian *kshatrapas* (satraps) dedicated by rich hetairae and decorated with elegant reliefs of the Tīrthankars, with their symbols, columns and stūpas.

Stray Sunga sculptures have turned up also at various other places; Śunga terracottas, of an amazing wealth of subject (yakshīs, musicians, priestesses, Jataka stories, etc.) have been discovered all over Northern India, from Bangarh and Tamluk in Bengal to Ahichhattra, Bhītā, Rairh and Mathurā in the west, and Timbarwa (Gujarat) in the south.

A most lively procession of chariots incised on a brass water vessel (now in the Victoria and Albert Museum, London) may convey a faint idea of Sunga painting.

SĀTAV ĀHANA ART — Early Indian art went through its golden age in the Śātavāhana Empire of the Northern Deccan. The Śātavāhana kings had risen in south-eastern Maharashtra on the decline of the Mauryas or Śungas somewhere between 200 and 100 B.C., had extended their power to Central India about the middle of the 1st century B.C., were repulsed between 80 and 125 A.D. by the Scythian Kshaharāta Satrap Nahapāna of Western India, recovered Mālwa, under Gautamīputra Sātakarni in the early 2nd century A.D., but were then pushed back for good into the Deccan; instead, they extended their power along the valleys of the Godavarī and Krishnā to the eastern coast. Though very little is known of its political history, the Śātavāhana empire was a great commercial and cultural power. To its western ports there came the Roman fleets in search of spices, diamonds and pearls, and the wars with the Kshatrapas were fought mainly over the control of these ports. From its eastern coast ships sailed to Ceylon, Burma, Malaya, Java and Annam. And its prospering merchants presented Buddhist shrines and monasteries near the capital, Pratishthāna (Paithān south of Aurangābād), along the trade routes over the Ghāts to the western coast, near the river ports of the east and, of course, also in the conquered Śunga territory of the north. When the Kshaharāta and later the Kārddamaka Satraps of Western India annexed part of the Śātavāhana empire, they, too, patronized the influential monks and, bringing no art of their own, had more monasteries built by the masons and sculptors who had already worked under the Śātavāhanas. When the Śātavāhana empire disintegrated early in the 3rd century A.D., its art was still cultivated for some time by some local dynasties of the eastern coast, the Ikshvākus and the Brihatphalāyanas.

After their defeat of the Śungas the Śātavāhanas had annexed Mālwa. The stūpas of Sāñchī were completed under their rule in the second half of the 1st century B.C., by the addition of four gates (toranas) to the Great Stupa (I) and of one to Stupa III. These gates are generally counted amongst the greatest masterpieces of Indian art. They consist of two stone pilasters ending in groups of elephants or dwarfs (yakshas) which, in their turn, support two vertical posts ending in Tri-ratna symbols (i.e. the Wheel of Law and a Trident symbolizing the Buddha, his teachings and his monastic order) through which posts three slightly curved horizontal stone beams seem to pass. These gateways are as elegant as if they had in fact been constructed of timber; the architects achieved this miracle by erecting statues of tree goddesses, yakshas, horsemen, lions, etc. which seem merely to form part of the symbolic decoration, but which in reality act as supporting brackets. At the bottom the pilasters carry figures of protective yakshas. Where the posts cross the horizontal beams, there are lion, horse and elephant groups, with or without riders. On the posts there are reliefs of stūpas or of the goddess Śrī-Lakshmī, of the Heaven of Indra, or of the Tushita Heaven of the unborn Buddha. On the pilasters and beams various Jātakas are described, or the chief events in the Buddha's life in which, however, he is always indicated merely by symbols.

*The gates of Sāñchī*

These scenes are a real delight. In comparison with the Bhārhut sculptures, how easy, how natural everything is! Natural, but not naturalistic! There are still many conventions, the composition is still dictated by decorative considerations, many figures are awkward, the customes are still rural. But all this has become unconscious. What obsesses the

Northern gateway of the great Stūpa (I) at Sānchī (inner side). On top of the posts the *Triratna* ('Three Jewels' = symbols of *Buddha, dharma* and *samgha*). In the centre a damaged 'Wheel of the Law' (*dharmachakra*) and a yaksha. On the top beam a representation of the 'Story of the Six-tusked Elephant'; on the middle beam the Buddha's Enlightenment; on the lowest beam the 'Story of Prince Viśvantara' (who gave everything away, even his wife and children). At the ends of the middle beam peacocks (the escutcheon of the Maurya emperors); on the panels of the posts flower vases (pūrnakalaśa), a symbol of fertility and also of the Buddha's nativity; also the goddess Lakshmī and a stūpa, symbol of the Buddha's death. Ist century B.C.

artists, is the discovery of a world not long ago haunted by magic and demoniac forces, a world now, however, friendly and interesting since the Buddha has overcome the forces of evil. What observation of nature, what charming landscapes, what a loving description of plants and animals, what an acute sense of the expressive gestures of men, women, gods and goddesses! There is grace, a spirit of solemn joy, reminding one of Italian art in the age of Masaccio and Fra Angelico, however far apart in time, space and tradition both arts may be. It was these masterpieces which set the model for the art then springing up in the heart of the Śātavāhana empire, the Deccan.

Of the ancient towns there (e.g. Paithān, Karhād, Kolhāpur, Maski, etc.) we know hardly more than a few excavated house foundations and potsherds, though even here finds of Roman coins, bronzes, terra sigillata and glass testify to an intensive international trade. But where the Deccan plateau falls down to the western coast in wild gorges and cliffs, Buddhist monks settled in cave monasteries along the trade routes from Kalyān, an excellent river port north-east of Bombay, via the Bhor, Nānā and Thāl passes, and also further south. For the broad horizontal strata of alternating hard and soft stone lent themselves excellently to the excavations of caves (lena, gumpha), well protected from the heat of the summer and from the rains of the monsoon, exposed to cool winds and in the most beautiful scenery. Such caves were not only inhabited by monks, but served also as summer retreats and places of amusement where the young rich enjoyed the dances and favours of courtesans (lenaśobhikā).

*The cave monasteries of West India*

The excavation of these rock-retreats was achieved, in the absence of explosives, by driving rows of vertical holes into the bottom of parallel tunnels, then wooden bolts were inserted and soaked with water, thus detaching huge stone blocks. This process was repeated until the general excavation of the cave was about finished, after which the finishing off and the sculptures were done with a chisel.

The design of the caves imitated brick and timber structures of the time, but varied according to local conditions and time. The cells of the monks were generally cut out beneath overhanging rocks, or along cliff ledges, sometimes accessible only by means of ladders, bridges and tunnels. First they consisted of a small, simple or pillared hall with stone benches for beds, or surrounded by cells, while by the side of the entrance an underground cistern was dug out, fed by a complicated catchment and aqueduct system. In later times big square pillared halls, with about a dozen cells and a porch, were preferred.

A vast hall with long, low stone tables served as a refectory. At a suitable spot there opened a vast chaitya hall ending in a small stūpa. Nearby, more stūpas are often found, and even cemeteries for the ashes of the deceased monks.

There exist some dozen similar cave settlements, and the number of individual caves goes into many hundreds. Exact figures cannot be given because there exist many, half-forgotten, caves, difficult to reach and of little artistic interest. The greatest group is that of Junnār, on the Deccan plateau due east of Bombay, consisting of 150 caves, the second is that of Krishnagiri (Kanheri) north of Bombay, comprising 87 caves; then come those of Ajantā and Ellora (Elūrā) having 27 and 33 (partly later and also Brahmanical and Jain) caves. Most consist of about six or a dozen excavations.

*The Bhājā caves* The earliest cave settlement in the Western Ghāts is that of Bhājā (near Lonavla) of the 1st century B.C. to 1st century A.D. where the entrance of an open chaitya hall with a projecting vault (imitating timber construction) is framed by high towers, balconies and dormer windows, going over into two storeys of monks' cells. The sculptures in the oldest hall, representing guards with swords and spears, the sun-god Sūrya driving in his chariot over a cloud demon, and the god Indra on his elephant, are curiously clumsy and primitive, compared with the contemporaneous reliefs at Sanchi. The chaitya hall of Bedsā, 6 miles east of Bhājā, is very similar, also that of Kondāne (in the grandiose gorge north of Khandala) the figural sculptures of which, however, are much better.

Yet the chaitya halls of Kanheri and Kārle (opposite Bhājā) reveal a considerably later stage (1st century B.C.—early 2nd century A.D.). The slightly sloping octagonal shafts of the columns in the earlier caves have made way for powerful vertical pillars rising on pot bases and ending in round cushion capitals, whose steplike projecting abacus slabs carry groups of divine couples sitting on elephants (as on the Sānchī toranas). At Kārle there is still a wooden ceiling inside the rock vault! The apse is occupied by a small stūpa rising on a high cylindrical base. In front, the hall is enclosed by a screen surmounted by a music balcony above which the broad "chaitya-window" lets in a flood of light on the stūpa inside. Between the three arched entrance doors of the screen, lifesize groups of donors are represented in high relief, skilfully, though somewhat naively modelled; unassuming, but of a natural dignity. But this is not yet the façade proper. For there is an anteroom, at Bedsā, enclosed by heavy pillars bearing groups of elephants, and at Kanheri and Kārle by another screen of two pillar storeys. At Kārle this is decorated with a false front of many storeys resting on elephant groups; at Kanheri huge Buddha statues were later added there. Outside there follows a court fenced off by a balustrade in which stone columns, topped by lion groups, once carried the "Wheel of the Law". The Kārle hall in particular is a masterpiece of a solemn grandeur, affirming life, notwithstanding the Buddhist message of renunciation. Life was regarded as imperfect, but not as necessarily sinful. And it was enjoyed, until its pleasures lost their attraction, on this earth and in successive heavens. Asceticism was merely a short-cut to the desireless bliss of Nirvana.

The last stage is represented by the Pandu Lenā caves near Nāsik (early 2nd century A.D.). There is here a rather small chaitya hall with a rich entrance, consisting of one central door under a projecting arched roof, and a huge chaitya window in the middle of a false front where small stūpas and arches fill the spaces of a colonnade of fully developed columns (like those at Kanheri); and the monasteries of Ushavadāta and Gautamīputra Sātakarni have rich front halls of full-fledged columns which rest on inverted abacus-plus-pot bases and end in cushion capitals bearing even richer abaci and lion (Kshatrapa symbol) or elephant (Śātavāhana symbol) groups, interconnected by balustrades above a frieze of dwarfs. At Junnār the Ganeśa Cave has very similar pillars. The Mānmoda cave (erected by a "Greek" Chanda) has a half-lotus above the entrance, the petals of which bear the image of the goddess Śrī-Lakshmī.

*The Pandu-Lenā caves*

Other groups of caves are further south in Mahārāshtra. Others are north of the capital Paithān (especially at Aurangābād, Ajantā and Pitalkhorā) of which those of Ajantā especially have become world-famous. At that time, however, Ajantā was still a small monastery consisting of two chaitya halls (nos. 9 and 10) which contain the only preserved remains of Śātavāhana painting — Jātaka stories rendered in a very naturalistic style similar to that of the reliefs around the Sānchī stūpas (unfortunately in very bad condition) — and three monks' quarters (nos. 8, 12, 13). Similar caves have been found also in Mālwa (Dhamnār and Kholvi) and in Saurāshtra (Sanā, Jūnagadh and Talājāh), but none are of special interest.

The Śātavāhanas had conquered the eastern coast probably in the years about the beginning of the Christian era and had moved the centre of their empire thither when their power in the west declined. Here conditions were very different. Wide river valleys emerged into

*The stūpas of the east coast*

Maya's Dream and the Birth of Buddha. Marble relief from the Stūpa of Amarāvatī, c. A.D. 100. 5′2″ × 3′2″.

a coastal plain, where only occasionally hills presented a site for a monastery. Remains of such monasteries, partly carved out of the rock, partly built up in dressed stone, have been discovered at Śankaram, Gurubhaktakonda and Durgakonda (near Rāmatīrtham), Vijayavāda (Bezwāda), Salihundam and Sengamedu, etc. Much more interesting are the ruins of the great stūpas and monasteries in the plains, at Guntupalle, Bhattiprolu, Goli, Gudivāda, Gummididurru, Ghantaśālā, Jaggayyapetta, etc., but especially at *Amarāvatī* and *Nāgājunikonda* on the lower course of the Krishnā. Most of these stūpas have been utterly destroyed; but excavations have been able to trace at least their ground plan and many of the richly sculptured marble slabs with which they were once decorated; and as quite a number of the Amarāvatī reliefs have representations of the great stūpa as it looked in successive stages of its history, we can form a fair idea of those once splendid monuments. The core of these stūpas was no longer massive; only the centre containing the relic chamber and the encircling buttress wall supporting the upper circumambulation passage (*pradakshināpatha*) were constructed of bricks. The space between, divided into a series of compartments by radiating walls, was filled with rubble. Behind the usual railing the stūpa rose on top of two storeys of marble reliefs. At the point where at Sānchī the toranas had been placed, a fenced-in forecourt, flanked by lion columns, led to a huge relief of a protective snake deity (Nāgarājā), later of the enthroned Buddha, behind which a balcony bore five slim columns (Āryaka), symbolizing the five heavenly Buddhas (Dhyānibuddhas).

The reliefs depict not only Jātakas, but the life story of the Buddha as glorified in the later scriptures (e.g. the Lalitavistara) now represented in human shape, surrounded by hosts of gods and genii, a glorious prince surrounded by thousands of beautiful women and servants, to become at last the wise world teacher before whom the gods are no more than poor, helpless beings. All the episodes of his career are elaborated in scenes of numerous figures, framed by richly decorative lotus roundels, animal friezes, etc. The earliest reliefs are almost as awkward as those of the oldest Bhājā cave. But then the style develops

*The life story of Buddha*

59

rapidly. The next stage represents the eastern counterpart to the architecture and sculpture of Kārle and Nāsik (elaborate pot-and-cushion columns decorated with reliefs of yakshīs and bearing lion and elephant groups, donors, etc.), and of Sānchī. At the same time life-size statues, in the round, of the standing Buddha and of his next disciples also turn up. Thereafter, however, the figures become excessively slim and elongated, drawn in very low relief. The zenith is reached by the middle of the 2nd century, in the reign of Pulumāvi Vasisthīputra, showing an impressive virtuosity in the treatment of the individual elegant figures, gracious movements, complicated composition, and an almost illusionary scenery. It is certain that the artists were acquainted with contemporary Roman art. For occasionally Hellenistic-Roman figures turn up, sometimes even slavishly copied; likewise figures of foreign Scythian mercenaries. And the composition has evidently learned from the no less complicated scenes on Roman sarcophagi and triumphal reliefs. The Roman trade port, Poduké Emporium (Arikamedu-Virampatnam near Pondicherry) was in the neighbourhood, and also overland trade was intensive with Rome, Parthia and the Kushāna Empire of Northern India. However, this Roman influence should not be overestimated. Śātavāhana civilization may be regarded as perhaps the most productive and freely creative phase of Indian culture, and such foreign elements as it absorbed were in the line of its own natural development.

*Ivory reliefs of Begrām* That this artistic exchange was mutual, is proved by some minor, but very beautiful finds: in Gujarāt a small à-jour bronze relief of two girls (late 2nd century, Baroda Museum), probably part of the decoration of a throne; in Begram, the ancient Kushāna summer capital Kapiśi in Afghanistan, numerous ivory reliefs (early 2nd century, Musée Guimet and Kabul Museum), once parts of the jewelry chest of a princess, in the most variegated techniques — bas relief, sunk relief, à-jour work, engraved drawings, sculptures in the round — most of them describing scenes of harem life, occasionally with some traces of Roman influence; and finally the ivory statuette of the goddess Śrī-Lakshmī (1st century), excavated at Pompeii, probably brought from India by some merchant, as the Indian form of Venus Stella Maris, the protectress of seafarers.

*Ikshvāku style* The last phase of Śātavāhana art belongs to the small dynasties (Andhrabhrityas) who inherited the eastern provinces of the disintegrating empire after c. 227 A.D. At Jaggagyapetta and Nāgārjunikonda the family of King Purushadatta of the Ikshvāku house donated sev-

Two girls. Panel from the ivory chest of an Indian Princess. śātavāhana work, 1st century A.D., from Begrām in Afghanistan. About original size. *Musée Guimet, Paris.*

eral stūpas, monasteries. Āryaka pillars, chaitya halls. These monuments are just as opulently decorated, but they are modest in size, their reliefs are small (about 1′ high; 2′—3′ under the Sātavāhanas), their workmanship becomes increasingly careless and mannered, and their character increasingly erotic. At Nāgārjunikonda the adjoining monasteries had large pillar halls (*mandapas*) but rather small chaitya halls, with apses and cult stupas, yet without arcaded naves. One monastery there served also as a hospital consisting of four stūpas as radiators of beneficent magic influences surrounding the rooms of the physicians and the laying-in rooms of the patients. There were a theatre and an arena, and in the palace a vast enclosure for the complicated ritual of the *asvamedha* (royal horse sacrifice). Along the river stood several temples of yakshas and of the god Kārttikeya; their sanctuaries resembled chaitya halls but were enlarged by a pillar hall in the centre of an enclosed court with a gateway and with (or near) a sacred pond (tepe kulam). The characteristic features of the later South Indian temple, all, turn up here for the first time in the 3rd century. Similar Siva temples, shaped like chaitya halls, have survived at Ter and Chezarla (4th—5th centuries), and they have also been the prototype for one part of the later Pallava temples (7th century).

KALINGA ART About the same time as the Sātavāhanas built up their empire in the Deccan, the Meghavāhanas or Chetis formed a kingdom in Kalinga (Orissa) which under Khāravela (1st century B.C. — 1st century A.D.) for some time became a considerable power. Its capital was Kalinga-nagara, probably identical with the strong fortress of Sisupālgarh, the mighty square fortifications of which, with eight gates and broad moat, can still be seen south-east of Bhuvanesvar (now the capital of Orissa) near the Maurya provincial capital of Tosali (Dhauli). In its centre a group of 16 monolith pillars is the last remnant of the grandiose royal palace. At Bhuvanesvara, probably on the spot of the present Lingarāja Temple, Khāravela erected a huge Jain temple, enclosing a beryl hall decorated with painted walls and ceilings. Although this temple has disappeared, the retreat for Jain *arhatas* (hermits) on Kumārī (now Udayagiri) hill, 6 miles north-west of Bhuvanesvar, donated by him (Hāthigumphā inscription), his queen (Chhota Hāthigumpha), his probable father Vakradeva and his probable successor Vadhuka, is still a favourite tourists' centre. Some of the caves (Hāthigumphā, Mañchapurī or Rānī-kā Naur) imitate the shape of houses, with courtyard, two storeys, balconies, guardian or elephant statues at the entrance, and comfortable rooms inside. But several of the hermitages have curious entrances, shaped like the head of a tiger (Vyāghragumphā), cobra, boa constrictor or frog. Inside, the larger caves have false arches and balconies, and very lively, but loosely composed sculpture friezes, representing the story of a Jain saint, with domestic, hunting and war scenes. Their style reminds one of the reliefs on the Sānchī toranas, though the figures are bigger and more robust. The Ananta cave on the adjoining Khandāgiri hill has similar sculptures. Of the later history of the Cheti dynasty we know nothing; Śiśupālgarh declined in the 3rd century and was abandoned in the 4th.

Both the Kalingas and Āndhvas were enthusiastic seafarers and traders whose ships travelled as far as Ceylon, Burma, Malaya and even Cambodia and Annam. On Ceylon Śātavāhana art had a lasting influence. Though the kings of Anurādhapura had already begun to build palaces, monasteries and stūpas in Aśoka's time (Tissamāhārāma, Yatthāla Dāgaba; Mihintale; the Tissa Weva (lake), the Bodhi Tree and Thūpārama at Anurādhapura), the most important monuments were erected by Dutthagmani (161—137 B.C.: Thūpārama, Mirisvetīya Dāgaba, Ruvanveli Seya,Lohaprāsāda = Brazen Palace), Vatthagāmani Abhaya (89—77 B.C.: Abhayagiri Dāgaba, Elāla Sohone, Nuvara Vewa) and Mahāsena the Great (334—361: Minnerīya Lake, Jetavana Dāgaba and Monastery). These buildings slavishly copied the earlier and later Śātavāhana monuments, enlarging especially the dāgabas (stūpas) to gigantic dimensions (Ruanveli 300 feet high, Abhayagiri 350, Jetavana 400). Their sculptures represent an adaptation of the Amarāvatī style, endlessly repeating a few types ("moonstones" = door sills decorated with lotusses and the animals of Aśoka pillars; Nāgarājā = snake king stelas, pūrnaghata, etc.) even as late as in the Middle Ages (Polonnāruva and even Kandy), inventing or transmuting hardly anything, merely adding later loans in the course of time. But sculptures in the Amarāvatī tradition have been discovered also outside Ceylon in Malaya, Sumatra, Borneo and even Annam.

Support of same ivory chest of an Indian Princess. A yakshī, riding on a griffin, emerging from the mouth of a dragon. śātavāhana work, 1st century A.D., from Begrām in Afghānistān. About 7″ long.

*Musée Guimet, Paris.*

# IV. CLASSIC ART

When early Indian art reached its apogee and end on the eastern coast of the Deccan and overseas under the Sātavāhanas, another, more mature art tradition emerged in North-western India from the political and cultural confusion which the conquest of the decrepit Achaemenian empire by Alexander the Great had created.

The Greeks and Macedonians were numerically too weak to hold those immense Asiatic territories for long, and Hellenistic civilization was too alien to affect more than their Mediterranean fringe and some trade centres in the interior. On the other hand the Hellenistic impact generated a national reaction which was soon to weaken the position of Alexander's successors, the Seleucids. And this weakness offered to the Central Asian nomads an opportunity of conquering Turkestan, Afghanistan, Iran and Northern India. As they had no notable civilization of their own, these nomads took over from the Greeks, Persians and Indians what they needed for their new role as a ruling aristocracy. Thus a syncretistic culture developed in these semi-nomadic empires — Iranian-Greek, then Iranian-Indian in daily life, Zoroastrian or Buddhist in religion and literature, Greek in art. However, the foreign domination in its turn aroused an indigenous political reaction in Iran and India, creating a consciously nationalistic culture in Iran under the Sassanians, and in India under the Gupta emperors. Both were the result of a revision and reinterpretation of their traditional culture on the defensive against foreign influences; aristocratic-clerical-capitalistic, conservative in principle, but very active, refined and very open to new ideas and developments, as long as these could be integrated as ostensible age-old national traditions. On the defensive against new hordes of Central Asian Barbarians, both ended in militaristic chaos. The Sassanians finally collapsed before the Muslim Arabs while the Gupta Empire disintegrated under the onslaught of the Huns and their allies. The Sassanian tradition continued to be the model for Islamic Asia, though disguised by Arabic ideology. Gupta civilization became the ideal prototype for all later Hindu tradition, claiming to be old and timeless, preached by the gods and the *rishis* (saints) of yore. The Middle Ages had set in.

NEW CURRENTS

The Seleucids soon moved their capital to Antiochia near the Mediterranean and were content with a loose control over their provinces in Iran and beyond. Already in 304 B.C. Seleukos Nikator (321—281 B.C.) ceded the Panjab and Afghanistan to the Mauryas and granted considerable autonomy to Bactria (Turkestan and Northern Afghanistan). His successors lost Northern Iran, then all provinces east of Syria to the Parthians. Thus the Greek Satraps of Bactria, in order to strengthen their position, conquered Afghanistan and North-Western India with the help of mercenary armies composed of Greeks and Bactrians. But they were too weak to impress Hellenistic civilization on India, except in their excellent coins, and occasional monuments, e.g. the semi-Greek capitals from Mathurā and Sārnāth. The older coins, especially those of the conqueror Demetrius (c. 200—165 B.C.) and of Eukratides (c. 170—155 B.C.), are very beautiful, in the best tradition of Praxiteles and Lysippus. After Menander (c. 155—140 B.C.) however, the Greeks, being mixed with Iranian and Indian blood, began to lose their identity. They adopted the Persian instead of the Attic monetary standard, their coin portraits lost freshness and animation, designs of Eastern motives were introduced on the reverse side, the Greek inscriptions were increasingly superseded by ones in the Irano-Indian Kharoshthi script. In 140 B.C. Greek rule collapsed in Bactria, and about the middle of the 1st century B.C. in India too.

However, this proved to be not the end, but the beginning of the influence of Hellenistic art; for with the fall of the Greek empire its art was no longer associated with foreign rule and became a convenient medium for the needs of the new conquerors, first the Indo-Parthians (c. 19—65/78 A.D.), then the Scythians and Kushānas, both Central Asian nomads (85 B.C.—19 A.D., and 65—230 A.D.; in Kabul, Kashmir and the Western Panjab again c. 390 A.D.—3rd quarter of 5th century). The Parthians, though Iranian nomads, were "Hellenophiles", i.e. they encouraged Hellenistic civilization and art in their empire. The Parthian satrap of Śakastān (Seistān), Gondophares, who founded a short-lived Indian empire, did the same at his Indian capital Takshaśīla (Taxila).

*Taxila*

Taxila, an old trade and university centre, situated in the pleasant Haro Valley, 20 miles north-west of Rāwalpindī at the foot of the Hazāra mountains, was occupied by Alexander the Great after his victory over Porus and was a provincial capital under the Mauryas. It was the residence of Indo-Greek, then Scythian kings, and afterwards of Gondophares; and it continued to be an important town until it

Indian coins.
*Top left:* Silver coin of Euthydemos II of Bactria (about 200 B.C.).
*Top right:* Gold coin of the Mughal emperor Jahāngīr (1605—1627) with the portrait of his aged father Akbar the Great.
*Bottom left:* Gold coin of the Gupta emperor Kumāragupta (414—455) attacking a rhinoceros, possibly referring to his invasion of Kāmarūpa (Assam) *Bottom right:* Gold coin of Kushāna emperor Kanishka (1st half of 2nd century). Original sizes. *British Museum, London.*

was destroyed by the Huns in the 5th century. The investigations of
Sir Alexander Cunningham and the excavations of Sir John Marshall
at the beginning of this century have demonstrated that the site of
Taxila moved considerably in the course of time. The irregular old
town seen by Alexander and the Maurya prince-governors occupied
the low Bhir mound on the farthest western end of the Hathiāl ridge
to the south of the Haro Valley. But Aśoka had already built several
stūpas in the neighbourhood, that of the "Sacrificed Head" at the
northern end of the valley (Bhallar Stūpa), another in memory of his
blinded son Kunāla, victim of the lovesick Queen Tishyarakshitā, at
Sirkap, and the great Dharmarājika Stūpa in the Tamrā valley east of
the old town. The Greeks then founded another town, on the Sirkap
plateau bounded on the west by the lower course of the Tamrā, as
they could there use the last peak of the Hathiāl ridge as an acropolis.
The Scythians abandoned the lower town (Kachcha Kot) of Sirkap
and strongly fortified the upper town which was also the residence of
Gondophares. The Kushānas finally abandoned Sirkap, constructing
a strongly fortified rectangular camp town in the plains. A considerable portion of Sirkap has been excavated. Outside the town (at Jan-
diāl) was a great Greek temple *in antis*, in the *opisthodomos* of which
a broad staircase led up to what seems to have been a sort of small
Babylonian temple tower (*zigurrat*). Though the temple is mentioned
by Philostratus in his life of the Hellenistic prophet-preacher Apollonius of Tyana as the place in which Apollonius and his companion
Damis spent the night, awaiting the king's permission to enter the
town, we do not know to which deity it had been consecrated; it was
probably a Zoroastrian fire temple. From the North Gate the main
street, crossed at a right angle by a number of smaller streets, led
straight to the acropolis. On both sides there were the houses of
prominent citizens, Buddhist temples and stūpas and also what seems

*Royal palace*  to have been the *royal palace*. From the Thirteenth Street one passed
into its Public Courtyard, which was surrounded by an audience hall,
offices and guest rooms; a corridor led to the Private Audience Chamber, guard rooms and various reception halls; north of these there
extended the harem, adjoining a Buddhist shrine. The architecture
of Sirkap is a queer mixture of pure Indian, Iranian and Greek forms.
For instance, the plinth of the so-called "Shrine of the Double-Headed
Eagle" (a stūpa) is decorated alternately with miniature reliefs of
toranas, chaitya-hall façades (crowned by the same eagle) and Greek
aedicula, between short Roman pilasters. It is not surprising that the

other finds reveal a similar cultural mixture, e.g. a white marble pillar with an Aramaic inscription in honour of a high official, a statuette of the Egyptian child god Harpokrates, a silver repoussé head of Dionysus, beautiful golden and silver jewelry (much of it lost during the disturbances in 1947), drinking goblets, lamps, terracotta figurines, shields, swords, caskets, scent bottles, finger rings, etc. For miles around the town there are monasteries and stūpas, the earliest ones of which have already been mentioned. As they were also increased, enlarged and embellished in the subsequent centuries, they belong, in the condition known to us, mainly to the Kushāna period and will be discussed in that context.

Typical *Parthian (i.e. Iranian) art* has not been discovered at Taxila. *Parthian art* This style, however, is amply represented by the red-polished pottery found in Western India, and even more by the stamped bricks which cover the floor of the Hārvan monastery in Kashmir. Curiously enough, these latter belong to a considerably later time (4th—5th century), so that the relief figures of Parthian horsemen, women, heads and busts appear side by side with early Gupta motifs.

About 65/78 A.D. the *Kushānas*, a horde of Central Asian tribes, GANDHĀRA overthrew the Indo-Parthian empire and established themselves as ART lords of an empire extending from Lake Aral to China and most of Northern and Central India. Their first princes, Kujala Kadphises I and Vīma Kadphises II, had been rather uncouth barbarians. But in *Kushānas* the 2nd century, under Kanishka the Great and his successors, Huvishka and Vāsudeva, the Kushāna empire became a first-rank political and cultural power. Thereafter it began to disintegrate; about 230 A.D. the Sassanians conquered the Central Asian provinces, whereupon most of the Indian vassals also made themselves independent. For some time the Sassanian crown princes, styling themselves Kushān-Shāh, ruled over a host of Kushāna princelings, until about A.D. 390 a related tribe, the Kidāras, who had occupied Bactria, emigrated before the advance of the White Huns to Kābul and reestablished for another century a Kushāna kingdom confined to Eastern Afghanistan and the Western Panjab.

As all the great trade routes (silk, gold and spices) of Asia, from China and India to Iran and Rome, passed through the Kushāna territories, the commercial towns there grew rich and quickly recovered from all political crises. Though the local culture in Khorezm (Khīwa), Sogdia and Bactria (Turkestan) was Iranian, in Afghanistan predominantly Hellenistic and in the Indian plains Indian, a certain cultural mixture was unavoidable and proved highly fruit-ful.

*Kushāna coins*   The *Kushāna coins* best mirror this syncretism. They were generally modelled on those of the Roman Empire, retaining, however Indo-Greek, Graeco-Bactrian and Parthian motifs, and evolving new Zoro-astrian and Indian features. On the obverse side, the head, bust or whole figure of the emperor is represented, standing, or sitting with crossed legs on a couch, in thick riding boots, wide, sagging trousers, a long stiff overcoat, with a pointed Scythian cap or mitre on his head, armed with spear, mace or bow, or holding a sceptre. A halo sur-rounds his head, and flames issue from his shoulders; for the emperors were regarded as *daivaputras* (sons of the gods). But on the reverse side a pantheon of Greek, Iranian and Indian gods appears in amazing confusion. There are still a few Greek names and figures — Zeus, Heracles, Helios, Hephaistos, Sarapis, Selene; but their very selection proves that they stand for indigenous deities. The Indian gods are not numerous — Buddha, Skanda (under several names), Śiva (Oesho). The majority of names, however, are Iranian — the sun god Mihira-Mitra, the moon god Māo, the wind god Vāta, Atsho the fire god, the war god Verethraghna, the Great Mother Nana(ia) or Anāhitā, and a few Zoroastrian abstractions like Kingly Glory, Perfect Rule, etc. However, a few types predominate: Mihira; Oesho-Śiva, standing, a trident in hand, in front of his sacred bull, sometimes four-armed and three-headed; Nana, sometimes also standing for Śiva's consort Pār-vatī; and the Iranian goddess of fortune, Ardokhsho, oft enalso meant to represent the Indian Hāritī or Śrī-Lakshmī. Individually, how-ever, the emperors had their personal inclinations. Kanishka was one of the greatest patrons of Buddhism, Vāsudeva bore the name of the Hindu god Vishnu-Krishna (not found on the coins), and the Kidāras were devotees of Śiva.

*Buddhism*   Although the image of the Buddha is found only on few coins, the archaeological monuments reveal to us that *Buddhism* was the most influential religion of the time. It had penetrated Afghanistan already in Aśoka's time, and in the Graeco-Iranian milieu soon began to evolve a distinct character of its own. It built up a whole set of new legends according to which the Buddha himself had visited his holy land "Gandhāra" (= Kandahār), consisting of the valley of the Kābul river, and also the neighbouring districts, the Swāt Valley (Udyāna), Taxila and Kashmir. Its character also changed. Instead of liberation from passions and salvation in the Nirvāna, active charity inspired by pity (karunā), and devoted faith in these divine beings exercising such charity, became the central dogma. Though an absolute Godhead was never acknowledged, a whole system of Bodhisattvas (beings qualified for Buddha-hood, but renouncing Nirvāna in order to help all living beings) and other deities was associated with the historical Buddha and his supposed predecessors and successor. These saviours assumed all the features of Iranian light deities and were represented standing or sitting on open lotus flowers (a Hellenistic-Egyptian symbolism), with flames emerging from their shoulders, and halos of light surrounding their heads. The most important of these gods were the future Buddha Maitreya, and the Bodhisattvas Vajrapāni (yaksha of Rājagriha and transformation of the old Vedic thunder god Indra), Avalokiteśvara the saviour par excellence, in later times Manjuśrī and finally Amitābha, "the Endless Light", with his western Paradise, Sukhāvatī. But as in India, so here the common people preferred more humble and homely deities — the yaksha Panchika, bringer of wealth, and his consort Hāritī, protectress of children.

Already under the early Indo-Scythians and Indo-Parthians the construction of stūpas and monasteries had begun. Now, thanks to the protection of the Kushāna emperors and the financial support of the wealthy merchants, they dotted all the hill sides of the Peshāwar, the Swāt, the Kābul valley, even the valleys of Baluchistan (Tor-Dherai) and beyond the Hindukush, up to Bactria (Balkh) and Bukhārā (= Vihāra, monastery). However, as the brittle schist (phyllite) of these mountains does not lend itself for caves, they were generally constructed as courts enclosing stūpas, on ascending terraces connected by stairs. Around Jalālābād (Fīlkhāna), Kābul, at Bāmiyān in the Ghorband Valley, at Kakrak, Mohin, and Aimak on the Tāshkurgān Road, and in the Tarim Basin of Central Asia, real cave temples and monasteries were also excavated. The older stūpas of Scythian, Parthian and early Kushāna times still resemble the Indian ones. But only that of Chakpat (near Chakdarra in the Swāt Valley) is a simple hemisphere on a platform. The others, like the Shpola on the Khyber Pass, those of Bīmarān, Bār-Robāt, Passanī, Deh-Rahmān, Gadara, Shinase, Amlūkdarra, the Surkh Tope, and those of Manikyāla (16 miles east-south-east of Rawalpindī) and Ushkur (Huvishkapura, near Barāmūla in Kashmir) consist of a low square platform, on which the stūpa proper is raised on a drum of approximately the same height as the platform. The platform and the drum are decorated with small Roman pilaster colonnades like those on the Double-Eagle Stūpa in

Taxila (Sirkap). It seems probable that this square platform was inspired by Hellenistic mausolea (which, in the last instance, had also developed from prehistoric tumuli); the colonnades, on the other hand, were merely the successors of the old balustrades, now merged into the wall (like those, in a different manner, in the late Andhra stūpas).

In the stūpas of the later and most common Gandhāra type e.g. at Hadda near Kābul, Alī Masjid in the Khyber Pass, Sultānpur, Nundara, Chahār Bāgh, Tope Darrah, Jamālgarhi, Takht-i Bāhī, Shahr-i Bahlol and Chārsadda (Pushkalāvatī or Peukaleotis) in the Peshawar plain, Mingora and Abbasahibchīna in Swāt, Pippala and Mohra Morādu near Taxila, the platform became much smaller, but also much higher, and was even duplicated. A monumental flight of steps led up to a rather narrow circumambulatory way round the stūpa proper, now a rather small hemisphere sandwiched between a tower of one to four successive drums, and a high set of umbrella roofs emerging from a conspicuous harmika.

*Stūpa of Kanishka* The extreme form of this type was the famous stūpa of Kanishka at Peshāwar (Purushapura), whose huge foundations (285 feet from side to side) were excavated in 1908—09 from the Shāhjī-kī Dherī mound nearby. Though the stūpa proper has disappeared, we know its approximate shape from the descriptions of Chinese Buddhist pilgrims, especially of Hiuan-Tsang (7th century). For it had been one of the wonders of its time, the highest tower in Jambudvīpa (India), as another famous pilgrim, Fa-Hian, says. It consisted of five storeys of stone (apparently the drum tower and the stūpa proper) rising to a height of 150 feet, then a richly carved wooden "harmika" of thirteen storeys and iron mast (400 feet high), the whole monument thus rising to a height of 638 feet, i.e. almost three times the height of the famous Qutb-Minār at Delhi.

In the numerous stūpas of the last Gandhara style (e.g. the Bhallār stūpa north of Taxila, the Hadda stūpas west of Jalālābād, the Shevakī stūpa south of Kābul and most of the stūpas in Swāt) the drums and the hemisphere are contracted into one round tower standing on a rather broad, square platform. Thus a stage was reached from which the Far Eastern pagoda could develop, though transformed under the influence of indigenous ideas. With the stūpas big columns (*stambha*) were occasionally connected, like the Minār Chakrī near Kābul.

In the monasteries (of which the best known are Shāh-Dherī — possibly the oldest one —, Bagh-Gāi, Haibak, Shotorak, Jamālgarhi and Takht-i Bāhī) the new stūpa type completely ousted the great chaitya hall. Instead, the principal stūpa was surrounded by a square or circle of small chaitya halls enclosing small stūpas or Buddha images, which were, in fact, no more than subsidiary chapels. The cells of the monks, the refectory, a square assembly hall, a scullery, kitchen and bath, generally formed a separate block in front of the great stūpa and its chapels. In the open space between, devout visitors erected a number of small stūpas. The cave monasteries (Bāmiyān, etc.) had cellas and rectangular, octagonal or round domed shrines and assembly halls interconnected by tunnels and decorated with statues and sumptuous paintings.

Very few shrines of other religions have been traced. The only ones of importance are the fire temple of Surkh Kotal in Bactria (2nd century), and the sun temple on the Khair-Khāna pass (4th century) near Kābul, both rather plain buildings, except for a few sculptures. Remains of Hindu temples, likewise very rare, belong to a much later period. This may seem surprising, in view of the opposite evidence of the Kushāna coins. But Buddhism then revered stūpas, monasteries and images, so much so that to the Zoroastrians and Muslims the name of the Buddha came to mean an idol (*būt*), and international traders had money to spend on such visible expressions of their faith. But most of the dominant Iranians attached little importance to the temple cult, and only the rulers were interested in fire or sun temples. Only when the orthodox Zoroastrianism penetrated under Sassanian overlordship, more attention was paid to temples (e.g. Khairkhāna). The local Hindus were probably content with modest shrines at the confluence of rivers, under odd rock formations, etc., such as we still see in the Himalaya. *Other religions*

Of civil architecture we know very little. But a number of fortifications are attributed to the Kushāna period, e.g. Begrām (the ancient Kāpiśi) near Kābul, Bīrkot and Udegrām in Swāt, the Northern Kāfirkot at the entrance of the Khurram valley, several other Kāfirkots (i.e. "forts of the heathens"), Giri, east of Taxila, and especially Sirsukh (the last city of Taxila). These latter ruins prove that the fortified rectangular camp so common, for instance, in Khorezm (Khīwa) was introduced by the Kushānas in India too. The walls of Sirsukh are 18½ feet thick, further strengthened, inside and outside, with a heavy buttress. Along their whole length these walls had two rows of loopholes for archers, the lower row being only five feet above *Civil architecture* the ground; but access to these loopholes was blocked by fire from the flanks, coming from huge bastions projecting at regular intervals of 90 feet. The excavation of the royal palace at Begrām has yielded the already mentioned Śātavāhana ivory box, Hellenistic plaster models, bronzes and Alexandrian glasses, but has not yet provided us with an idea of the palace as such.

*Gandhāra sculpture* The Buddhist monuments were decorated all over with innumerable statues and reliefs. They filled the intervals between the Roman pilasters and Indian columns in the walls of the stūpa platforms. They enclosed, in successive circles, the drums of the stūpas themselves; they crowded the chapels under trefoil arches and steep gables. The Buddha (and Bodhisattva) statues of the chapels generally reach half, occasionally full life-size, the figures of the reliefs vary between one to five inches. Jātakas are still represented; but much more common are the events of the Buddha's life, his antecedents in heaven, his miraculous birth, his marvellous deeds as a boy, his life in the harem, his flight and exchange of clothes with a beggar, his austerity, his victory over Māra "the Lord of this World" and his enlightenment, the first sermon at Sārnāth, many miracles and episodes, healing of the sick, resurrection of the dead, taming of mad elephants and dragons, but especially his multiple appearance at Śrāvastī, his conversions, and finally his death at Kusinagara.

All these statues and reliefs are executed in a straightforward provincial Roman — or more correctly late Hellenistic-Syrian — style. For this purpose the Hellenistic figure types were adapted. Zeus became Śakra (Indra), now a divine devotee of the Buddha; Apollo was transformed into the Buddha or a Bodhisattva; Heracles became Vajrapāni, Panchika, Indra or Śiva; the classical orator a monk; Athena a female harem guard; Silen Vajrapāni or a Yaksha; Tykhe Hāritī, Ardokhsho or Nanaia; the nymphs Yakshīs; the Dryad queen Māyā giving birth to the Buddha; the Atlantes Yakshas; and Nike angels in flight (*devatās*). The donor figures, of course, were taken from real life. Most of them are Indians with complicated turbans, though their dress has to some degree been affected by Syrian fashions; the ladies especially seem to have been influenced by Syrian hair styles. But there appear others too: primitive barbarians in riding breeches and pointed caps, or in tunics and flat caps, others in Indian costume, but with unmistakable Iranian or 'Gallic' features. Whole scenes are often just adapted from the repertory of the Hellenistic artist, in others there is evident inspiration from real life. In the landscapes

The Bodhisattva (the future Buddha) leaving his sleeping wife in order to renounce the world. In the background his groom Chandaka brings his turban. Stucco relief, originally painted, from Hadda, Afghanistan. 5th century. *Musée Guimet, Paris.*

one feels the Alexandrian nostalgia for nature, notwithstanding the Indian details, lions, monkeys, etc.

At first, scholars believed that the sculptures in the best Hellenistic style were the oldest, after which a progressive degeneration set in. Sir John Marshall then developed the theory that the schist reliefs were of imperial Kushāna and the painted stucco figures of Kidāra-Kushāna times. As a matter of fact, there seem to have been continuous imports

Stucco head of the Buddha, from a stūpa at Hadda near Kābul. The mark between the eyes (*ūrnā*), originally a hole, was later believed to emit rays of light, like the third eye of śiva and Devī. The hole in the forehead was probably formerly filled with a piece of rock crystal, mounted on gold. 4th—5th century.
*Rijksmuseum voor Volkenkunde, Leiden.*

of sculptor's models (like the great set excavated at Begram) and repeated immigrations of Hellenistic masters, as the continued contact with new style developments in the Roman Empire proves. But these masters had to rely on the collaboration of numerous indigenous sculptors of very different background and dexterity. Schist sculpture was restricted to the area where phyllite was common, and the prevalence of stucco on later Kushāna art was rather due to a shift of artistic activities to areas where schist was not available (Kashmīr, Taxila, Kābul, Bāmiyān, Central Asia). The quality of Gandhara sculpture, therefore, varied extraordinarily. There are great masterpieces by the side of clumsy apprentice work. The latter is in an overwhelming majority, because the few masters could not cope with the enormous demand for devotional reliefs, and because for the general decoration of the monuments the quality of the minor reliefs did not matter. To some degree, however, the brittleness of the schist was also responsible; for since very delicate work was impossible, the figures in the small reliefs had necessarily to be short and thick-set, and their modelling poor. But even in the best sculptures we feel a strain between the realistic approach of Western art and the mystic spirit of Buddhism.

By early Kushāna times a stylization had already set in. When the Sassanian victories weakened the contact with the Roman world where, since the 3rd century, sculpture had been quickly degenerating, other tendencies made themselves felt — Iranian and especially Indian. Mathurā sculptures and sculptors had from early times occasionally found their way to Gandhāra (e.g. the Hāritī of Skarah Dherī); later the ripe Mathurā style asserted itself; and when Gupta art rose in the 4th—5th centuries, its harmonious proportions, clearcut surfaces and serene expression made a strong impression on late Gandhāra art. However, in its last stage the latter made itself independent. The stucco statuettes of Hadda (near Kābul), Akhnūr, Ushkur (both in Kashmir), and other places (5th century) reveal a sort of Baroque impression strongly reminiscent of the best works of the Pergamene school — dead for many centuries — but in other cases also of the high Gothic art, which was many centuries ahead. The phenomenon of these striking parallels is still unexplained, but the enchanting beauty of the small statues and reliefs (many now in the Musée Guimet in Paris) is beyond question.

In the meantime Gandhāra sculpture (in painted stucco, a method introduced from Alexandria) had spread deeper into Central Asia. At

*Mathurā style*

Bāmiyān (on the route to Herāt and Balk) a group of cave monasteries had been excavated from the vertical cliffs of the Ghorband Valley. In the 5th/6th centuries several gilt Buddha colossi were carved out in trefoil niches, decorated with paintings of the sun and moon, or with flying minor deities. Though of little aesthetic merit, they impress by their overwhelming size (the two standing statues are 174 feet and 112 feet high; the sitting Buddha at the nearby Katrak 39 feet high) and are all the more conspicuous since stairs in the rock and a passage from the top of the cliffs make it possible to climb up to their heads. They have inspired similar statues in the Far East (Yunkang and Lungmen caves in China) as well as in India (the Buddha colossi of King Lalitāditya at Srīnagar and Parihāsapura in Kashmir) and beyond (Polonnāruva, Ceylon; Pagān, Burma; Chienmai and Ayūthia, Siam). Similarly the peculiar folds of their robes (made by hanging ropes over the huge bodies and then covering them over with stucco) have been copied by Buddhist artists in China. Still later (7th century) is another sanctuary at Fondūkistān, halfway between Bāmiyān and Kābul. Its clay sculptures covered by painted stucco represent the last, over-ripe phase of the Hadda style — slim, elegant figures in over-ornate costumes, sophisticated and yet weak and tired. In the Tarim basin, settlements of cave temples and monasteries line the trade routes between the Taqlamaqan desert and the mountains north and south of it. Other stūpas and temples, constructed in brick, wood and plaster, penetrated the desert along the rivers which lose themselves in the sands. Their stucco sculpture, done with moulds, shows a progressive degeneration.

*Gandhāra painting*
Of early Kushāna painting we know only the murals round the stūpa of Mīrān near the Niya oasis in Eastern Turkestan (2nd century). The winged angels emerging from a garland, the groups of monks and scenes from the Vessantara Jātaka are the work of "Tita" (Titus) and remind one of Pompeian frescoes, at any rate when compared to other Asian painting. In the much later murals at Bāmayān the Iranian element predominates while those at Dukhtar-i Noshirwān are almost pure Sassanian. Finally the murals of the cave temples of the Tarim basin (Khotān, Kashghar, etc.; the richest group is at Ming-Oi, near Kuchā), combine Gandhāran with local Iranian and Gupta-Indian features.

*Applied art*
Some Siberian bronzes found in the Hazāra district, as well as occasional foreign ornaments on Gandhāra sculptures are the only remains of the national art of the conquerors. Otherwise we find Hel-

lenistic work like the "Bīmarān Reliquiary" (now in the British Museum), a golden casket set with costly stones, showing, in embossed work, the Buddha and his devotees in pointed round niches, very much as later became the fashion in early Christian art. Its discovery together with coins of the Scythian (Śaka)) King Azes, as well as its style, place it in the first century B.C., just before the foundation of the Indo-Parthian Empire. The Kanishka Reliquiary, found in the foundations of the gigantic Shāhji-kī Dherī stūpa, is a golden cista, encircled by a frieze of lively Erotes holding a garland behind which the meditating Buddha, the sun god and moon god and minor deities appear scattering flowers. In front Kanishka himself is standing. This garland frieze is very similar to the angel frieze at Mīrān. Around the lid there runs a frieze of flying *hansas* (swans), while on its top the figures of two Bodhisattvas flank the preaching Buddha. The work-manship of "Agiśala" (Agesilaos), i.e. again a Hellenistic Greek, is rather crude. Though he must have had excellent models for the

Terracotta figurine of a girl wrapped in a sārī.
Mathurā, 1st—2nd century. 5" high.
*Baroda Museum.*

friezes of hansas and erotes, the Asiatic figures, which he had to do himself, are clumsily executed, completely out of proportion and with monkey faces.

CLASSICAL INDIAN ART In Afghanistan, Hellenistic art was the dominant cultural force for about a thousand years, and its final echoes (in Kashmir) lasted until the 10th century. In Central Asia its influence was decisive until the 7th century, and it was responsible for many aspects of early Buddhist art in China and Japan. But in India proper it spent itself in the Western Panjab, Mānikyāla, east of Rāwalpindī, being its easternmost outpost. Beyond that it can be traced up to Mathūra on the Jumnā, but merely as an undercurrent within the national Indian tradition. And yet the influence of Gandhāra art must have been immense, not as a practical medium and model, but as a challenge to be overcome, stimulating Indian aesthetic consciousness.

*Mathurā* The principal scene of this encounter was Mathurā. Here the highroads from Central Asia via Taxila, from the Indus Valley via Mīnnagar, and from the gulf of Gujarat via Ujjayinī and Madhyamikā (Nagarī near Chitorgarh) ended in the fertile North Indian plain. Mathurā, therefore, was an old and important town, capital of the Saurasena tribe, later of a Nāga kingdom, provincial capital of the Mauryas and Śungas, a wealthy mercantile centre, one of the most holy places of pilgrimage for Hindus, Buddhists and Jains, and a great centre of art and learning. Yet it was for centuries under foreign rule, a capital of Greek, Scythian and Parthian war lords and a winter residence of the Kushāna emperors. Here the foreigners were not passing adventurers, but everyday neighbours, who could not be ignored and against whom the Indians had to marshal all their cultural resources. At Mathurā, therefore, classic Indian art was born.

Unfortunately, for these same reasons, Mathurā has been destroyed and rebuilt many times. But the mounds surrounding the present small town cover (badly disturbed) ruins of a number of once-famous monasteries and temples, e.g. that of Jamālpur, the Buddhist monastery of emperor Huvishka; the Katra; the Yaśa Monastery; the Saptarshi Tīlā, the Guha Monastery; Bhūteśar a Buddhist and Kankali Tīlā a Jain stūpa; while at Māt, some 7—8 miles to the north, a family temple of the Kushāna emperors yielded portrait statues of Vīma Kadphises, Kanishka and of their vassal Chashtana, the founder of the Kārddamaka dynasty of Western Indian satraps, as well as a number of unidentified Scythian portrait heads. Though no ruin has hitherto been properly excavated, stray architectural fragments and

Bust of a lady. Red sandstone, Mathūrā. 2nd century A.D.. *Museum voor Volkenkunde, Leiden.*

representations on reliefs prove that local buildings of the time were built in a late form of the Śunga-Āndhra style, though with a light sprinkling of Hellenistic motifs, e.g. Roman pilasters along some plinths, or door frames vaguely imitating the Roman-Syrian scheme, though every detail was related to the pure Indian tradition.

We can observe the same approach in the sculptures. The already mentioned Kushāna and Scythian statues may be set apart as a foreign intrusion connected only with the imperial court; they are purely Iranian, hieratic in attitude, and very simply modelled, minor details being engraved in thin lines. Though closely related to the obverse reliefs of the imperial coins, they had no influence on either Gandharan or Indian sculpture, but are most interesting precursors of the Sassanian royal statues and investiture reliefs. It is uncertain whether we may add to this group the Sphinx capital from Chaubāra as well as several other horned heads.

*Sculpture* Typical Gandhāra works are the stūpa drum from Dhruv Tīlā, the Hāritī statue from Saptarshi Tīlā and a relief of Heracles with the skin of the Nemean lion. Roman prototypes are also seen in several triton reliefs, various Buddhist torana lintels and some Bacchanalian groups (connected with the Yaksha cult). The heads of a married couple on a pilaster from Īsāpur remind one immediately of Roman tombstones. And yet, if you look at the detail, nothing foreign can be detected either in the torana lintels or in the Īsāpur relief; the Roman prototypes have not been imitated, but completely transposed into the Indian style. And the overwhelming majority of the Mathurā sculptures are in the purest Indian style. As a matter of fact, the sculpture of Mathurā, for centuries under foreign rule, is less affected by Hellenistic art than the reliefs of Amarāvatī or Nāgārjunikonda to which the Greeks and Romans came only as individual mariners and traders. And this resistance apparently was conscious. For in the reign of Kanishka Mathurā sculpture underwent a curious change. The previous sculptures had followed the general course of early Indian art, from very clumsy to lively compositions, like the votive relief of the courtesan Āmohinī (14 A.D.) and elegant works such as the so-called "Holī" relief (late 1st century A.D.), or an Ayyagapatta (Āryakapatra) dedicated by another courtesan, representing a towerlike stūpa surrounded by yakshīs and flying angels. Thereafter, in the slim and elegant, finely worked and polished figures of the yakshīs, *mithunas* (erotic couples) and genre scenes on the pillars of the Bhūteśar balustrade we witness the same development as at Amarāvatī — but with a difference. The figures are generally bigger, the scenes simpler. There is nothing of the naive freedom of the Āndhra compositions. The postures as well as the anatomical details of the figures, the composition of the groups, their balance, the mutual relations of all details are carefully studied. We can make the same observation about the sculpture in the round, in the statues of Buddhas, Bodhisattvas, Yakshas, Nāgas, Hindu gods, etc. They start from the old yaksha statues, soon grow into vigorous figures standing or in the yoga posture, become temporarily disorientated by the impression made by the Gandhāra Buddhas, absorb and transform some iconographic details (e.g. the folds of the monk garment and the short curls on the head) and at last grow into a really grand conception of the Enlightened One in which nothing of the Gandhāra and, in the last instance, of the Hellenistic

Head of a young man (Bodhisattva?). Stucco work from a stūpa in Hadda, 4th—5th century. *National Museum, New Delhi.*

style can be discovered. And yet, this whole change is intelligible only as a result of the contact with Hellenistic art which by that time had became highly formalized, possessed a theory of art and an elaborate canon of proportions, a system of poses and postures, and a fairly fixed stock of types and compositions. However, what we encounter here is not an imitation of the Hellenistic theory and canon, it is an Indian counter-theory and counter-canon with very different ideals. It is sufficient to have a look at the Buddha from the Katrā Mound or at his companions, with their bodies completely controlled by the spirit, or at the yakshīs of the Bhūteśar balustrade, very sexy and yet motherly, to experience the complete difference in outlook between Mediterranean and tropical man.

*Rise of a*
*national culture*
As a matter of fact, Mathurā sculpture was only one aspect of a general cultural revolution then in full swing, which in the end resulted in the birth of the classic national state, the Gupta Empire. This revolution had already begun under the last Mauryas and had been supported by the Śunga and Kānva emperors, and also by the Śātavāhana kings who, in restoring the popular customs suppressed by the Mauryas, reinstalled the brahman priests. But for the time being the disorganized mass of local cults and sects, of mythical and epic traditions was merely a popular undercurrent, in no way a match for the well-organized Buddhist and Jain monk-orders which had the support of the wealthy merchants, of some of the ministers and of many ladies in the royal families. But as time went on, these cults began to coalesce. The leading Hindu sects, the Bhāgavatas and the Pāśupatas, began to annex innumerable local yaksha cults, declaring these minor deities to be no more than local forms or human incarnations of their own chief deities. The foreign invasions gave a further impetus to this development. Greeks, Scythians and Kushānas understood only theistic cults, with images, sacrifices and a simple faith. Most of them were converted to Vaishnavism or Śaivism; moreover they introduced the cult of the sun god Mihira-Helios who was identified with the Vedic Surya.

Thus the foreign conquerors found themselves in accord with the indigenous aristocracy which gained increasing importance during these endless wars. For the foreign domination tended to do away with all surviving democratic trends above the level of parochial autonomy. By and by another ruling class of officials and officers evolved who, in their turn, formed a more or less closed aristocracy, together with the millionaire financiers. Thus the many comparatively democratic tribal societies were slowly submerged by a new aristocracy of a much broader and, at the beginning, rather international outlook. This new society, and especially the foreigners, needed a common lingua franca. But already before the time of the Buddha the living Sanskrit language of the early feudal period (the background of the Mahābhārata War and of the Brāhmana-Upanishad literature) had broken up into about a dozen folk dialects. The brahman priests and the bards, on the other hand, had conserved the ancient language and literature, and the more their influence grew again, this rather simple language was turned into an artificial, but clear medium of cultured communication. It was popularized amongst the aristocracy through the recitation of the great national epics , the Mahābhārata and Rāmāyana, religious hymns and philosophical and political literature gradually incorporated into these epics. In the centuries between the fall of the Mauryas and the rise of the Gupta Empire they found their final form.

In the 2nd century A.D. the sophisticated classical Sanskrit had in most parts of India become the carrier of a refined court culture different from that of the masses. It was understood at the court of Kanishka, as the works of his poet laureate Aśvaghosha prove; it was no less familiar at the Mahākshatrapa court, as the Girnār edict of the Great Satrap Rudradāman shows. Whoever wanted to belong to "society" had to absorb this upper-class culture, its refined manners, its affected language, its artificial poetry, its snobbish art interests Fundamentally it was a secular movement, and amongst its principal protagonists were the great courtesans (ganikā), rich and elegant, living in beautifully decorated houses full of statues and murals, accepted at court (as in the Italian Renaissance), good musicians, dancers, actresses. But this secular movement would not be intelligible without the background of an intensive theological and philosophical activity. Under foreign rule, however, such a cultural movement, capable of challenging foreigners with an equivalent, if not greatly superior civilization, inevitably aroused a national spirit (as in Germany in the time of Schiller and Goethe). An Indian dynasty describing this cultural renaissance on its banner, had every chance of uniting the Hindu world because it would be enthusiastically welcomed by all patriotic Indians. This dynasty was found in the Imperial Guptas.

The Guptas had been an obscure feudal dynasty which, in the days of Kushāna supremacy, had gained control of the former imperial cap-

*Classical Sanskrit*

THE GUPTA
EMPIRE

ital, Pātaliputra. By his marriage with Princess Kumāradevī, heir of the Lichchhavi state, Chandragupta I became lord of the whole of Bihār, added to it parts of Bengal and of the Ganges plain and began the Gupta Era as a sovereign ruler in A.D. 320. His successor Samudragupta (c. 328—76) conquered most of Northern India, made Assam, Nepal, Kumaon and the tribal kingdoms in the Panjab (independent since the decline of the Kushānas) tributary, invaded the north-eastern Deccan and successfully weakened the Satraps of Western India. Chandragupta II the Great (376—414) annihilated the Western Indian satraps in a long campaign (c. 400—409), probably invaded Afghanistan as far as beyond the Hindukush (thus opening the way to Kābul for the Kidāras) and joined the Vākātaka and Kadamba kingdoms of the Deccan to the Gupta political system by marriage. Under Kumāragupta I (415—55) the Gupta Empire at last reached its zenith of power and spendour. Thus, within a few decades the Gupta emperors united all the parts of India which, though centres of the Hindu cultural renaissance, had hitherto groaned under foreign rule. Beyond, in the South, their leadership had no appeal. And indeed, the Guptas were themselves representatives of the Hindu renaissance, devotees of Vishnu, poets, musicians and great patrons of all the arts. During the war in Mālwa with the Western Kshatrapas and his stay at Ujjain after it, Chandragupta II rallied around him the famous "Nine Gems", the greatest intellectual lights of his time, and it was there that the characteristic Gupta style of life and art was born — consciously refined, a synthesis of sensitiveness, method, learned training and self-control. Under Kumāragupta's peaceful rule it spread over the whole empire and was accepted as authoritative by all the associated courts in the same manner as in the 17th and 18th centuries Versailles set the model for all European courts. Never was

*A golden age* India so happy, so rich, so refined. But after Kumāragupta's last year the decline of the empire set in. From outside it was attacked first by the Maitrakas, then by the White Huns and their Gūrjara allies, barbarian nomads from Central Asia who, massacring, burning and looting, extended their raids as far as Bihār and Mālwa. Thus the real power got into the hands of the generals who dominated Skandagupta's (455—67) weak successors and set emperor against emperor. In the 6th century the empire dissolved into a number of military states, under Vishnuvardhana Yaśodharman, the Maukharis, Maitrakas, later Guptas, Pushpabhūtis, etc., and fought the Nalas, Bhojas, Katachuris, Kadambas, etc. in the Deccan. The imperial coinage of pure gold was completely devaluated. The big cities shrank to a fraction of their former size, the depopulated districts were resettled with defeated and deported barbarians, the capitalistic merchant class disappeared, and with it Buddhism and Jainism lost their influence, art became a misused instrument of crude pomp and irresponsible luxury, literature became pedantic, religion turned towards mysticism. Gupta civilization twice seemed to recover, under Harshavardhana of Thānesar (606—647) and Yaśovarman of Kanauj (c. 700—752), but at last collapsed as a result of the conquest by Lalitāditya of Kashmir (c. 725—756).

The decisive innovation of the Gupta period is the Hindu temple. Small shrines of yakshas, of Vishnu, Vāsudeca and Śiva had been known for a long time. In the Kushāna period, possibly already in the later Śunga period, they developed into tower-like structures several storeys high, if we may draw conclusions from the controversial so-called "Patna Plaque" and reliefs at Sānchī and Mathurā. But their type became fixed only in Gupta times. The simplest variety is a square cella (*garbhagriha*) with a flat roof of stone slabs (*bhūmikā*). In front of it there is sometimes an open porch of two to four pillars (e.g. at Udaypur and Udaygiri in Mālwa, temples no. 17 and 31 at Sānchī) or of two columns between two lateral walls (templum in antis, e.g. at Tigowā). The entrance resembles that of Syrian-Roman shrines and there are other parallels which witness an inspiration from the West. But as at Mathurā, such inspirations were completely translated into Indian forms, and the general development of the Hindu temple went in a very different direction, though likewise inspired by novel ideas from the West, especially by Babylonian astrology. The further evolution of the Hindu temple was determined by four factors: 1) It was raised on a broad platform (*medhi*) like the Buddhist stūpas, with steps leading up on one (at Bhumarā) or all four sides (at Deogarh, later also at Bhītargāon and Gop). In the course of time these terraces were increased in number and the flights correspondingly extended until a tower on a cross-shaped ground-plan developed (at Ahichhattra, Nandangarh, Pahārpur, Masrūr, and the temples in Greater India). 2) A covered circumambulatory passage (*pradakshinā-patha*) was provided around the shrine, either a corridor lighted by windows or a pillar hall (at Nāchnā-Kuthārā; Deogārh; Lād Khān, Kontgudi and Meguti at Aihole in the Deccan; Gop in Kāthiawār). 3) By the addition of one or more storeys the cella became a tower rising above the pradakshināpatha. 4) Finally subsidiary chapels were added, either by the side of the steps leading up to the platform (Bhumarā), or on the four corners of the platform, e.g. the *panchāya-tana* temple at Osiān, 8th century) or on three sides of the sanctuary, the fourth being occupied by the porch (e.g. at Bajaurā in Kulū, 8th century). Instead of chapels of this kind reliefs on the three available façades of the temple served the same purpose (already at Deogarh). A fifth feature, the cult hall *(mandapa, vimāna)* did not become prominent before the Middle Ages.

*Microcosm of the world*

Probably already in the late 5th century the central idea emerged which was to guide the whole later development of the Hindu temple: The *Śikhara*. Like the Buddhist stūpa the Hindu temple too was interpreted as a sacrificial microcosm of the world. Its plinth was regarded as an altar, its superstructure the mythical world mountain Meru on which the gods lived. Its cella was a cave *(guha)* in which the image of the deity was hidden, like the brahman in and beyond the material world *(prakriti)*. The cella was surrounded by the chapels of other deities in their cosmic order, and its entrance had to accommodate further divine beings.

However, this concept was not fully elaborated before the 7th/8th century, and was worked out in all its implications only in the Middle Ages. The plinth, first no more than an unobtrusive platform, developed into a miniature house façade, consisting of a diminutive plinth, a pillared wall, a cornice and a miniature roof with dormer windows. The outside decoration of the cella developed in successive phases. First niches were introduced with scenes from the myth of the god worshipped in the temple, then real chapels or chapel-like niches, crowned by a chaitya-window as a gable, with blind doors or, more often, the images of those important deities which otherwise would have found a place in the subsidiary shrines on the platform or by the side of the flights of steps. For in a time of syncretism one did not like to displease any of the great gods, Śiva, Vishnu, Brahmā (or Kubera) and Sūrya, and later the Devī and Ganeśa in place of the last two. In the next stage the niches were reserved for the eight protector gods of the horizon (Parivāra Devatās) or World Guardians (Lokapālas or Dikpālas), old Vedic gods such as Soma or Kubera in the north, Īśāna (Śiva) in the north-east, Indra in the east, Agni in the south-east, Yama in the south, Nirithi or Virūpāksha in the south-west, Varuna in the west, Vāyu in the north-west. At last, in the Middle Ages both systems were combined — the important gods in projecting chapels, the Parivāra Devatā along the adjoining sections of the temple walls.

The decoration of the shrine entrance consisted of 2—7 step-like projecting friezes of scroll work (*Kalpalatā*) growing from the navel of
yakshas, and friezes of various deities. In the 5th century these were
yakshas like those on the Buddhist balustrade pillars, but reduced to
small erotic groups (mithuna). In the 6th century the Mithuna were
pushed aside (to the bottom or on additional friezes) by the figures of
the goddesses of the two holy rivers, Gangā (Ganges) standing on a
crocodile (makara) and Yamunā (Jumna) on a tortoise (the finest
examples being in the temple at Kharod, Madhya Pradesh, and the
two terracotta statues from Ahichhattra). Gangā and Yamunā soon became accompanied by parasol bearers and other attendant girls, but
were in their turn relegated to the bottom of the door posts or to their
upper corners. For now the friezes had to depict, in miniature chapels,
the Nine Planets (*Navagraha*), i.e. Sūrya the sun, Chandra the moon,
Mangala — Mars, Buddha — Mercury, Brihaspati — Jupiter, Śukra —
Venus, Śāni — Saturn, Rāhu the increasing, and Ketu the dwindling
shadow of the moon. In the 8th century the figures of kings, disguised
as divine shrine-guardians (dvārapāla) and queens, disguised as river
goddesses, were introduced into the richer and richer designs of the
sanctuary doors. Their lintel was at first decorated with mithunas,
later with flying minor deities, carrying garlands or playing musical
instruments in honour of the deity of the shrine, depicted on a projecting central coping-stone (or its accompanying animal, *vāhana*).
The development of the temple entrance was further complicated by
the introduction of a purely indigenous type — a miniature roof
(*pancharama*) supported by two slim columns (*stambha*). This roof
soon was dissolved into a sequence of 3, 5, 7 or 9 chapels in which
groups of gods or the planets found a place. These temple doors are
often of considerable size (e.g. those of the Telī-kā-Mandir, Gwalior,
are 35 feet high), as the late Gupta period had a predilection for huge
metal images which could be seen from a distance when the doors
were opened, especially when the temple possessed a high substructure or was situated on a hill or mountain.

The most conspicuous feature of the temple, however, was the spire
(*sikhara*). It developed from the upper storey of the early shrines,
through a progressive increase in number (on the average up to 9) and
amalgamation of storeys. These were reduced to mere decorative
façades, each with its plinth, wall, cornice and roof; then the plinths
and cornices, and finally the walls as well were eliminated so that only
a sequence of innumerable roofs survived, provided first with image

niches, then mere dormer windows (*gavākshas*) from which the heads of indeterminate gods looked down. The whole was crowned by a cupola (*śringa*) or a wagon roof (e.g. the Jagesvar temples, Telī-kā Mandir, Vaitāl-Deul at Bhuvaneśvar, and several temples in Greater India), or by a heavy wheel-shaped stone block (*āmalaka*). In the 8th century the outline of the spire became parabolic and its storeys often disappeared completely, being superseded by a maze of dormer windows, now reduced to a meaningless band of ornament.

Of course, the great monuments of the Gupta period have long since disappeared. What has survived, is provincial shrines, the greatest group of which has been discovered in the jungles of Central India, especially in Bundelkhand and Baghelkhand (Bhītargāon, Garhwā, Nāchnā Kuthārā, Bhumarā, Tigowā, 5th century); then in Mālwa (Pathārī, 6th—8th centuries, Mukunddarra, Udaypur, Deogarh, 5th century), in Gwālior (the huge Telī-kā-Mandir, c. 750) and its neighbourhood (Naresar, 8th century; Pawāyā, 5th century), in Rājasthān (Nagarī near Chitorgarh, 5th century; Chitogarh, Mandor near Jodhpur, 8th century), in Saurāshtra (Bileśvar, Gop, Gumli, Kadvar, Mādhavapur, Sūtrapāda, Thān, Viśavāda), in the Himālaya (Jageśvar, 6th—9th centuries; Masrūr, 8th century; Bajaurā, 8th century; Brahmor, 7th century) and in the old Vākātaka kingdom, along the upper course of the Mahānadī (Sīrpur, Rājim, Khārod, 6th—8th century). The monuments of Aihole, Bādāmī, etc. in the Deccan will be discussed later.

*Buddhist architecture* Buddhist architecture of the Gupta period, as we know it from the great centres of pilgrimage at Saheth-Maheth (Śrāvastī), Basārh (Vaiśālī), Sārnāth near Banāras, Bodh-Gayā, Sānchī and Kasiā (Kusinagara), as well as from the ruins of the great Buddhist university of Nālanda in Bihār, and finally from the ruins in Sind (Mīrpur-Khāss, Depar Ghangro, Thūl Mīr-Rukan) is much less interesting. On the one hand it followed the developments in Gandhāra, translating them, of course, into Gupta forms; on the other it took over, with slight adaptations, the new Hindu temple type. For in practice — though not in theory — Buddhism had now become a theistic religion. The stūpas became towerlike buildings, with chapel niches on four sides (e.g. the Dhamek stūpa at Sārnāth), or in fact a real tower of several storeys, decorated with image niches, on top of which a bellshaped *dhātugarbha* of modest proportions was placed (Nālanda). These stūpas were similarly often set on high platforms, at the corners of which smaller stūpas were provided. From this combined type the

The Mahābodhi temple in Bodh-Gayā, the upper storey consisting of the central shrine and four corner chapels. Erected in A.D. 526 above the Vajrāsana, the throne of the Buddha's enlightenment.

pagodas of Burma and the Borobudur in Java were later to develop. But temples now became equally common. A good example is the early Gupta temple no. 17 at Sānchī; another one, a shrine at the foot of the great stūpa at Nālandā. Two-storeyed chapels formed an integral part of every monastery, standing opposite the now rather monumental entrance building or occupying the centre of each side of the court yard. A brick temple on a substructure of several high terraces, approached by four long flights of steps arose in the centre of Pahārpur monastery (Somapurī Vihāra) in Central Bengal (c. 5th—9th centuries). At Bodhgayā the emperor Bālāditya (probably Narasimhagupta) built in A.D. 526 the huge Gandhikūta ("Mahābodhi Temple") around the Vajrāsana (diamond throne) of the Buddha, a Panchāyatana temple, 180 feet high, on a platform (26½ feet high) accessible via two vaulted staircases, which lead to a circumambulatory passage (13 feet broad) with four chapels, and the central sanctuary. The walls are organized in storey upon storey of chaitya-window niches, framing Buddha images. In spite of many repairs by the Burmese (A.D. 1105 to 1881) the impressive building still looks more or less as it did when the Chinese pilgrim-scholar Hiuan Tsang admired it in 635. The monasteries had the same groundplan as in Gandhāra, though sometimes (e.g. at Nālandā) they were several storeys high. The last chaitya hall still standing is the one at Sānchī (no. 18), a pious restoration of an older building. For otherwise chaitya halls had gone out of fashion.

*Cave monasteries* Under the Vākātakas, and even more under their successors, especially the Katachuris (and their vassals, the Mauryas of the Konkān) and later the Chālukyas of Bādāmī, Gupta civilization spread to the Deccan. Here cave architecture continued to be in fashion, not only because it was so suitable to this part of the country, but also because many of the old Buddhist monasteries had been excavated at local cult centres, some of which were now reclaimed by the brāhmans and also by the Jains. Even the old Buddhist monasteries (e.g. at Bhājā, Kanheri, Junnār and Nāsik) underwent considerable alterations in order to be adapted to the new dogmatic and ritualistic needs. The chaityaśālās of Śātavāhana and Mahākshatrapa times were redecorated with reliefs of the preaching Buddha surrounded by Bodhisattvas, and with murals in the Gupta taste. New chapels were carved out, devoted to the cult of the saviour Avalokiteśvara and to the Buddhist Madonna, Tārā. And many new monasteries were added to the old ones, in the modern taste of course, with vast square halls surrounded by colonnades and monks' cells, opening in front into a veranda, and ending at the back in a chapel full of huge Buddha and Bodhisattva statues. There is little ascetic spirit to be felt. Balustrades and railings are carved with figures not only of the Buddha, but even more with those of erotic couples (mithunas), and with ornaments of every imaginable type of jewelry. Walls and ceilings are painted not only with scenes from the Jātakas, the life of the Buddha and the celestial Buddhas and Bodhisattvas, but also with dancers, musicians, charming young couples in dalliance, etc. Had part of this decoration been taken over from the caves of the Lenaśobhikās (cave hetairae) and from the houses of the expensive city courtesans? The few late chaitya halls (cave 19 and 26 at Ajantā and Viśvakarman cave at Elūrā, 6th–7th century) also look very different, walls and pillars being covered with big reliefs of the sitting or standing Buddha, with or without attending Bodhisattvas, on a lotus held up by Nāga kings, or of the Master's Temptation by Māra, and his Parinirvāna, of innumerable smaller Buddha figures and a multitude of flying deities and erotic couples (the former yakshas), all immersed in a flood of jewel-like ornament. In the Viśvakarman cave, even the big chaitya window has been superseded by the pediment above the porch of Hindu temples, following the development of the time. The most important of these new cave monasteries are those at Ajantā (5th–8th century), so well protected in a narrow gorge that they were rediscovered by chance practically intact, after more than a thousand years, by a party out shooting, 63 miles north of Aurangābād; then Ghatotkacha (9 miles west of Ajantā, 6th century), Aurangābād (7th century), Elūrā (5th–7th century), and in western Mālwa those of Bāgh (halfway between Indore and Dohād in Gujarat, 5th century).

But by their side, or independently, the Hindus also laid out cave temples, generally in honour of the god Śiva. Their plan was to some extent adapted from that of the later Buddhist caves. The commonest type consists of a pillar-supported veranda, behind which one to three sanctuaries, sometimes surrounded by a circumambulatory passage, were cut out of the rock. In other cases this cella, now with four entrances, formed the centre of a vast pillared hall opening on three sides to antechambers and courts. The decoration is much simpler but also much more grandiose than in the Buddhist caves. The walls are plain or sparsely ornamented, and the pillars are rather sober. Lifesize or even bigger relief panels with mythological scenes embellish the walls, and the entrance to the sanctuary is guarded by

*Cave temples*

gigantic deities (dvārapālas). The most important examples of the first type are most of the cave temples at Elūrā, especially the beautiful Rāmeśvaram cave, the earlier caves (nos. 3—4) on the island of Elephanta (Ghārapurī) in the Bay of Bombay, the Udaygiri caves near Bhīlsā (Mālwa, 402—6), those of Lonād, and Ainkai-Tankai, Pātna, Karusa, Jogai Ambā, Dhokeśvara, etc. The earliest and richest example of the second type is the Jogeśvar cave near Bombay, a masterpiece of the best Gupta style, but, with the exception of a few reliefs, in a deplorable condition due to the far-gone erosion of the soft rock by the humid coastal climate. The others are the famous great cave temple (no. 1) at Elephanta, the Bhāmburda cave temple at Poona (much damaged by the Muslims), the Dumar-Lena or Sītākī Nahāni at Elūrā and the Bādāmī caves, all of which well be better discussed in a different context.

*Secular architecture* — Of the secular architecture of the Gupta period nothing is preserved. For the excavations at Bhītā and other places have yielded only foundations of lower and middle-class houses. But the classic authors, such as Kālidāsa, Bāna, Dandin, etc. have left us descriptions of gorgeous palaces, full of sculptures, murals and richly decorative carvings, though in most cases they were probably constructed merely of bricks and wood. But the "worldly" cave monasteries of Ajantā, Bāgh and Elūrā give us a good idea how these palaces looked. The wall paintings there also depict light garden pavilions of brick and slim wooden columns and roofs. A small summer palace of the 8th century, with columns decorated with loving couples, still stands near the bottom of a deep cistern at Osiān, north of Jodhpur. The best examples of military architecture still standing are the walls and moats of Aihole in the Deccan, and the almost inaccessible cliff forts defending the Chālukya capital Bādāmī (ancient Vātāpī) on the north and south sides; however, from the point of view of fortification technique they cannot compare with the Kushāna curtain walls and bastions of Sirsukh (Taxila).

*Architectural forms* — Certain architectural forms are common to all these buildings whether Buddhist or Hindu, religious or secular. The style is no longer an imitation of wood construction, but conceived in terms of dressed stone. The round forms have almost disappeared, everything consists of horizontals or verticals. The arch of the chaitya window has been reduced to the small dormer window (*gavāksha*), and even that is transformed into an ornament without tectonic function, a spiral, a band motif which can be duplicated, triplicated, broken up, ex-

94

panded into a surface decoration, without beginning or end. Only a small chaitya window was occasionally retained on the pediment above the temple porches until the 8th century, when it was transformed into the frame of a relief representing the deity of the shrine, most commonly Śiva as the heavenly dancer (Natarājā); later, filled with a demon mask (kīrtimukha) or a threefaced head, it became just another ornamental motive (bhadramukha). The genuine stone arch, though known (Bodh-Gayā, Bhītargāon, Mūl-Dvāraka, Mārtānd), is seldom to be found. Everywhere the construction consists of pillars and pilasters, horizontal beams and lintels, and ceilings of alternating stone slabs placed diagonally; the keystone is generally a big stone slab, sometimes of gigantic dimensions and enormous weight. Where vaults could not be avoided, corbelling was the rule; brackets, later often in successive rows, were preferred to arches. The columns were *Columns* much more complicated than in the previous period; but no strict canon was developed and varieties are legion. There were square pilasters, octagonal, sixteen-sided, and round columns, plain, fluted and helical. The base had disappeared, and instead the cushion or pot-and-foliage capital and brackets were richly developed. Normally the Gupta column is of a combined type. A simple variety consists of a square pilaster changing, by means of lotus half-roundels, into an octagonal or sixteen-sided shaft, to return in the same way to its original form. Most common is a square pilaster changing into an octagonal, then sixteen-sided, then round shaft ending in a cushion or pot-and-foliage capital supporting a cubic abacus and a simple or cross bracket. In many cases the round or fluted shaft is contracted beneath the capital, thus permitting the latter to deploy itself more freely. Often ornamental bands encircle the shaft at every transition, while the angles between the square, octagonal, etc. sections are filled with small figures of various genii. The sides of the brackets, finally, are most commonly allotted to flying angels and amorous couples; or tree goddesses or mithuna groups serve, themselves, as brackets. The relation between all these pillar parts varies immensely, as do the general proportions of the pillars — short and heavy in caves, in length about 6—10 times the diameter in average buildings, very slim in light wood constructions. The beams were decorated with lotus rosettes and reliefs, the ceilings with scroll friezes, flying angels and amorous couples in the corners, and big lotus rosettes in the centre.

The process of conscious formation already so evident in the Mathurā *Gupta sculpture* school of sculpture during the Kushāna period, reached its consummation under the Gupta emperors. It was the collective product of the poets and priests who provided the imagery, of the actress-hetairae who explored the potentialities of expression through the medium of the human body, and lastly of the sculptors who had a perfect knowledge of anatomy, but could never regard that latter as a means of expression by itself.

As the reader must already have realized, erotic scenes play a most prominent role in Indian art. The embrace of a beautiful, amorous woman was generally regarded as the highest bliss to be hoped for on this earth as well as in the lower heavens. Poetry thus elaborated female beauty in every detail — the scented hair, the languid eyes, the full breasts, the slim waist, the broad hips; and also all the refinements of diaphanous clothes, glittering jewelry, perfumes, make-up, mirrors and combs, pet-birds; and every movement, every slightest gesture betraying the passions of the beloved. But these observations were in their turn saturated with the old fertility symbolism connected with the yakshas and yakshīs, and, in reverse, penetrated religious art when the yaksha couples became an integral part of stūpa and temple decoration — the Kalpadruma and Kalpalatā ("Tree of Paradise"), the lotus and lotus-pond, the water-vessel (*pūrnaghata*), the tree goddess (now reduced to the Śalabhanjikā, the girl leaning against a tree and causing it to blossom by the very touch of her foot), the heavenly musicians (Gandharvas), Śrī-

Buddha statue from the Mahābodhi temple, Bodh-Gayā, 5th century. *Banāras Museum.*

96

Lakshmī the goddess of beauty, and later the Great Goddess in her many aspects as virgin and mother, goddess of lust and goddess of death.

The representation of the gods proved more difficult. Like other religions, Hindu religion visualized them primarily, but not always, in the idealized image of man, as heavenly kings and queens, or as ascetics and uncanny figures of the forest and cremation ground. But Hinduism was still developing, and Buddhism had suffered a far-reaching transformation. The religious imagery of the Mathurā school, therefore, never outgrew the experimental stage. It needed the four centuries of Gupta civilization to evolve a clearly defined iconography; and even that continued to have an experimental fringe. For a multitude of deities had to be assimilated, by declaring them special aspects of the leading gods, or their consorts, children, attendants and servants; and as four great systems were struggling for power, a number of gods changed their allegiance several times. Art represented the character of the various gods by a system of symbolic poses (*āsana* and *sthāna*), gestures (*mudrā*), weapons and instruments (*āyudha*) and attendant figures. Several heads were an expression of omniscience, many arms (and also legs) one of omnipotence. Yoga posture (*yogāsana*) with stiff body and crossed legs was a symbol of transcendence, an easy posture (*lalitāsana*), sitting on one leg, the other dangling down or drawn up, denoted the merciful presence of the deity, sitting in European manner (*pralambapāda*) or standing (*sthānaka*) authority, jumping (*ālīdhāsana*) demoniac dangerousness. The crown was reserved for heavenly kings (*kirīta-mukuta*), ascetics' hair (*jatā-mukuta*) was connected with transcendency, different hair styles (*bandha*) and jewelry stated the ranks of goddesses as well as of queens. Various positions of the hands (*mudrā*) were the signs of protection, teaching, explanation, prayer, meditation, warning, threat, etc. The attributes in the hands were either cosmic symbols like the club (physical power), lotus (biological growth), disc (time), conch (space, sound, logos), or instruments indicating the function of the particular god, e.g. sacrificial instruments for Brahmā, fire for Agni the fire god, disc, lotus and arrows for the sun god, lute and book for Sarasvatī the goddess of wisdom and art, mirror and lotus for Lakshmī, the skull drum for all demoniac deities, weapons for terrible gods and goddesses. These attributes could be combined in many ways, as in principle the great deities were regarded as being beyond good and evil, appearing in a benevolent or terrible form as their momentary

Minor goddess bearing a *chaurī* (yaktail fan). Bronze from the Akota hoard. 7th-8th century. ¾ original size. *Baroda Museum.*

function or the mood of the devotee demanded. For God is gracious and terrible, creator and destroyer, male and female, because in the last instance neither the one nor the other, i.e. transcendent. And in this respect there is no difference between all Indian religions — Vishnuism, Śaivism, Śāktism, Jainism, Buddhism. Postures, gestures, crowns, costumes might be differently grouped, but basically they were, with few exceptions, identical.

The pantheon of the Gupta period was, however, much simpler than that of the Middle Ages. The deity most venerated by the Gupta emperors was Vishnu, the heavenly king, sitting on the sun-eagle Garuda, or in the company of his consort Lakshmī, or sleeping as Nārāyana (creator) on the snake Ananta (eternity). His favourite incarnations were Rāma, the great hero and idealised king of the past, Krishna Vāsudeva, the founder of the Bhāgavata cult, now increasingly identified with the local yaksha of Mathurā, Krishna (as the Lifter of Mount Govardhana and the Killer of the snake king Kāliya; all his later adventures were first represented in the 7th century), and the semi-animal forms of Varāha (boar) and Nrisimha (man-lion) which became popular especially during the wars with the Huns. Kalkin on his horse, the saviour of the future, seems originally to have been a mythological form of Yaśodharman-Vishnuvardhana, a dictator who annihilated the Huns early in the

6th century and temporarily made himself master of almost the whole Gupta empire. Far less important was the cult of Śiva. His most common representations were the *mukhalinga* (a male member decorated with a mask of the god, like a Greek *herme*), and Lakulisa (a young Pāśupata ascetic, born c. 125 A.D. in Gujarat, author of the Pāśupata-sūtras, who then disappeared at Ujjain). His more demoniac aspects were known, but did not begin to play a role before the 6th century when the troubles of the time drove people to mysticism. Śiva's consort, the Great Mother, turned up first as Umā-Pārvatī (the heroine of Kālidāsa's Kumāra-Sambhava), and as Durgā Mahishamardinī (the virgin slaying the bull-demon). For some time she had to compete with "the Mothers", seven or eight frightful deities to be appeased by human sacrifice. Kārttikeya-Skanda-Kumāra, later her son, was first connected with these "Mātrikas". The elephant-headed Ganeśa then made his first appearance in Northern India. Sūrya was the favourite god of the military emperors of the 6th—8th centuries. Buddhism was dominated by the Yogāchāra school which regarded all Buddhas and Bodhisattvas as emanations of the "void" universe and set up a complicated system of Dhyāni Buddhas and Dhyāni Bodhisattvas, corresponding to the elements, senses, etc., and of their consorts, the Prajnās (wisdoms), the Madonna Tārā, the queen of heaven Mārīchī, the Prajnāpāramitā ("Sta. Sophia"), etc.

These secular as well as religious figures and scenes were represented *Dancing* in an apparently natural, very expressive and beautiful manner. However, in reality none of these creations was spontaneous, but the result of endless study. At the terracotta reliefs of minor temples prove, the Gupta artists were quite capable of dashing off lively figures when they were not bound by the lofty ideals of court society. These ideals, however, demanded measured, harmonious movements, and a face never distorted by excessive passions. Thus expression had to be achieved by means of poses and gestures. And this was the research field of the dancer-actresses. Indian dancing has developed from the folk dance, and has a distant similarity e.g. with Spanish dances. But it differs from European dance in so far as the steps start from the heel instead of from the toes (a result of wearing *chappals*, i.e. leather soles, held merely by a strap across the toes). Stage dance by professional dancing girls developed very early at the courts and in connection with temple festivals. By the time of the Gupta emperors, Bhārat Nātyam (as this style of dancing, which was preserved in th South Indian temples, is called today) was already fully developed, at least in its basic approach and movements. It probably resembled in many respects the pantomime in Imperial Rome, and also modern Ballet, though choreography is much more elaborate than that of classical Franco-Russian ballet. It distinguishes postures of the body (*sthāna, bhanga, āsana*) and head, of the arms (*hasta*), of the hands (*mudrā*) and of the feet (*pāda*), even movements of the neck and eyes, appropriate for the expression of every sentiment or for the narration of every possible sequence of events. It is thus more than a rhythmic pantomime, for a flow of additional gestures describe an imaginary scenery as well or the actions of imaginary partners, etc., without, however, upsetting the principal pantomime. These additional gestures rather form an undercurrent comparable to the elaboration of moods, scenery, subconscious thought, etc. in modern music since Richard Wagner. However pedantic, even abstruse all these detailed distinctions and classifications may look on paper, when danced by a really first-class artist, they fuse into a fascinating masterpiece which keeps great audiences under its spell for days and nights.

*Stage and sculpture* In the Gupta period this body language of the stage was transferred to sculpture. Already the oldest theoretical treatise, the Vishnudharmottaram declares that sculpture and painting cannot be understood without a knowledge of dancing, and that, without music, dancing cannot exist at all. This explains why Indian art was never naturalistic in the crude sense of the word. Early Indian art did not care. Classical Indian art did not want naturalism. For it was too much permeated by a sense of harmony and rhythm, and saturated with the poses and gestures of the dance to envisage anything other than rhythmical idealized forms of a clear two- and three-dimensional structure, often approximating to abstract geometry, and yet living and tangible. However, this idealization started from a thorough, loving study of the human body, of animals and plants; and it was only in later, decadent times that textbooks and ready-made artists' models became more important than nature.

This classical style developed first at the court of Chandragupta II at Ujjain in the first decade of the 5th century. In the reigns of his predecessors, Chandragupta I and Samudragupta, a somewhat harsh imitation of the Mathurā school (e.g. the Mankuwār Buddha, Kārttikeya in the Banāras Museum, Samudragupta's horse at Lakhnau), even late offshoots of the Śunga style (e.g. the Trivikrama relief at Gwālior, the Śiva-Pārvatī group from Kosām, or the Krishna stele at Mandor) were still characteristic. However, their gold coinage, first

Vishnu-Nārāyana as the primordial Godhead on the snake of Eternity or Adantaśāyin. Lakshmī massaging his feet. Relief from the Gupta temple at Deogarh near Lalīpur, Central India, about A.D. 500. 4' 11" × 3' 10".

inspired by Kushāna-Roman models, soon evolved a great number of original new designs.

In the Udaygiri caves near Bhīlsā in Mālwa, in the first years of Chandragupta's campaign against the Mahākshatrapas of Ujjain, a remarkable imagination created the images of important deities, the Mukhalinga, Skanda, Ganeśa, Durgā, Vishnu, Nārāyana, dvārapālas, and especially the gigantic boar-incarnation of Vishnu raising the earth-goddess from the chaos in the presence of adoring gods and saints. But the style is brutal, sometimes even clumsy.

*Classic Gupta sculpture* And then, after the conquest of Ujjain, Chandragupta's coins reveal a new style, elegant and ornate. For the first time the masses of curls (in the 6th century in fact periwigs) and the elaborate, jewel-clad costumes so characteristic of classic Gupta art, turn up at the same time as Roman features in architecture. Under Kumāragupta's peaceful rule this style became generally accepted, but also soft and often somewhat effeminate. The wonderful Buddha statues found at Mathurā and at Sārnāth near Banāras are mild and gentle, and yet they are sustained by a real spirituality, a will to help and enlighten, inspired by a mind which has understood the basic evils of the world and feels endless compassion for the miseries of all living beings. In the Khoh *mukhalinga* the sexual member of the god has been reduced to an almost meaningless herme and instead, we are face to face with the bust of the god who is the origin and essence of the world, half ascetic, half king, a noble face, majestic, inexorable and yet mild, sunk in deep meditation, the great yogī whose very dreams are the stuff of this universe. This nobility is very common in Gupta sculpture of the 5th century, but it is rarely so spiritual, and remains vague, rather a matter of good breeding (viz. the mythological and epic reliefs of the Deogarh temple, Buddhist stelas (*urddhvapattas*) from Sārnāth and Garhwā, the statues of the snake-stūpa Māniyar Math at Rājgir, the Gangā relief from Besnagar, the reliefs from Dah-Pārbatīya in Assam, the Khijing sculptures, etc.). And soon it turned into a smooth superficial elegance (the Vishnu of Mathurā, the Bodhisattva in London, the Sultānganj bronze Buddha, the Brahmā statue from Mīrpur-Khāss in Sind, the Lokanātha of Sarnath, etc.). The relief scenes never achieve the freedom of the scenes at Amarāvatī and Nāgarjunikonda; they are like living pictures set on a stage without depth, but never in real scenery.

*Decline* With the decline of the Gupta empire this serenity disappeared. The sculpture of the 6th century (e.g. the Mandasor stelas and the Sāmlajī

Mother goddesses), are charged with nervous tension — heavy bodies, with stark light and shadow contrasts, but full of restlessness and a visionary mysticism behind the outward display of superhuman energy. In the 7th century, sculpture again became light and elegant, but careless and lacking internal structure and expression. It was the product of studios which apparently had quickly to satisfy the ever changing political powers of the time. In many cases it is quite evident that the artists merely used famous earlier creations as models and adapted them to their needs. For instance, one of the Deogarh reliefs (Nara-Nārāyana) was thus adapted, on a smaller scale, at Bādāmī, or the teaching Buddha on a lotus (e.g. Ajantā) was transformed by very slight alterations into Lakuliśa (at Chitorgarh, Elūrā and Elephanta). On the other hand the composition of the reliefs became richer, consisting of many over-elongated and richly dressed figures in an equally pretentious setting. In the 8th

A mother goddess (Nandā or Bhadrā?) Schist statue from Sāmlajī (North Gujarāt) 5th-6th century. 2′ 4″ high. *Baroda Museum.*

century this mannerism was unnaturally exaggerated, the modelling becoming hard like metal, the figures swinging excessively in their hips, the gestures pathetic but empty. However, individual great masterpieces can be traced (e.g. at the Telī-kā-Mandir at Gwālior, probably the funeral temple of Yaśovarman of Kanauj); but the majority of sculptures are clumsy, badly proportioned, static and lifeless. The competent masters still living could no longer train pupils who understood the spirit of Gupta art, but merely masons who faithfully copied the iconographic types without sensing anything beyond the most obvious crudities. In the temples of Naresar near Gwālior only a last flickering of the Gupta tradition can be discovered. But the same struggle between excellent Gupta models and barbarian local art can be traced in the 7th and 8th centuries over all the border areas of the Gupta world: at Brahmor in Chambā, Vasantgarh, Bhīnmal and Osiān in Rājasthān, Kapurī in Gujarat, Aihole in the Deccan, Nalatigiri in Orissa. The dying civilization handed its heritage on to young peoples just entering history — the Gūrjaras, Chālukyas and Oriyan tribes.

*Gupta painting* Most of what has been said about Gupta sculpture applies also to painting. It was just as artificial as sculpture, just as perfect during the golden days of the Gupta empire, and degenerated into equally dead mannerism in the centuries of decline. It was much more common than sculpture. For some training in painting and good judgment were part of the general education of the upper classes. Portrait painting and discussion of pictures, therefore, belong to the plots of the classical Indian drama (e.g. Bhavabhūti's *Uttara-Rama-Charitra*). And courtesans were expected to be able to paint well. Murals, and also panel pictures were found in every good-class house, temple or monastery. Wandering monks used pictures of the gods and Buddhas, their miraculous deeds and the tortures of hell painted on cotton cloth as illustrations to their popular sermons.

But very little has been preserved. Some fragments at Dengaposhī and Sītābhinjī in the jungles of the Keonjhār District, Orissa, are the only remains of the early Gupta style. Only the murals in the Bāgh caves in south-western Mālwa are classical Gupta. Those in cave monasteries nos. 16 and 17 at Ajantā belong to the reign of the last Vākātaka ruler, Harishena (c. 475—500). Some fragments in the Bhājā and Bedsā caves may also be of the Vākātaka period or slightly later. Ceiling paintings in the Do-Thal and Tin-Thal caves at Elūrā may be attributed to the time of Katachurī supremacy. Most of those at Ajantā were executed under the Katachurīs and the Chālukyas of Bādāmī, especially under Pulakeśin II (609—642). The real Gupta paintings have the same qualities as the contemporaneous sculptures. The outline predominates, but only slightly. The colours are applied with well-balanced, compact surfaces. But the lines are not emphasized, and discreet shading and transition by means of curls, or-

A flying goddes. Mural in cave temple No. 17 at Ajantā, end of the 5th century A.D. An example of the highly refined style of life and art in Gupta times.

A couple of lovers (*mithuna*). From cave temple No. 17 at Ajantā.

naments, etc. achieve effects coming very close to picturesque interpretation. The individual lines as well as the composition of whole
scenes is rhythmic and decorative. The scenery shows perspective, but
prefers a steeply rising stage with little depth, where the individual
scenes are grouped one above the other, though in apparently natural
transition. There is much loving observation of near nature, but no
feeling for landscape. We cannot judge what colour combinations
were favoured, as many of the paints have deteriorated. Today a deep
brown combined with a strong lapislazuli, turquoise green and white
predominates. The figures are very beautiful and sometimes full of
intense feeling. At Bāgh there is a bevy of girls dancing a folk dance
(*garba*) around a man, apparently a foreigner; at Ajantā a charming
group of heavenly musicians (*kinnarīs*); at Bāgh as well as at Ajantā,

loving couples and men in quiet discussion; at Ajantā the dignified promenade of a king and queen in their garden, surrounded by a circle of courtiers; at Bāgh a solemn procession on horseback; at Ajantā a dying princess in the arms of her despairing attendants; at Bāgh a deeply moving couple of weeping ladies. They are all great masterpieces.

In the 6th century a Baroque mannerism appears and a stronger accent on outline. Men are strong and women voluptuous with pathetic gestures and feelings. The Great Bodhisattvas of cave I and II at Ajantā, the processions of kings and queens, etc. make a profound impression.

*Mannerism*

In the Ajantā murals of the 7th century, already under Chalukya rule, the outlines resume their fluency, the figures show a lighter elegance. But the paintings tend to become coloured drawings. The mannerisms of the 6th century are exaggerated in the unnatural, sagging eyelids, curved arms, thin bodies with immense breasts, etc. And on a closer investigation one discovers that a good part of the work has been done with stencils. But all these weaknesses are glossed over by a-fashionplate sensuousness and masses of curled hair, jewelry, textile designs, etc., in glaring contrast to the ascetic ideals to which the monks were supposed to be devoted. The many loving couples have in most cases nothing to do with the Jātaka stories which form the official theme of the wall decoration. Did the artists, in their desire to complete their extensive work quickly, just introduce part of their accustomed repertoire for princely harems and courtesans' houses? Or had the moral discipline of the monks already become so lax?

Thereafter, in the late 7th and early 8th centuries the rapid disintegration can no longer be hidden. The lines are dead, the colours cold, the figures grotesquely misproportioned, and the stencils clumsily put together. Gupta painting was dying.

*Applied art*

Gupta industrial art is largely unknown. The majority of objects found in excavations reveal a certain affluence even among the non-privileged classes. In particular, great quantities of terracottas have turned up for minor temples and house-shrines, decorative bricks, bronze vessels, etc. But very little is of the high quality to be expected from the evidence of the literary sources. However we possess many seal impressions, showing the most beautiful workmanship, of monasteries, law courts, municipalities, etc. Some small jewelry pieces are marvels of delicate and tasteful workmanship; and there are also some ivory figurines. The high standard of textile production can be inferred from the cobweb-thin costumes and exquisite designs represented on sculptures. As a matter of fact, the forms and designs of Gupta applied art are best known to us as the canonical vestments of religious, especially Buddhist, images not only in India, but in South-East Asia, Central Asia and the Far East. They are based mainly on floral motifs with creepers, scrolls and flowers, often enclosing jewels or small holy images. Via a long detour over Central Asia, even our European crowns are an offshoot of the Gupta tradition.

*Decline of Gupta Art*

In the 8th century the spirit of Gupta art had long been dead. For in the three centuries after the death of Kumāragupta it had turned from a national ideal into a religious dogma. We have already seen how closely Gupta nationalism was linked with the rise of Hinduism, i.e. the synthesis of the national folk cults. Innumerable contradictory, sometimes wise, sometimes silly local myths had to be brought into a coherent system, and had to be harmonized with the Vedic ritual and the philosophy of the Upanishads and of the Yoga. This was achieved in the Purānas (Old Stories) — religious books pretending to be revelations as old as the Vedas or even the gods themselves, preached by the gods or by some *rishis* in a hoary past. Though they contain, no doubt, masses of old folklore as well as ritual, they were all composed mainly in the late Kushāna and the Gupta period, and even their oldest sections cannot claim to go further back than the time of the late Śunga or Kānva emperors. These Purānas claimed to be compendia not only of mythology and ritual but of all aspects of life, and thus chapters on history (in the form of ancient prophesies) and art were also incorporated. Hitherto, fine art had been treated as some of the Sixty-four Kalā's ("arts", or better "skills"), being placed alongside hairdressing, make-up, erotic caresses, flower arrangements, social manners, puns and jokes, medicine, mechanics, chemistry, etc. But the priests had a different approach. For them art was part of magic and ritual. A house could not be built without a number of ceremonies to protect it against fire, water, demons and other bad influences. A temple was an elaboration of a sacrificial altar, with all the complicated magic relations between its individual stones and the universe. An image (*mūrti*) was of interest only as an idol (*pratimā, archā*) or an attendant figure to an idol. It had value only insofar as its iconographical details expressed the underlying theology, and insofar as magic ceremonies had opened it to the presence of the godhead. A painting had to fulfil the same conditions. Its proportions stood in a relation to magic diagrams, its colours were symbols of cosmic forces.

These ideas were not new, but hitherto they had been a harmless undercurrent, because cultural life, religious ideas and artistic forms were in a constant flux. But Gupta civilization had attempted to set an authoritative, and therefore not very flexible ideal. When it broke up, when the imperial authority was shaken, when the cultured classes were impoverished and the masses uprooted, when the cultural tradition was in danger of being annihilated by the barbarians, people took refuge in religion, the emperors and nobles tried to bolster up their authority by means of divine sanction, and the priestly class became all-powerful. What had been theoretical discussion of aesthetic principles or textbooks based on practical experience (e.g. the chapter in the Brihatsamhitā), now became dogma. And the artists, forced into cheap mass production and grown accustomed to the use of models and stencils, submitted to a theological art theory and detailed rules of construction and composition claiming to be divine law. We have such art textbooks from the later Gupta period (the Vastu Śāstra for architecture, the Śilpa Śāstra for sculpture and painting), the oldest being the Vishnudharmottaram, the Bhārata Natya Śāstra and the Mānasāra.

Yet even in its death-throes Gupta art enriched most of Asia. When North India was overrun by barbarian raiders and the armies of Indian war-lords, innumerable artists became unemployed. Many turned to the south, and them we have to thank for the second blossoming of Gupta art in the Deccan during the 6th and 7th centuries. Others went to Nepal and Tibet, laying the foundations of religious art there; in fact, Nepalese art is but an independent branch of 7th century Indian art, influenced in the 9th—12th centuries by innovations from Bihar and Bengal, and thereafter developing independently. In Tibet King Sron-tsan-gampo imported Indian and Nepalese art in the 7th century, together with the Buddhist religion; and his successors invited more Buddhist missionaries from Bengal as well as from Kashmir. Other Indian artists found employment with the barbarian warlords of the North-west. In the 6th and 7th century Gupta art began to penetrate into the Central and Western Panjab, Kashmir, Afghanistan and Central Asia. In Kashmir it got a foothold under the Kārkota kings (7th—8th centuries); in the buildings of the great conqueror Lalitāditya (c. 725—56), especially at Parihāsapura, Mārtānd and Malot, Chinese and late Gupta sculpture were combined with a Roman-Gandhāra-Bengali architecture. In Afghanistan and Central Asia late Gupta sculpture and painting were no more

*Colonial Gupta Art*

than contributors to a hotchpotch of styles, mainly Gandhāran and Irānian, which became Chinese in the 8th century. In the Tarim Basin the Gupta element is most conspicuous in the murals of Ming-Oi (Kuchā). Via Central Asia, as well as directly, through the Chinese pilgrims who brought home small-size copies of venerated Buddhist images, Gupta-Buddhist art came to China and even Japan. The images of the Tien-lung-shan caves are merely a slightly Chinese version of Gupta sculptures; the same is the case with several stone sculptures and bronzes of the time of the "Six Dynasties", found in Southern China. Buddhist painting under the T'ang emperors, especially the murals of the Tun-huang caves at the western end of the Chinese Wall; and those of the famous Horyūjī temple in Japan (destroyed by a fire some years ago) are based on a Gupta tradition which seems to have been much more grandiose and sublime than the Ajantā murals which, in their time, had been no more than provincial products.

*Overseas colonies* The most important new field of Gupta art developed, however, in the overseas colonies of India — in Ceylon, Burma, Siam, Cambodia. During the later Anurādhapura period (until the 8th century) the Gupta fashion was taken over by the royal court and the Buddhist orders tending towards the Mahāyāna. To the first group may be attributed the palace (Ratnaprāsāda) of Mahāsena the Great (334—361), the Queen's Pavilion (resembling the wooden pavilions on the Ajantā murals) and Queen's Bath (Kuttam Pokuna), the royal pleasure gardens and baths near the Tissa Weva, a *pokuna* near the Loha Prāsāda, and the statue of a king near the Ruanveli Dāgaba, all at Anurādhapura. Further Sīgirīya, the residence of King Kassapa I (479—97), a town and vast garden palace strongly fortified with huge walls and moats, in the centre of which rises a unique volcanic cone, almost an imitation of the palace of the gods on Mount Meru, to which a ramp hidden behind a gigantic brick lion and a narrow passage along the vertical cliffs, painted with "cloud maidens" (or a procession of queens) once gave access. These grandiose ruins alone offer us today an idea of Gupta (or early Pallava) imperial palaces. And the Sīgirīya murals are the finest Gupta paintings outside India, more virile than those of Bāgh or Ajantā. The Kantaka Chetiya at Mihintāle had a relic chamber decorated with painted deities floating around the small dāgaba-shaped reliquiary placed on top of a stone model of the Meru. At Anurādhapura several monasteries (one with thunderbolt capitals), the Gedige and Daladāga relic shrines, and especially the Isurumuni Vihāra with its beautiful Gupta rock chapel and sculptures, have to be mentioned. Further, a number of heads from Mihintāle (Anurādhapura Museum), bronze statuettes of Bodhisattvas from Anurādhapura, Badullā and Palonnaruwa, possibly also the well-known brass figure of the South Indian goddess Pattinī Devī (a deified chaste wife) in the British Museum, finally murals discovered at Pulligoda Galkande near Polonnāruwa Hindagale, etc.

In Siam Gupta remains have turned up especially on the Malayan isthmus, at that time a shortcut on the sea-route to the Far East, at Takuapa, Jaiya (especially a fine Lokeśvara) and Nakon Srī Tammarat; then in the area of the ancient kingdom of Dvāravatī in Southern Siam (mainly Buddha statues of the 6th—7th centuries), occasionally also at Rājaburī, Prapathom and Chantaburi. On the watershed between the Menam and Mekong the most important town was Śrīdeb. Further east, the principal areas of Indian influence were the Mekong Delta (Funan) and Champā (the Annamese coast). In Funan, the sanctuaries of Preikuk, Hanchei and Āśram Mahā Rosei follow the early Gupta type; that of Prasat Bayang is reminiscent of the Baitāl Deul (Bhuvaneśvara), the Telī-kā-Mandir (Gwālior) and the Naresar temples. Bakong stands on a pyramid of terraces, thus forming the transition to the later Khmer shrines. Of the many sculptures from Angkor Borei, Prapatom, Vat Koh, Phnom Da, Kuk Trap, Romlok, etc., the so-called Stoclet Lokeśvara and the Harihara of Prasat Andet have become very well known. In Champā the temples of Mison (near the present Tourane) have śikharas with offset terraces, a wagon roof with pronounced endpieces and reliefs in the Gupta "folk style". Monuments in the Gupta taste

Cloud maiden. Mural in a recess in the cliff along the path to the top of the mountain fortress of Sīgiriya. Gupta style of painting in Ceylon. End of 5th century.

have been found at Kedah, Perak, etc. in Malaya; and on the volcanic Dieng Plateau in Java. The latter are a set of temples in which the genesis of the Gupta temple from the step tower to the śikhara can be readily studied. East of Malaya Indian art was quickly adapted to the local mentality. But even in the dreamy, sensuous reliefs of the Borobudur or the vigorous scenes of Parambanam in Java, the Gupta heritage is still strongly evident. However, the peak period of Indian influence in South East Asia was only to come later, and its principal source was classical and mediaeval Indian art in Bengal and Southern India.

**THE SOUTH
INDIAN
RENAISSANCE**

The national awakening pervading Northern India spread also to the Drāvidian peoples of the South. Nevertheless the Gupta renaissance found little response. The Drāvidas had never been under Greek or Scythian rule. Hellenistic art was known only as an exotic curiosity. The Prākrit-Sanskrit controversy did not concern them, both being foreign languages. North Indian civilization was, in its entirety, an alien import, though not so foreign as Hellenistic and Iranian civilization to the North Indians. It had been absorbed, but merely as an aristocratic culture.

Politically therefore, the South went its own way, and culturally it accepted the Gupta ideals, but without much enthusiasm, later discarding them in favour of a national brand of civilization which differed according to the degree in which Gupta civilization had been absorbed — least of all in the plains of the south-east, much more in the Southern Deccan (Karnātak). The Pallavas of Kānchī (Conjeevaram near Madras) expanded their rule over the whole peninsula except the farthest South, then under the tyranny of the Kalabhra-Kalavar tribes. When King Vishnugopa was defeated at the Krishnā by Samudragupta, the Kadambas became independent in the Western Deccan, but the Gangas of Maisūr remained loyal to the Pallavas. When the Gupta emperors conquered the provinces under Kushāna or Mahākshatrapa rule, many Jains no longer felt happy in the new atmosphere of the Vaishnava-Śaiva revival and emigrated to join their co-religionists who had settled in Southern India in pre-Christian times. And soon they became influential at the Kadamba, Ganga, Pallava and Pāndya courts. Thus, though Sanskrit became the court language in the South as well, Gupta culture was no more than a court fashion.

*Śiva and Vishnu*  But in the 6th century the South too began to ferment. The brahman policy of syncretistic assimilation which had shaped Hinduism in the

North, began to bear fruits also in the South. A popular religious movement, spread in the Tamil language by the Nāyanār and Ālvār saints, aroused a passionate devotion for the god Śiva as well as for the god Vishnu. Despite repeated tussles, Saivas and Vaishnavas were in accord in their positive attitude. God is great, glorious, gracious! God's works are wonderful! God is Love! Even where God appears as the great destroyer, He is so overwhelmingly adorable that His beings can but sing hymns in His glorification. Man can have only one attitude towards God, i.e. loving devotion. Both sects merely differed in their imagery.

To the Śaivas God is the Great God (Mahādeva), the creator (Sadāśiva,) Lord of the universe (Jageśvara), the eternal yogi (Yogeśvara), the supporter of the moon (Somanātha, Chandraśekhara) and of the heavenly Ganges (Milky Way: Gangādhara), the divine dancer (Natarājā), the victor over the giants (Tripurāntaka) and over death (Mrityunjaya), the Gracious (Śiva) and the Terrible (Bhairava), the Great Black One (Mahākāla), lord of the demons (Bhūtanātha). He is also the loving husband (Kalyānasundara) of the Great Goddess (Mahādevī, Maheśvarī), the glorious (Gaurī), fire-faced (Jwalamukhī), love-eyed (Kāmākshī, Mīnākshī), great beauty (Mahālakshmī), the mountain-daughter (Pārvatī), devoted wife (Satī), virgin (Kumārī, Durgā) and mother (Umā, Ambikā), the great force (Mahāśakti) of creation (Māyā), the great yogini (Yogeśvarī), and also the terrible (Bhairavī) black (Kālī) lady of death (Chāmundā) and epidemics (Sītala). Their children are the six-headed Kārttikeya (Skanda, Kumāra, Viśākha, Subramanya) and the elephant-headed Ganpati or Ganeśa (lord of demons), their attendants the divine hosts (Gandharvas) and saints (rishis) as well as the demons (ganas, bhūtas) and witches (yoginīs, dakinīs). Thus Śaiva iconography has a glorious and an uncanny aspect. One is the court of the Lord of the Universe on Mount Kailāsa, surrounded by adoring gods, minor deities and saints, while in the depths of the mountain the demon king Rāvana is kept captive; Parvati's struggle for the hand of Siva, the incineration of the God of Love (Kāma) and the lamentations of the goddess of lust (Rati), Śiva's and Pārvatī's wedding and happy family life, their marital quarrels, chess games, Pārvatī's fright when Rāvana rumbles in the depth, to be silenced by a slight pressure of Śiva's toe, Śiva's and Durgā's victories over the giants, etc. The other aspect reveals the divine pair in ascetic's guise, black and naked, smeared with funeral ashes, their dirty, matted hair wound up in a high crown, with skulls, corpses and snakes

*The śaivas*

113

as ornaments or loin cover, dancing on corpses in drunken ecstasy to the sound of drums made of human skulls, drinking human blood from cranium-bowls and gnawing the flesh from human limbs, in the company of demons, witches and skeletons among the fires of a lonely cremation ground. Here is all the fear-obsessed imagery of in the jungle, of demons, tigers, elephants, snakes, and yet deprived of its terror because the devotee knows also the glory of the same deities and regards them merely as two inseparable aspects of the one transcendental Godhead, like light (*satya, rajas*) and darkness (*tamas*), life and death. For Śiva and Bhairava, Gaurī and Kālī are the same, even the Great Goddess is no more than an aspect of the Great God, who is male and female (Ardhanārīśvara), because ultimately neither one nor the other.

*The Vaishnavas* The Vaishnava movement was much less revolutionary, more or less accepting the Gupta mythology and iconography. But it evolved the imagery of God's glory in heaven, the creator on the snake of eternity (Nārāyana-Anantaśāyin) from whose navel the lotus grew which produced Brahmā, the demiurge of this world (Padmanābha), the essence of all forms (Viśvarūpa), the lord of paradise (Vaikunthanātha), the lord of the goddess of beauty and life (Śrīnātha, Lakshmīnātha, Lakshmī-Nārāyana), appearing in twenty-four divine forms (Keśava, Madhusūdana, Damodara, Samkarshana, Vasudeva, Pradyumna, Aniruddha, Purushottama, Achyūta, Janārdana), taken over from the older Pancharātra theology, but venerated especially in the form of his earthly incarnations (Avatāra). Of these the child Krishna (Bālakrishna), the prankish son of Devakī and foster-son of Nanda and Yaśodhā, the leader of the Ābhīra cowherd boys of Gokula and adored lover of the milkmaids (gopī) of Vrindāvana, overshadowed his aspect as the mature hero of the Mahābhārata, the lord of Dvāraka (Dvārakanātha), the husband of Rukminī and Teacher of the Bhagavadgītā (Pārthasārathi). Rāma (Raghunātha) became the lord of the most sacred Vaishnava temple of the South, at Śrīrangam. The Gupta cult of the Varāha and Nrisimha avatāras of Vishnu was accepted also in the South, but lost much of its importance.

To this religious outburst the Jains could oppose only a rather sober intellectual ethics, but they controlled economic life and the courts. However when the reformers succeeded in winning over several kings, the Jains and Buddhists were persecuted, impaled or expelled, and some of their temples and property confiscated. And those dynasties who supported this popular religious reform, rode on it to power, as the Guptas had risen on the crest of the North Indian national movement.

These were the Pāndyas in the farthest South, who late in the 6th century shook off the Kalabhra tyranny and extended their power over Kerala (Travancore and Cochin); the Pallavas of Tondai Mandala (the country round Kānchī-Conjeevaram near the present Madras) who became overlords over the Chola country (Tanjore) and for some time also of South-Āndhra (the country between, and north of the estuaries of the Godavarī and Krishnā) as well as most of the Eastern Deccan; and finally the Chālukyas of Bādāmī who conquered the whole of the Deccan and the western sea coast from Maisūr in the south to Gujarat in the north.

Of the art of the early Pāndyas we know hardly anything. As far as we can risk some conclusions from early monuments in Kerala, e.g. the temples of Vizhinjam and the Guhanāthasvāmin at Cape Comorin, the caves of Kaviyūr and Chitrāral, a few early bronzes or the murals of Tirunandikkara, they did not evolve an art of their own, but were under the spell of the Pallavas who were the actual originators of an independent South Indian art, while the role of the Chālukyas was more that of mediators between North and South, responsible for the shaping of the Deccan style and the indirect inspiration for the final formulation of South Indian art under the Cholas in the 10th century.

In the last quarter of the 6th century King Simhavishnu (c. 574–600) had restored the greatness of the Pallava kingdom by the conquest of Āndhra and Coromandel (Chola-Mandala, i.e. the Chola country). His peaceful successor Mahendravarman I (c. 600–630), called Vichitrachitta "the Original-Minded", was interested in the pleasures of life and in religious problems, art and literature, had Bhāravi (the author of the *Kirātārjunīyam*) as his court poet and was himself an amateur painter and dramatist (author of *Mattavilāsa*). After having persecuted the Śaivas in the name of Jainism, he was converted by Appar Nāyanār, a great devotional poet, and manifested his new zeal by the erection of so many temples in honour of Śiva that he was called Chetthakāri ("the temple builder"). After centuries of construction in brick, wood and metal, he resumed building in stone (Mandagapattu inscription). Though none of these stone temples has survived, we know at least a great number of cave temples founded by him, from Madurai in the south to the Krishnā estuary in the north. But he was no match for the great Chālukya conqueror Pulakeśin II (609/10–642) who besieged him in Kānchī (Conjeevaram) and deprived him of Āndhra. His son Narasimhavarman I Māmalla (the "Great Fighter", 630—668) was able to storm the Chālukya capital Vātāpī (Bādāmī) in 642, on which occasion Pulakeśin II perished; but Āndhra he could not recover. Instead, he developed the maritime power of the state, founded an important port with many temples at Kadalmalai, renamed Māmallapuram (Mahābalipuram or "Seven Pagodas" south of Madras), sent two naval expeditions to Ceylon and, tolerant towards the Buddhists then strong in Ceylon and Indonesia, encouraged an intensive trade with South Eastern Asia. His peaceful second successor Parameśvaravarman (670—80) was in 674 ousted from Kānchī by Vikramāditya I who had restored the Chālukya empire. The capital was badly damaged, but at last Parameśvaravarman succeeded in reestablishing his authority. Narasimhavarman II Rājasimha (c. 680—720) and Parameśvaravarman II (c. 720—31) had peaceful reigns during which the capital was rebuilt and endowed with many fine temples, while Māmallapuram and other towns also received new shrines. With Nandivarman II (731—95) a lateral branch of the dynasty ascended the throne after a civil war during or shortly after which the Chālukya Kīrtivarman II stormed Kānchī, sparing its temples however. Though Nandivarman II was an able ruler, the royal power had been shaken and had to rely increasingly on alliances with other states, especially the Rāshtrakūtas (successors of the Chālukyas). At last, in 897, King Aparājita was overthrown by Āditya I (879—907), founder of the Chola Empire.

*Pallava architecture*  The first stage of the Pallava style is represented by the cave temples of Mahendravarman I, in the neighbourhood of Kānchī, at Pallāvaram, Vallam and Tirukkalukkunram near Chingleput, Dalāvanur, Mandagapattam, Singāvaram and Melacheri near Gingee (Jinjī), Kilmavilangai near Arcot, but also in the south at Tiruchirāpalli (Trichinopoly) and in the north at Bhairavakonda near Nellore and at Vijayavāda (Bezwāda), Undavalli and Mogalrājapuram on the Krishnā. These caves are linga shrines, consisting of a simple anteroom or pillar hall in front of one or several sanctuaries. The elements of this architecture are taken from contemporaneous "Gupta" art in the Northern Deccan; simple pilasters of square, then octagonal and then again square cross-sections, supporting equally simple, slightly indented brackets. Beneath, there is a simple Gupta plinth; on top a low, rounded-off roof with *gavaksha* windows. More than life-size reliefs of guardian deities (*dvārapālas*) serve as decoration. But then the style developed quickly. The main cave at Undavalli now has several storeys and many pillars, and there are also small memorial shrines imitating free-standing buildings, the plinth raised on a plain base, slim pilasters flanking the entrance, and a top-storey set on the low roof, with another plinth, an arched dormer window and a heavy dome. At Bhairavakonda one not only finds fully developed Gupta columns, but these are placed on the heads of sitting lions, while other lion statuettes decorate the brackets and the roof.

The second stage of the Pallava style is represented by the Rathas and cave temples erected by Narasimhavarman Māmalla at his overseas port Māmallapuram. The old city has completely disappeared. Only two low ridges of cliffs rise from the sandy plain ending in single boulders emerging here and there. The bigger one was transformed into the citadel of the town, with tanks and fortifications of which at present only the levelling of the rocks once supporting the bastions can be seen. Attached to this citadel were a huge rock relief representing the "Descent of the Ganges" and cave temples cut into its escarpment, or *"rathas"* modelled from single large boulders, while smaller ones were transformed into statues of monkeys, lions, elephants, etc. The earliest caves (Dharmarāja Mandapa, and Kotikal Mandapa) are still in the simple Mahendravarman style. Cave temple no. 3 has Gupta columns like the Bhairavakonda caves. But in "Rāmānuja's Mandapa" (a later name) and the Mahishāsura Mandapa a distinct Pallava architecture begins to develop which assumes its full shape in the Varāha, Ganeśa and Valaiyankuttai Mandapas, and in the *rathas*, i.e. sculptured imitations of temples constructed in dressed stone. Its most characteristic features were the column and the *Kudā*, i.e. the North Indian *gavūksha*, further evolved by a bizarre exaggeration of the individual elements of Gupta art. The column was placed on the head of a sitting, later of a jumping lion; while its shaft, contracted (*kalaśa*) beneath the capital, became slimmer and slimmer, the capital developed into a broad cushion (*kumbha*) resting on some ring moulds (*tadi*) and a broader abacus (*palagai*) resting on a low "flower-cup" (*idaie*) on top of which a huge cross-bracket (*bodigai*) was placed. In the further development of this "order" the bracket too was dissolved into a floral ornament (*pushpa-bodigai*). In the *Kudu* the "chaitya-window" motif was neglected in favour of its apex which was decorated with a trident-headed Śiva image (almost like those on the Mohenjo-Dāro seals), and later by the mask of a lion or demon. The five *rathas*, later called — like so many other old monuments — by the names of the Pandavas (the principal

Elephant group from the great rock relief of the 'Descent of the Ganga' at Māmallapuram, south of Madras. 7th century. The relief probably depicts the climax of the 'Kirātarjunīya' of Bhāravi, court poet of king Mahendravarman Pallava. This poem was based on a story in the Mahābhārata describing how the hero Arjuna besought the god śiva for his bow. The god, in the disguise of a Kirāta (jungle hunter) provoked Arjuna to a shooting contest and after finding him worthy, revealed himself and presented his divine weapon to the hero, kneeling in veneration. The picture shows the other gods and the animals witnessing śiva's self-revelation.

heroes of the Mahābhārata), give a good idea of the development of the temples. Draupadī's ratha imitates a house, whose slightly curved, pyramidal roof rests on twelve slim columns. Bhīma's ratha reproduces an oblong, two-storeyed house, covered by a wagon roof; around the upper storey there is a balcony with a balustrade composed of a series of small house models (Pancharam). In Sahadava's ratha we have a three-storeyed temple with porch, two Pancharama galleries and a roof like a chaitya-hall. Arjuna's and Dharmarāja's rathas represent similar buildings, three and four storeys high, with a square ground-plan and crowned by a dome (*śringa*). However, all these buildings merely imitate structures of several storeys; in reality only the colonnades and the sanctuary of the ground-plan are genuine, the rest is mere decoration.

And yet after the destruction of Kāñchī in 674 the Pallavas erected some temples of several genuine storeys. Narasimhavarman II Rāja-simha built the magnificent Kailāsanātha (Śiva) temple at Kāñchī, the "Shore Temple" (also dedicated to Śiva) at Māmallapuram; Ma-hendravarman III, the Mahendravarmeśvara (by the side of the Kai-lāsanātha), Nandivarman II, the Matangeśvara and Mukteśvara (ded-icated to Śiva) and the Vaikunthaperumāl (dedicated to Vishnu) at Kāñchī. To these there have to be added several small temples of Rājasimha's time at Panamalai, Māmallapuram, Tiruchirāpalli and Sāluvankuppam, and other of the last period at Oragadam, Tiruttani and Gudimallam. The big temples were the carriers of new religious ideas, such as the cult of Śiva as Somaskanda, i.e. in the company of his consort and children, or of Vishnu, for whom Narasimhavarman I had already built several shrines at Māmallapuram. These were provided with entrance buildings (*gopura*), courts, pillar halls (*mandapa*) for the cult, subsidiary shrines and circumambulatory passages. The "Shore Temple" merely pretends to have several storeys, but the Kai-lāsanātha and especially the Vaikunthaperumāl really possess a pyra-mid tower (*vimāna*) of up to four storeys. Their style is fairly baroque, because of their high plinths, the chapels, *pancharamas* and *śringas* strongly projecting from the walls or raised above conspicuous drums, the huge lions rampant and dvārapāla figures along the walls. And theses characteristics were also retained in small temples (generally of the "Sahadeva Ratha" type) of the decadent period, the walls of which are rather plain, whereas the upper storey is a veritable orgy of baroque, eccentric decoration.

Gupta art seems to have stood also at the cradle of Pallava sculpture. There is reason to believe that there had been rather good sculptors at Mahendravarman's court. But in the surviving provincial cave temples one feels nothing but a very distant echo, even fainter than that in the early Chālukya temples at Aihole. Only the Gangādhara relief at Tiruchirāpalli reminds one of the sculptures in the brah-manical caves of the Western Deccan. It has power, volume, life and a strong rhythm, though no cohesion. But there is nothing of that care-ful study of the human body, nothing of that inner tension which had been essential qualities of Gupta sculpture. And the other sculptures,

The Shore Temple at Māmallapuram, south of Madras. Built by the Pallava King Narasimhavarman II.
Rājasimha. 680-720.

even at Tiruchirāpalli, mostly dvārapālas, at Kilmavilangai a relief of Vishnu, at Undavalli another of Vishnu and Lakshmī, Nārāyana and the Ālvārs, are crude (at Undavalli due to barbarian restoration). The dvārapālas especially, with buffalo-horned caps or voluminous matted wigs on their heads, leaning on their heavy clubs, look more like visions of the jungle.

But at Māmallapuram we encounter a very different world. There are many reliefs: dvārapālas, portraits of King Mahendravarman and his queens, Brahmā, Śiva as such or in the guise of Somaskanda, Durgā adored in glory, standing on the killed buffalo, or on her lion attacking Mahishasura and his host of demons, Vishnu adored by the gods, as Nārāyana, Varāha and Trivikrama (conqueror of the three worlds, i.e. heaven, earth and the nether world lost to the demon king Bali), as Krishna lifting Mt. Govardhana, and Lakshmī sitting on a lotus, surrounded by elephants and nymphs. There is the huge rock relief alternately called "The Descent of the Ganga", or "Arjuna's Penance", in fact an illustration of Bhāravi's Kirātārjunīya, describing the encounter of Arjuna, the great hero of the Mahābhārata, and of Śiva disguised as a primitive jungle hunter, a Kirāta. On both sides of a cleft through which the surplus water of the rock plateau can fall into a tank beneath, a multitude of figures has been carved out; snake deities (of the water) in the cleft, at the left a small Siva temple surrounded by ascetics, on the right elephants. And, above, the god Śiva reveals himself in his glory to Arjuna, amidst a host of flying gods and various animals. For fun, there is also a cat (regarded as a hypocrite) which has joined the ascetics to do penance. And finally, there are sculptures in the round, of bulls, elephants, lions, and also a charming group of monkeys hunting for lice. All these are very lively, elegant figures, with exaggeratedly slim bodies, in dresses so thin that they are often not visible at all, wearing very high crowns, indeed often like cylinders; the gods and goddesses magnificent, the kings and queens charming and fashionable. Based on the best later Gupta tradition, the figures take up and absorb likewise the ideals of the Amarāvati style, no less elegant, but much stronger, healthier and more monumental.

In comparison with these works the sculptures of the Kānchī temples mark a visible decline. They are shorter and much more agitated, the composition becomes rather overcrowded and restless, the number of subjects has grown to a comprehensive pantheon as well as to historical cycles (Nandivarman's II rise to power and royal career, on the walls

*Kānchī temples*

121

of the Vaikunthaperumāl temple). But on the other hand the figures
often become grotesque, the faces are dull, poses without verve, the
compositions become stereotyped. There is nothing of the charming
ingenuity and joy of life, nothing of the originality of the sculptures
of the Māmalla period.

*Pallava painting*
At Śittanavāśal (in the former Pudukkottai State, c. 35 miles south of
Tiruchirāpalli) some fine murals of the time of Mahendravarman
have been discovered in a Jain cave temple. Their style can well compare with the best works of the 6th century at Ajantā. The figures,
though elegant, are strong and healthy, the mood shows a subdued
joy of life, the drawing is very sensitive, though sometimes sketchy.
Most of them, rather faded, are naturalistic lotus flowers or circular
ornaments, but there are some figures. Whether they were executed
before or after Mahendravarman's defection from Jainism, we can no
longer tell. But they represent the spirit of art under "Vichitrachitta"
much better than the crude Śaiva caves of his time. Later fragments
in the same tradition have been traced in the Kailāsanātha at Kānchī,
at Tirumalaipuram (7th century) and Malayadipatti (c. 788—840).

*Spread of
Pallava art*
With the naval power and maritime trade of the Pallava empire its
art also spread to Ceylon and Greater India. King Mānavarman of
Ceylon had been installed on the throne of Anurādhapura with the
help of Narasimhavarman I Māmalla. It is, therefore, not surprising
that a number of Buddha statues of decided Pallava character have
been found there. The other two centres of Pallava influence were the
Isthmus of Ligor on the Malayan Peninsula at Takuapā and Jaiyā
where Pallava Buddhist as well as Hindu statues have been discovered; and the Empire of "Funan" on the lower course of the Mekong, where Pallava sculpture (at Prasat Andet, Vat Pan Morai, Tre-
pan Phon, Kompon Cham, etc.) competed with sculpture in the
Gupta style. Its influence spread to the interior, up to the ancient
town of Śrīdeb, on the watershed to Siam, and it was far more decisive
in the formation of national Khmer art than the Gupta model. On
land, on the other hand, Pallava art played a considerable role in the
formation of Chālukya and Rāshtrakūta art.

*The Chālukyas*
The Chālukyas had been a small vassal family in the Karnātak which
was able to strengthen its position during the many political changes
of the 6th century. Pulakeśin I Satyāśraya (c. 535—66) made himself
independent and moved his capital from the small country town of
Aihole to the strong Vātāpī (Bādāmī). Kīrtivarman I (566—597/8)
overthrew the Nalas and Kadambas, then the dominant dynasties of

the Western Deccan, and the Mauryas of the Konkān, Mangaleśa (597/8—610/11) defeated the Katachuris and thus extended his rule over the Northern Deccan. Pulakeśin II (610/11—642) conquered Maisūr and Gujarāt, repulsed an attack of Harsha, the mighty emperor of Northern India, expelled the Vishnukundins and Pallavas from Āndhra, but was at last defeated by Narasimhavarman I Māmalla and fell during the defence of Vātāpī. For about a dozen years the Chālukya empire seemed extinguished. But Vikramāditya I (655—81) restored the empire, took the Pallava capital Kānchī, invaded the Chola country in the south, and re-occupied Gujarāt (lost by Pulakeśin to Harsha). Vinayāditya (681—96) invaded even Northern India, though with disastrous results. Vijayāditya (696—733), Vikramāditya II (733/4—744/5) and Kīrtivarman II (744/5—757) were so completely bogged down in the war with the Pallavas, that they had to leave the northern defences of their empire to their Rāshtrakūta viceroys who soon became semi-independent. Weakened by the invasion of Lalitāditya of Kashmir (736—47), the last Chālukya was annihilated by the Rāshtrakūtas between 754 and 760. However, the Eastern Chālukyas of Vengi, the descendants of Pulakeśin II's younger brother, Vishnuvardhana, survived until the 11th century. Maintaining neutrality in the wars of their cousins with the Pallavas, they defended themselves heroically against the Rashtrakutas in the 8th and 9th centuries, were almost ruined in the 10th century by internal dissension kindled by the Rāshtrakūtas and were finally saved by the Chola emperors of the South. In 1061 the Chālukya Rājendra Kulottunga I, a Chola on his mother's and grandmother's side, founded the second dynasty of Chola emperors.

The Chalukyas were not so much creators as mediators in the field of art. In the north they came in contact with the provincial Gupta civilization of the Deccan and the later imperial civilization of Gujarat and Northern India, in the south with the Andhras, Pallavas and Cholas, in the west in trade relations with the Sassanian empire via the ports of the Konkān and of Gujarāt, and with Indonesia via Āndhra, and were later involved in wars with the Muslim governors of Sind. Chālukya art thus passed through several phases.

The first was that of the early 6th century, at the earliest capital *Aihole* Aihole on the Malprabhā river. It is a small town, hardly more than a village, surrounded by an almost circular wall with bastions and moats, at the foot of a ridge occupied by a citadel. But the place and its neighbourhood are full of interesting temples. The oldest Śiva shrines, i.e. the Kontgudi group and the so-called "Lād Khān" (after a former peasant occupant) are mere adaptations of the later Buddhist monastery type: a front colonnade, a square hall, and against its back wall the sanctuary proper. It is very heavy work with simple plinths and cornices, plain walls, heavy pillars and pilasters with simple brackets, the central roof, formed by horizontal stone slabs, surrounded by slightly sloping slabs. On top of the Lād Khān there is a small chapel like an early Gupta temple, and on one of the Kontgudi shrines, a sort of Pancharama storey. Sculpture is sparse; the pillars have crude lotus roundels, "pearl-hangings" and scroll work, the windows *jālīs* (perforated stone screens) imitating wood construction, the balconies reliefs of water vessels. On the pillars of the front gallery of the Lād Khān there are three-quarter life-size figures of the river goddesses and of yaksha (Gandharva) mithunas, in Gupta costume and imagery, but in their general character descendants of the relief groups in the old Śātavāhana cave temples. Clumsy, poorly proportioned, they nevertheless have the charm of a naive honesty and directness.

*Durga temple*   The most remarkable monument of this style, however, is the Durga (Fort) temple, an adaptation of a Buddhist chaitya hall, raised on a high plinth, the inner colonnade transformed into the sanctuary, the enclosing wall turned into an open colonnade. The temple was completed much later, in the 7th century, so that its sculptures cover all the transitions from homely figures in the manner of the Lād Khān to great masterpieces of the later Gupta style. In the subsequent temples, e.g. nos. 7 and 11, and the Mahākūtesvara (south of Bādāmī), the Gupta style is developing; the artists evidently had good models, but the imitation is pathetically weak. In temples nos. 53 and 9, the Huchchimalligudi, and the Nāganātha at Nagrāl (Bījāpur District) of A.D. 601 the Gupta style is at last mastered. And at the same time the plan has changed: an open porch, an oblong *vimāna* and at the end the sanctuary, with or without a circumambulatory passage and crowned by an orthodox North-Indian *sikhara*. In the Meguti temple in the citadel the best Gupta style triumphs. Indeed, it was erected in 634/5 in honour of Jinendra, as we are told by a most important inscription of the donor, Pulakeśin II's court poet Ravikīrti, who therein claims equality with the great Kālidāsa and with Bhāravi, the protégé of Mahendravarman Pallava.

*Vātāpī (Bādāmī)*   But the Gupta peak phase of Chālukya art is connected mainly with Vātāpī (Bādāmī), the later impregnable capital founded by Pulakeśin I and Kīrtivarman I. The scenery alone of Bādāmī is magnificent;

a valley between two cliff spurs at the western end of the same mountains, at the eastern end of which Aihole is situated; forts on those vertical cliffs; a lake between, retained by a huge dam across the valley; further out in the plain the remains of the bastions and moats which in Chālukya times connected the hill forts, thus protecting the royal town along the lake; in the valley and on the cliffs, temples; and in the escarpment of the southern cliffs a group of four cave temples, dug under Kīrtivarman I and Mangaleśa (inscription of 578). The first two, dedicated to Śiva, remind one of the last caves of Ajantā. Cave III, the biggest of all, dedicated to Vishnu, is a fairy world of sculptures, mighty figures of Vishnu in all his power, and gentle goddesses and mithunas on walls, pillars and brackets; indeed, these latter are among the most ravishing creations of later "Gupta" art. Important fragments of murals have also been discovered, in an equally attractive style. The free-standing temples, especially the Malegitti Śivālaya and the temple on the Northern Fort, reveal the Gupta style of sculpture at its zenith, but their architecture reminds one rather of Pallava architecture in the transition period from the Mahendra to the Māmalla style, though without the exaggerations of the latter. The temples of Gop in Saurāshtra and Lakrodā in Gujarāt were built at that time, and the last Ajantā caves (nos. 1—5, 21—27) were dug out of the rock and painted, one mural even representing the embassy sent by the Persian king Khusrau II to Pulakeśin. The latest Buddhist caves at Aurangābād, cave 17 at Nāsik, and some of the early Buddhist caves (nos. 5—9) at Elūrā are also of this period.

The Pallava occupation after the death of Pulakeśin II in 642 is probably responsible for a Pallava monument, the small but very fine Śaiva cave temple at Aihole, with sculptures and painting in the best Māmalla style (with one of the earliest reliefs of Śiva Natarājā, lord of Chidambaram, between Pondicherry and Tanjore).

After the restoration of the empire by Vikramāditya I (654/5) a split in Chālukya art set in. In the northern provinces where the early Rāshtrakūta governors enjoyed a considerable autonomy, the Gupta style underwent a transformation very similar to the art of Kīrtivarman I and Mangaleśa in the Bādāmī caves, carried by the same spirit *Elūrā* of enthusiastic devotion to the great Hindu gods. It is a grandiose art, in a way even more impressive than the creations of the Gupta Empire. The cave temples dedicated to Śiva at Elūrā (Rāvana-kā-Khai, Dumar-Lenā), at Elephanta and Mt. Pezir (Mandapeśvar, near Borivli, north of Bombay), and likewise the Mahāyāna-Buddhist shrines

in imitation of them at Elūrā (nos. 1—5, 11—12) are conceived on a mighty scale. The principal hall of cave temple no. 1 at Elephanta for instance measures 130 × 130 ft and is 15—17 ft high; and adjoining it, there are two courts with smaller shrines. The Dumar-Lenā (or Sītā-kī-Nahānī) at Elūrā, opening on a gorge where in the rainy season a waterfall plays, is of about the same size. Their interior is rather plain, but impressive because of the mighty guardian figures and reliefs which adorn the shrines and the walls. These statues are of an admirable perfection of form and a superhuman serenity, very sensitive and yet completely self-controlled. These reliefs, telling the most famous myths of Śiva and Pārvatī, are immensely impressive. The great deities, charged with energy and passion in their visible form, and yet basically unconcerned in their transcendental stillness, dominate a scene where a restless life of minor gods, demons and attendant animals whirls about in the twilight of the background. At the back of the great Elephanta cave, however, behind the linga shrine, there is the world-famous Trimūrti relief, a gigantic head with three faces, terrible, majestic, gentle, once interpreted as the Hindu Trinity (i.e. Brahmā, Vishnu, Śiva combined), in reality Śiva in his three fundamental aspects. The Buddhist Do-Thal and Tin-Thal are two-, and three-storeyed caves, in the pillar halls of which long rows of solemn Buddhas, Bodhisattvas and Tārās, hieratically sitting on lotus flowers, evoke the image of later Buddhist temples in China and Japan.

At Elūrā this cave architecture and sculpture continued to flourish until the 10th, even the 12th century; but already in the later 8th century it was becoming rare, and after the 10th it disappeared. And even the most famous monument of the Rāshtrakūta empire at Elūrā, the Kailāsanātha, is not understandable without reference to the temple architecture in the southern provinces of the Chālukya empire. For the Kailāsa at Elūrā is an elaboration of the Kailāsanātha at Kānchī, via the temples of Pattadakal.

Pattadakal is a holy Tīrtham, 10 miles south-east of Bādāmī, where a *Pattadakal* Vishnu temple in the style of the later Aihole shrines or of the Northern Fort temple at Bādāmī had been erected, probably in the reign

Dvārapāla (guardian deity) resting on his club. Relief on a pillar at the entrance of the Virūpāksha temple, Pattadakal. 746-7. Almost life-size.

of Vikramāditya I. Some decades later it was re-dedicated to Śiva Pāpanātha (Lord of Evil) and enlarged by a closed hall (*vimāna*) of sixteen columns. In about 725, King Vijayāditya added the Vijayeśvara (the present Samgameśvara) temple. After Vikramaditya II had taken Kānchī in about 740, his queens Lokamahādevī and Trailokyamahādevī had in 746/7 the Lokeśvara (present Virūpāksha) and Trailokyeśvara (present Mallikarjuna) temples built by the architect Gunda, in commemoration of this great victory and with the help of masons deported from Kānchī.

In all these temples as well as in those nos. 39 and 53 at Aihole, one can observe the progressive replacement of the Gupta-Chālukya by the late Pallava style. In the Pāpanātha the Aihole-Bādāmī tradition is enriched merely by a well-developed North Indian *sikhara* and by relief niches crowned by North Indian pediments. However, the Samgameśvara has a Pallava tower, and the Virūpāksha and Mallikarjuna temples are in the best Pallava style, though adapted to the Chālukya taste insofar as all the bizarre exaggerations have been avoided. The ground-plan has no court, the cult hall (*navaranga*) has three open porches (in front and on both sides), the sanctuary is enclosed by a broad circumambulatory passage and surmounted by a tower of three storeys, not exceeding however the average Chālukyan size, much smaller than those at Kānchī. The plinth, though richly sculptured with lions, hansas, etc., retains its basic Gupta character. The walls consist of alternating projections, with image niches crowned by *makaras*, and recesses with windows of nicely perforated stone slabs. But the rhythm of projections and recesses is subdued and the columns framing the projections differ only slightly from the late Gupta type. In the same way the *pancharams* along the roof and the storeys of the tower form a closed outline, notwithstanding their opulent sculpture. The heavy pilasters of the interior, decorated alternately with figurate roundels and half-roundels, and vertical as well as horizontal figure friezes, bear plain indented brackets. The shrine entrance follows the Gupta type, yet with certain deviations, i.e. late Gupta columns crowned by makaras supporting a roof lintel topped by a big *kudū*. The sculptures display the same manifold deities as the later Pallava temples, but their style retains the elegant dignity of the Gupta tradition of Pulakeśin's time, though more mannered and far less monumental.

With those five monuments, the Telī-kā-Mandir at Gwālior, the Mārtānd temple in Kashmir, the Pahārpur temple in Bengal, the temples

*End of classical art*

of Kānchī in the Tamil South and the temples of Pattadakal in the Deccan, classical art faded out. Here we are faced with the first mediaeval cathedrals, huge structures decked with the innumerable figures of a complicated iconography in a strictly prescribed and mannered style. Here the development of mediaeval art set in, the art of "Mystic India". The creative phase of ancient Indian art was over, the era of the elaboration of a fixed canon and typology had set in, which continued until its ultimate degeneration into a lifeless mass production of merely iconic or ornamental art. What had begun as one of the most noble conscious efforts in human history to achieve an unsurpassable national ideal of formal beauty, human nobility and religious vision, ended, under different social conditions, as a ready-made professional formula to serve the pomp and luxury of an exclusive military and priestly aristocracy.

# V. MEDIAEVAL HINDU ART

Gupta society in the 4th—6th centuries was secular mixed, aristocratic-capitalistic, and its centres were the great cities. The leading class consisted of members of former ruling houses — some claiming divine or semi-divine origin — reduced to governors and generals, professional warriors from the old kshatriya ranks as well as indigenous and foreign soldiers of fortune, officials of a mighty bureaucracy and finally rich bankers, merchants and industrialists. But between the 6th and 8th centuries this society underwent a radical change very similar to that in the later Roman Empire: It became aristocratic-theocratic. The emperors and kings surrounded themselves with all the glamour of religious sanction. They occupied a privileged position in religious life, being admitted to temple ritual inaccessible to the public. Later in the Middle Ages they often behaved as mere agents of the state deity, having presented their kingdom to this deity and received it back in divine trust. Their palaces became imitations of the Kailāsa, the mountain of the gods. The aristocracy became an exclusive caste, claiming as their ancestors not merely the old Kshatriya class, but a few famous kings and heroes of the Mahābhārata and Purānas. They were divided into Sūryavamśīs (descendants from the sun), Chandravamśīs (descendants from the moon) and Agnivamśīs (descendants from a magic fire by the saint Vaisishtha in order to ward off the asuras). The overwhelming majority of these claims were fictitious and at first vague and often contradictory, as most of the claimants had been soldiers of fortune, even barbarians and jungle tribesmen. But the claims were acknowledged by the priestly class, bribed by rich endowments to temples and monasteries, and were enforced by a systematic arrogant exclusiveness.

This military aristocracy arrogated all the power, all the wealth, all the beautiful women, all the luxuries of life, fighting endless bloody wars for short-lived conquests, but rarely dispossessing their opponents completely. Defeated kings or nobles were deprived of their vassals, subjects and most of their treasure, and were thereafter reinstalled as vassals; nobles were deprived of their army and court offices and of part of their fiefs, but they continued to be nobles. The ruling class was sacrosanct, it could be slain in battle, deprived of the

*The aristocracy*

131

fruits of its valour, but not exterminated. And thus those endless wars were more or less inconclusive, an up-and-down of supreme power, but never a stable empire. Within a few years a state could rise from a district to an empire comprising a large part of India, fall back into obscurity and rise again. The bill had to be paid by the looted cities and by the harrassed peasantry, all of which, however, enjoyed a considerable autonomy, as the military aristocracy was not interested in administration and the royal bureaucracy was corrupt, oppressive vis-à-vis the weak, and powerless vis-à-vis the great lords.

*The priests* The only class profiting most of the time were the priests of the innumerable big or small temples, on which the rulers showered gifts in order to win their support. Every noble aspiring to royalty would found a number of modest temples in order to set up a clique of priestly supporters; every successful ruler would build huge temple cathedrals or enlarge the already existing ones. And, conversely, the great hierarchs would make and unmake kings. As a result there was keen competition between the various cults, supporting and seeking the favour of princes, queens, ministers, etc., and sometimes stooping very low in order to advertise their special brand of religion. The ordinary people, excluded from public life and enmeshed in endless rituals and caste duties, became fanatically interested in the feuds of those religious parties; political pretenders often sought to obtain the support of some sectarian movement, and in such cases the normally peaceful co-existence of the various sects flared up into cruel persecution.

As a matter of fact there was not much difference between the loyalty to princes and feudal lords, and the adherence to this or that religious sect. The gods kept court like the kings and nobles. After the theory had been accepted that the idol (*archā*) was not only symbolically, but in the most tangible reality the locus of the divine presence, i.e. an incarnation of God on earth, the obvious consequence was that it had to be honoured and treated like a living being of the highest rank, i.e. it needed a palace, servants, concubines, dancers, musicians, ministers, soldiers, etc., and the daily routine of levée, breakfast, public reception (*darśan*), luncheon, afternoon nap, evening amusements, dinner, and nightly rest. Around these, an additional cult ritual developed. For these purposes the temples had to be enlarged and embellished. Whatever nice distinctions the educated classes, initiated into the sublime flights of Hindu philosophy, might draw, this concept degenerated for most people into a gross idolatry, while to the upper classes it opened a back door to secret rituals in which symbolic concepts, dragged down to the material level, eventually offered an excuse for orgiastic excesses. The indignation of the Muslims over Hindu idolatry was thoroughly justified. And the Hindus themselves started a reformation which, however, gained momentum only after Muslim iconoclasm had smashed the priestly-aristocratic vested interests in these malpractices.

While the masses were taught to renounce the vanities of this world and to seek refuge with this or that deity by means of an austere life, all the luxuries of life were enjoyed at the royal as well as at minor princely courts, costly treasures were collected in the temples, education was exclusive to the priestly class. Poets and scholars worked for the amusement and the glory of the kings or in the service of the temples, and artists and artisans worked for temples and palaces, under the strict control of a scholastic tradition which prescribed and censored every detail of their work and private life.

In theory Mediaeval Hindu art had no chances of growth and development; in practice it had quite a number, at least for half a millennium. The scholastic theoreticians evolved a very sensitive aesthetic theory. Though originally evolved by the poets, especially the dramatists, it was also applied more or less to the fine arts. Based on Vedāntic philosophy, it co-ordinates the aesthetic qualities (*rasa*) of the object of contemplation with the mental state (*bhāva*) of the onlooker. The result is enjoyment (*bhoga*), a state of enraptured slf-forgetfulness in the contemplation of the work of art. This self-forgetfulness, however, is a mental state similar to that of the devotee in the contemplation of the Divine, where he identifies his own self (*jīvātman*) with the cosmic Self (*paramātman*). For beauty herself is an aspect of the Divine, one of the attributes of its revelation. This reaction of the onlooker results from *dhvani*, the deeper meaning of artistic expression achieved through the technical skill (*lakshana*) of the poet, sculptor, painter, dancer or musician.

*Theory of mediaeval Hindu art*

But over and above this, the theoreticians also prescribed practically every detail, size, plan, decoration of the temples, the various figures of gods, goddesses, demons, etc., their proportions, the characteristics of their bodies, their symbols, their hair style, their colour, the moods of expression, and surrounded them with a ritual of prayers, invocations, ablutions, etc. But the priestly class, well entrenched in its prebends, had time for speculation, and thus continued to develop the initial concept into more and more complicated details, adducing, in good scholastic manner, innumerable quotations from ancient religious texts, few of which had originally had anything to do with the main body of argument. Every new religious current tried to find expression for its own theology by means of special combinations of divine symbols and re-ordering of divine figures, new interpretations of myths, etc. And for these reasons alone the shape of the temples went on changing, together with their imagery.

On the other hand the theologians were not interested in all aspects of art; they were indifferent to the ideal human type represented by sculptors and painters, and they left the artist a free hand wherever scenes from ordinary life were introduced. And here the influence of the kings, queens, ministers and nobles who financed the building of the temples, was felt; here the influence of secular court art came in, of which we know much from literary sources, but little from original documentation. For in the endless wars, palaces and mansions were destroyed time and again, and what survived through the Middle Ages, was sent up in flames when the Muslims conquered India in the 13th—14th centuries.

*Court life* The life of the courts, however, was luxurious, and this is shown in the different fashions. Like the courts, the temples too had to be fashionable. If the great gods and goddesses loomed in inaccessible holiness, the host of heavenly nymphs (Apsaras, Surasundarī) and minor deities (Gandharvas) accompanying them could be shaped to the image of the court ladies and gentlemen. As the official religion became more superficial in the later Middle Ages, so did beautiful young prostitutes (veśyakumārī) become the fashion as temple dancers (devadāsī) and partners in secret Tāntrik rituals, and so also were statues of fashionable sexy females used to adorn the walls, columns and ceilings of the temples. During the last centuries before the Muslim invasion many of these figures were portraits (in a few cases they can even be identified), and in the last stage even frankly obscene groups were not rare.

And finally there was a purely secular section in the art of every temple: donor statues and reliefs, representations of the court assembly or of the victories of the donating or founder king, and finally the "Nara Thara". For as the temple was intended to be a microcosm of the world, there also had to be scenes of all aspects of human life: wars, processions, jousts, home life, sports, hunts, educational activities, etc. Here the artists had complete freedom, and while they often filled these friezes with merely conventional scenes, in other cases we find very interesting and important revelations about the life of the time.

Beyond those common characteristics, however, there existed in immense variety of style, typology and imagery. As has already been described, the renaissance of the South had developed on different lines from those of the Gupta national civilization in the North. The Deccan differed from the lowlands of Tamilnād and Malabar. In Northern India there were great differences of cultural level as a result of the immigration of barbarian tribes in the wake of the Hūna invasion, now, however, claiming to be "Rājputs" (sons of kings, i.e. kshatriyas). In the east, Bengal and Bihār, loyal to Buddhism and the Gupta art tradition, formed a cultural province almost distinct from the rest of India, but closely connected with Nepāl, Tibet, Burma and Indonesia. In the west, Kashmīr, the last outpost of Hindu civilization, encircled first by semi-barbarians, then by the Muslims, developed its own style of art, mixed and archaic.

In the chaos following the collapse of the empire of Lalitāditya of Kashmīr after 753/6, the people of eastern Bengal had elected Gopāla, an indigenous kshatriya and Buddhist as king. His successors, Dharmapāla (c. 770–810) and Devapāla (c. 810–850), expanded the kingdom over most of Northern India, but were driven back to Bihār by the Pratīhāras of Rājasthān and the Rāshtrakūtas of the Deccan. In the late 9th and 10th centuries it fell into obscurity, squeezed in between the Pratīhāras, Chandellas and Kalachūrīs in the west, and a number of local dynasties in the east. But Mahīpāla (c. 992–1040) renewed the kingdom, and it reached the peak of its glory under Rāmapāla (1084–1126). Then the Pālas were superseded by their vassals, the Senas (c. 1150–c. 1280), originally brahman immigrants from the Deccan and zealous champions of Hindu orthodoxy, whose most famous ruler was Lakshamasena, a great maecenas of the arts, expelled from his capital in 1206 by the Muslims.

Bengal had been accepted into the Hindu cultural fold rather late. The originally matriarchal, indigenous population, semi-Mongoloid, adhered to a cult of mother goddesses (especially Kālī), in which sexual rites and bloody sacrifices played a great role. They were despised by the brāhmans as low-caste, hated the brāhmans in their turn, and accepted Buddhism. But it was the late Buddhism with its system of divine emanations and feminine deities as expounded in the Guhyasamāja Tantra. From this the Tāntrik Vajrayāna developed in Bengal, Orissā and Assam, with its innumerable, frequently terrible

NORTH INDIA

*Pālas and Senas*

135

male and female deities and its extreme mysticism, couched in an often highly erotic, symbolic language. The number of deities is practically endless, each growing from the "Void" (*Śūnyatā*), i.e. the formless transcendental, into a mystic syllable (*bīja*) and then into a special god or goddess who, in turn, is the force behind some aspect of the world process. These deities whom the devotee had to evoke by hard meditation, individually or in a magic circle (*mandala*), are described in special texts, such as the Sādhanā Mālā and Nishpannayogāvalī.

The Senas installed a number of brāhman families who still form the aristocracy of Bengal. But the imagery of their orthodoxy, mainly representing Vaishnavism, though also Śaivism and Śāktism, was of the usual kind. Only the snake goddess Mānasā became popular with the masses; the cult of Kālī, now the most popular in Bengal, was only accepted vary much later.

*Architecture of the Pālas and Senas*

Of the architecture of the Pālas and Senas,, little has survived. Most of the country is a plain, inundated half the year by the Ganges and Brahmaputra, where villages and temples had to be erected on artificial mounds which, of course, were used again in later times. Towns had to be protected by dykes and moats. Only southern Bihār and the districts west of the Hūghlī (Burdwān and Bankūra) are drier; moreover the Pālas also made donations to all the old centres of Buddhism further up country: Banāras, Sārnāth, Kasiā, Sahet-Mahet, etc. The Pālas first resided in Bihār, later in Bengal, at Rāmavatī (Chandīpur) near the bifurcation of the Ganges and Hūghlī, whereas the Senas founded Vikramapura (Rāmpāl) and Lakshamanāvatī (Lakhnautī), and the Muslims Gaur.

Nālandā then became the most famous university of the East, to which students flocked from China, Central Asia, Burma and Indonesia. The Gupta stūpa was enlarged to huge dimensions, and new monasteries, several storeys high, were erected, among them that of King Bālaputra Śailendra of Yava and Sumatra for the students from his own country (in 778). Oddantapurī and Vikramaśīla (Pātharghāta near Bhāgalpur) competed with Nālandā, which was ruthlessly destroyed during the Muslim invasion. Somapurī (Pahārpur) was similarly rebuilt by Dharmapāla, a vast enclosure of monks' cells and minor shrines around the central temple on its cross-shaped step pyramid. Vestiges of minor Buddhist shrines can be traced everywhere. The temples developed from the tower-like Gupta stūpa by transferring the most important Buddha niche, in enlarged proportions, into the interior of the stūpa drum; and after a time the Pāla-

Buddhist temple became a mere variation of the Hindu temple, with a stūpa and its chhattrāvalī instead of the śikhara, and a round or trefoil sanctuary-entrance (developed from the halo — *prabhāmandala, prabhāvalī* — behind the "divine" figures). The late Gupta śikhara temple also existed (e.g. Tārā Temple at Bodhgayā). However, during the crisis of the Pāla empire in the 10th century its Mediaeval form was also introduced from Orissā (Siddheśvara at Bahūlarā). The Begunia temples and the (damaged) Sakeśvara and Salleśvara temples in the Barākar District already reveal a progressive transformation. The Ichaighosh temple at Gaurangapur (Burdwān), on the other hand, which is constructed not of stone, but of brick, with plain walls and a plain, very high śikhara whose sides project steplike in vertical "paga", may be regarded as its final, Bengalī form.

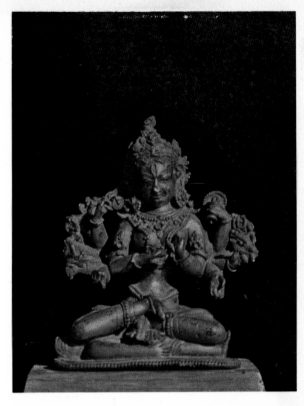

Chundā (Buddhist goddess) from Pattikera in Eastern Bengal. Bronze idol (²/₃ original size), 10th century. *Baroda Museum.*

*Pāla sculpture*

Pala sculpture (carved from the bluish-black slate of the Rājmahal hills, the only quarries on the Ganges) first imitated the Gupta style in a clumsy, boneless fleshiness. The rather simple idol stelas were rounded on top, the figures were heavy but easy moving and friendly. In the 10th century, costume, jewellery, background became richer, and the slender but powerful bodies and longer faces imbued with an intense life. But in the 11th century, and especially under the Sena kings, a superficial elegance prevailed: rigid, lifeless, over-elongated bodies, faces with a forced smile, consciously pretty poses and affected movements, luxurious dresses, crowns and jewels, long, slender, pointed stelas covered with a multitude of figures and masses of

God śiva and his consort Pārvatī, sitting in loving embrace on a lotus flower. On two smaller flowers their children Ganesa (left) and Karttikeya (right). Small bronze from Bengal, 12th or 13th century. About original size. *Museum of Fine Arts, Boston.*

elaborate ornaments. What had begun as an expression of genuine religious feeling, had become an icon, ritually correct, but without any inner life behind the mask of courtly sensuality. The bronze idols found in many places are also very beautiful; most of them, however, come from a few hoards rediscovered at Nālandā, Kurkihār, Rangpur and Jhewāri (Chittagong), and are of excellent workmanship, finely chased and inlaid with gold and silver.

*Painting*

Painting under the Pālas, Varmas and Chandras (but not under the Senas) is known from less than two dozen palm-leaf manuscripts of the Prajñā-Pāramitā,, Sādhana-Mālā, Pancharaksha and Karandavyūha, illustrated with small (c. 1—2 sq. inches), rather stereotyped miniatures of Buddhist deities, stūpas, famous places of pilgrimage all over India. Their style is based on that of the late Gupta period, passing through the same development as sculpture, from a simple, but warmly felt and rather picturesque, to a complex, affected and mainly linear expression. The Tibetan historians mention Dhīmān and Bitpālo as founders of the Pāla school of painting.

Pāla-Sena art had an immense influence. In India proper the Orissā temples (belonging to the Pratihāra-Rājput tradition) took over the Pāla idol-type. Nepāl was practically an exclusive province of Pāla art in the 9th—12th centuries, and it preserved this style, together with the preceding late Gupta tradition, piously until our own time. Its history is still little known, for in this Himalayan valley, temples and palaces were constructed of wood. Most of the monuments, the great stūpas of Śvayambhūnatha and Bodhinātha, the temples of the three capitals, Lalita-Pattana, Bhatgāon and Katmāndū, of holy Paśupatinātha and Chāngū-Nārāyana, etc., are not older than the 16th, rarely than the 15th century. Nepālese bronzes, gilt and encrusted with semiprecious stones, are found in most leading museums all the world over. Tibet adopted the Pāla tradition, via Nepāl and Kashmīr, both in sculpture, bronze art and painting; however, later on, Chinese influence became stronger and stronger, so that all minor scenes are done in the Chinese, and all strictly iconic ones in an elaboration of the Pāla taste. Another sphere of Bengal influence was Burma, not to speak of minor countries between, such as Comilla, Tripura (Tippera) and Chittagong. The great temples erected by King Anawrata (1040—1077) and his successors at Pagān: the Kyanzittha, Shwezigon, Ānanda, Nanpaya, Seinnyit, Pethaik, Thatbinnya, Mahābodhi, Mingalazedi, etc., display all possible variations of the Pāla-Sena temple type: the stūpa on top of a pyramid of terraces (Mingalazedi), the

temple with a pyramid roof ending in a stūpa (Bidagat Taik, etc.), a two-storeyed mixture of both: i.e. a high substructure ending in a pyramid of terraces, on which another monumental sanctuary with another pyramid of terraces and a stūpa are placed. The peak of this style is represented by the Ānanda pagoda, with its huge halls projecting on four sides. Old Burmese sculpture is, essentially, a slight mongolization of Pāla sculpture, and the same is true of the murals in the temples of Pagān. Through Northern Burma Pāla influence penetrated Northern Siam (Chiengmai). But by sea it also reached Southern Siam via Malaya (Jayā, Pakon Pathom, etc.), and found its strongest echo in Java and Sumatra, in the monuments of the Śailendra kings. The world-famous Borobudur in Java, though without a known prototype in India, is intelligible only in the light of Pāla-

*Java*

Buddhist theology. For it is an immense Mandala (magic circle) evolved from the terrace pyramid, ending in a central stūpa, surrounded by minor stūpas. The symbolism of this huge monument is remarkable, the successive circumambulatory passages (not visible from outside) where the pilgrim passed beautiful relief-cycles depicting a number of sacred texts, starting with scenes in hell, and ending in the abstract purity of the stūpas with their no less abstract statues of Dhyāni Buddhas. Just as beautiful, though smaller, are the monuments of Chandī Kalasan, Chandī Sewu and Chandi Mendut. The soft, dreamy sculptures are better than those of contemporaneous Bengal, as they have preserved much of the best Gupta tradition. In the bronzes, on the other hand, the Pāla influence is so strong that only very careful examination has revealed the slight differences from their Bengal models.

For in all those overseas colonies of Indian culture the influence of various parts of India worked simultaneously, thus tending to create a standard type. The older Indian inspirations, carefully cultivated, made themselves felt much longer, as the new fashions and styles coming from India, though eagerly accepted, infiltrated only sparsely, by way of individual visits, emigrating artists, pilgrims with souvenirs of bronzes and paintings. And last but not least the indigenous element made itself felt, though only unconsciously, through unacknowledged misunderstandings and misinterpretations. For to the natives of South East Asia both Buddhism and Hinduism were no more than new garbs for their own religious ideas, and they emphasized those features in Indian art which were congenial to their own ideas and experiences.

*Kashmīr*

While the Turks, successors of the White Huns, were hard pressed by the Chinese and the Muslim Arabs in Central Asia and Afghanistan, Kashmīr — hitherto under the rule of Parthians, Kushānas and Huns — became, under the Kārkota dynasty, the leading power in North-Western India. The empire of Lalitāditya (c. 725—756) reached from Maisūr to Mongolia, from Bengal and Orissā to Afghanistan. At the end of the 8th century Jayāpīda perished as a result of a fruitless effort to keep at least Northern India. The Utpala dynasty (c. 855—939) restored the rule of Kashmīr, lost during the preceding chaos, over the Panjāb and Afghanistan. But the Hindu-Śāhī kings who, in the middle of the 9th century, had superseded the Turkish princelings, made themselves independent and conquered the Panjab by the middle of the 10th century, merely to be overthrown by the

Turkish sultans of Ghaznī between 973 and 1026. In the 11th century the Lohara dynasty (1003—1171) again built up an empire in the Panjab Himalayas. Thereafter Kashmīr, weakened by internal strife, was an unimportant kingdom until its conquest by the Moguls in the 16th century.

Kashmīr, culturally very active, evolved her own systems of Śaiva and Vaishnava theology. Its chief contributions to Hindu iconography were the three-faced Vishnu image, combining the royal with the boar and lion aspect, and that of Sūrya (the sun) with several faces and many arms (found at Mārtānd in Sāsānian costume!).

The oldest Kārkota monuments are at Pandrethān (Purānādhisthāna, i.e. the "old capital"). But the real founder of mediaeval Kashmīr art was Lalitāditya, who built the great town of Parihāsapura (Paraspor, on the Srīnagar-Barāmūla road), much of old Srīnagar (since then almost completely destroyed), the mighty sun temple of Mārtānd, the temples of Wangāth (Bhūteśar), Narastān, Būniyār, on the Takht-i-Sulaimān, then Malot and possibly also some other temples in the Panjab at Kallār, Ketas, Kāfirkot (Bilot). His principal minister, Chankuna, a former Chinese official, erected the great stūpa at Parihāsapura and other stūpas at Pandrethān, decorated with sculptures in the Wei and T'ang Chinese taste. The great chaitya at Parihāsapura (of which the foundations have been excavated), like Chankuna's stūpa, imitated Gandhāra art; once it contained a huge Buddha image modelled on the Bāmiyān colossus. In the Malot and Mārtānd temples late Roman-Syrian architecture was combined with Bengalī *Temple styles* forms and late Gupta sculpture. In the other temples, however, those constituent elements are no longer recognizable, a new style having emerged, characterized by Gupta plinths, a Roman wall design, pilasters of plain, fluted or helical columns on Gupta bases, but with capitals faintly reminiscent of Byzantine ones, trefoil arches, Indian ceilings of intersecting squares, steep, often capped gables, and steep, often duplicated pyramid roofs. The temples are generally set on a pyramid in the centre of a court enclosed by small chapels between projecting bound columns. The somewhat smaller temples of the Utpala dynasty, those of Avantivarman (856—83) at Vantipur, and those of Śamkaravarman (883—902) at Pātan, however, are much more richly decorated, and Mediaeval Hindu and Sāsānian-Persian motifs have been incorporated in this decoration. The stone temples of the 10th—12th centuries are small and their decoration is simple. Wooden temples were built at that time in great number, whose

142

blockhouse construction seems to survive in the peculiar type of Kashmīrī mosques. Examples of their richly carved decoration survive only outside Kashmīr, at Marol (Udaipur) in Lāhul, and in some early Buddhist monasteries in Ladakh, Spiti (Tabo) and Gugé (West Tibet). They reveal the same façade design, but elaborated into a fragile filigree thronged with delicate figures in chapel niches or on lotus flowers.

The late Gupta style of sculpture degenerated under Lalitāditya into a barbaric brutishness. The figures of the 9th century, in a half Gandhāran, half Gupta costume, are more lively, more elegant, but look rather bloated. A big bronze frame found at Divsar for a Buddha image converted by Śamkaravarman into that of the Buddha Avatāra of Vishnu, is covered with the figures of the avatāras within flower scrolls, echoing the powerful sculpture of the Rāshtrakūtas with whom Śamkaravarman had allied himself against the Pratīhāras. Later Kashmīr sculpture, however, such as we know it from a Bodhisattva bronze dedicated under queen Didda (958–1003), or from the wooden frame of the Marol temple in Lāhul (under Ananta, 1028–63), is of an elegant effeminacy, with the slightly Mongoloid bloated features so characteristic of many early Tibetan works.

*Lalitāditya*

Kashmīr murals we know only from places outside the valley: the earlier style in part of the "Gandhāran" murals at Ming-Oï (Kuchā) in the northern Tarim Basin, the later, in the frescoes of Man-nan and of the "Red Temple" at Tsaparang in Western Tibet; and illustrated manuscripts have turned up in Tibet. The style of this "school of Hasurāja" has more vitality than the Bengal miniatures but a harder line, and brighter, but rather cold colours.

Kashmīr art spread outside the valley to Taxila and Hānsī in the Panjab, to Afghanistan beyond Kābul, to the Panjāb Himālayas up to Chambā, Kāngrā and Kulū, Lāhul, Spiti and Western Tibet. In India the three-headed Vishnu type was accepted as coming directly from Kailāsa, the mountain of the gods (e.g. at Khajurāho and in Gujarāt). But otherwise the Kashmīr style left no mark in India.

The princes who gave shape to mediaeval art in the countries in the heart of Northern India, were the Pratīhāra emperors of Kanauj, rulers over the Gūrjara tribes and the Rājput clans totally or partially descended from them, the Gūrjara-Pratīhāras (Parihāras), Chāhamānas, Kachchhapaghātas, Chapotkatas, Solankīs, Paramāras, Chandratreyas and Kalachūrī-Haihayas. In the late 8th century they were the leaders of restless, aggressive tribes along the Rājput desert trying to

*The Pratīhāras*

penetrate the rich agricultural provinces to the east. Nāgabhata II (c. 784—833) made himself master of Kānyakubjā (Kanauj), regarded since the Maukharīs (6th century) as the sacred imperial capital of the North. Ādivarāha Mihira Bhoja I (c. 833—885) consolidated this empire, which comprised all the provinces from central Bihār in the east to the Rāvi in the Punjab, from the valleys of the Himalayas to Gujarat, Saurāshtra, Mālva and Central India. Under Mahendrapala (c. 885—907) the Pratīhāra court reached its greatest splendour and refinement. But then the succession to the throne was contested; the empire was attacked by the Rāshtrakūtas of the Deccan and by the Kāshmīrīs, and Kanauj was taken by Indra III Rāshtrakūta between 915 and 918. Mahīpāla (c. 912—42) was re-installed about 930 by his great feudatories, but thereafter the Pratīhāra emperors were merely puppets in the hand of their Chandella major-domos, until Kanauj was taken in 1019 by Sultān Mahmūd of Ghaznī, and Rājyapāla was slain by Ganda Chandella. When, about 1030, the last scion of the imperial house disappeared, Northern India had already disintegrated into a number of "Rājput" kingdoms.

*Pratīhāra religion* The Pratīhāras claimed brāhman ancestry, though strongly mixed with Gūrjara blood. But even about the turn of the millennium their subjects were looked down upon as barbarians by other Indians. Pratīhāra religion, therefore, was rather impersonal, with a bent towards magic and the yoga of the Gorakhnāth (Kanphata) sect. The idols, as magic incarnations of the deities, and the temples, as cosmic-magic machines, assumed an excessive importance. The gods most venerated were Śiva, mainly in his terrible aspects, the sun, and Vishnu in his boar-incarnation. Vishnu as king of heaven only became more popular later on, superseding Sūrya first as Sūrya-Nārāyana, then as Lakshmī-Nārāyana. But the more common tendency was to offer almost the same respect to all gods, first in groups of temples, then in temples which provided chapels and images for all of them. As a result, the ideology of the Hindu temple was carried to its furthest conclusions. In the 8th—9th centuries an open cult hall (*mandapa*), covered by a flat or corbel-vaulted roof resting on columns and closed by a balustrade, was added in front of the shrine. The temple doors, therefore, could no longer be thrown open in order to show the, often colossal, idol to the outside world. Instead, a smaller image, artificially lit behind the dark *antarala* (the former porch), was revealed to the privileged few who were admitted into the cult hall. In the 9th—10th centuries a closed cult hall, an extension of the circumambulatory passage, came into fashion, probably as a result of contact with the Deccan during the wars with the Rāshtrakūtas. For in the Deccan *vimānas* of this kind had been in use since the Chālukya dynasty of Bādāmī. In the late 10th and early 11th centuries we find North Indian temples (in the Nāgara style) fully developed in and near the capitals of the succeeding Rājput kingdoms; but there are strong reasons for the assumption that this design was already fully elaborated in the golden age of Pratīhāra culture, under Mahendra-pāla (885–908) and his immediate successors, at the imperial capital of Kanauj, at Mathurā and Banāras, all of which have since then been destroyed so many times; of that at Kanauj only a huge mound is left, whereas the present monuments of Mathurā and Banāras are not older than the 18th, in some cases the 16th century.

This fully developed mediaeval temple-cathedral stands on a vast platform (*medhi*) and consists of several buildings: a flight of steps (*nal*), an open pillar hall enclosed by a balustrade (*ardha-* or *nal-mandapa*), a closed cult hall (*gudha-mandapa*) opening only onto a few balconies, a dark porch (*antarala, mukha-mandapa*) and the shrine (*prāsāda*) surrounded by a circumambulatory passage (*pradak-shināpatha, bhrama*) with three balconies of pillars standing on a balustrade (*vedi*). The open hall (*natya-mandapa, sabhāmandapa*), reserved for the performances of the dancing girls (*devadāsīs*), and the ritual dining-hall that is occasionally found (*bhoga mandapa*) are sometimes separate buildings. To these have to be added, also as separate structures, subsidiary temples, triumphal arches (*torana*) and holy baths (*kunda*, especially for the sun god). All these temple rooms are raised on a high receding plinth (*pītha*) within very thick walls (*man-dovara*) and are surmounted by a huge śikhara and a pyramidal roof. The walls are broken up into a system of pilasters (*janghā*) alternating with narrow recesses which are continued above the cornice (*chhajja*) as subsidiary śikharas (*paga*) flanking the central śikhara. Horizontally these pilaster walls are divided into the plinth (*pītha*) consisting of a series of friezes, of demon masks (*giraspati*), animals (*asvathara* and *gajathara*), and scenes from human life (*narathara*), all between various richly decorated angular or rounded mouldings (*bandhana*). On the level of the shrine and cult halls, niches and brackets project from the walls, carrying the figures of the principal gods and of the *Parivāra devatās*, accompanied by innumerable heav-enly nymphs (*surasundarī*); eaves and pediments form the transition to the cornice (*chhajja*), above which the śikharas and subsidiary śikharas rise like a huge mountain range to the coping stone (*āmala-ka*). And in fact, the whole building-complex forms one integral unit, ascending from hill to mountain, and at last to the highest peak of the "world mountain" above the principal shrine. In the interior, massive columns (*stambha*) support an octagonal entablature of brackets sculptured with divine dancing girls or cusped arches on which the low corbelled dome rests, decorated with circle upon circle of floral bands and flying gods, or with radiating ribs of heavenly nymphs. The pillars themselves are arcaded towers in miniature, in which gods and heavenly dancers posture. The walls are covered with image niches and images in consoles. The shrine entrance follows the same scheme as in the late Gupta period; but friezes and statues have multiplied. As a matter of fact, the Gupta architectural tradition is still alive, but, like the Roman tradition in Romanesque art, is reduced to ornamental motifs combined into new architectural forms.

*Gupta tradition*

The whole is an artificial heaven, formerly even more bewildering, when it showed in many colours, reflecting the light of innumerable brass or golden lamp stands, the idol seen shining through the opened shrine door beyond the pitch-black porch. In a royal temple the idol was of gold set with diamonds, rubies and emeralds, hung with crowns, necklaces, bracelets, anklets studded with costly stones; and beneath it untold treasures filled a cellar in the substructure. When His Majesty the Paramarabhattāraka Mahārājādhirāja attended the service accompanied by his queens, ministers and other relatives and friends, all in costly, fashionable attire, when a choir sang, accompanied by a great number of instruments, when beautiful dancing girls displayed their art before the idol, furtively throwing amorous glances at the visitors, it must indeed have been a magnificent spectacle. A spectacle, a masterpiece of refined showmanship built up around the divine presence in the idol. What it was worth as genuine religiousness, is another matter. But official religion in an aristocratic society always tends to develop in this direction, and did the same in Mediaeval Europe, China and Japan.

When at last the Muslims smashed mediaeval India and destroyed the Hindu temple cathedrals, they brought home treasures which can be compared only with those captured by the Spaniards from the Aztecs and Incas. But they could only demolish part of the temples; they proved too massively built: huge blocks, set one on the other without mortar, held together by their sheer weight or by metal clamps. Only later were these blocks sculptured in situ. For this reason also, very few mediaeval Indian sculptures except idols have found their way into foreign museums; they were too difficult to detach from the temple walls.

The number of extant Pratīhāra temples is not excessive, since, because of the low cultural standard of the Gūrjaras, most of them were of moderate size and many of low artistic standard. Thus many of them were later rebuilt, and only fragments indicate their former existence. These fragments reveal a complete disintegration of the Gupta ornament into a flat band ornament, not very different from the arabesque and inscription friezes of Islamic art; even a number of motifs of Central-Asian origin are identical. However, a number of fine temples has been preserved. The oldest are those of the early Gūrjara capital of Bhīnmāl (7th–9th century) and the vast camp town of Osiān in Rājputāna (8th–9th century): small śikhara shrines combined with an open mandapa whose late Gupta architectural and decorative motifs dissolve into a curious mass of clumsy incoherent detail. Related to them are the temples of Badoh and Pathārī near Bhīlsā, and ruins at Jagatsukh in Kulū, Agroha in the Panjab, Ghatiyālā near Osiān, Kadvār in Saurāshtra, etc. To the 9th century we can attribute the later temples of Osiān, and (mostly small) temples at Tinduli (near Āgra), Gwālior (Chaturbhūj, 875, also some Jain caves there), Auwā (Kāmeśvar), Sirwa (820), Pali (Pātāleśvar), Sādrī in Rājasthān, Vadnagar and Kārvan in Gujarat, Deogarh (where there is a Jain temple of 862), Gyāraspur (Ath-Khamba), Kālinjar and Khajurāho (Chaunsat Joginī) in Central India, Kāngrā Fort in the Himalayas. To the early 10th century belong the temples of Chambā, Brahmor (Mānimaheśa and Narsingh), Dvārahāt, Jageśvar and Lakha-Mandal in the Himalayas, the sun temple of Markherā and the Khokhai monastery at Ranod in Central India, and the central portion of the great sun temple of Modherā in Gujarat. We can only infer the magnificence of the imperial temples at Mathurā, Kanauj and Banāras, and also of the famous Somanātha temple in Saurāshtra from the poets and historians at the court of Sultan Mahmūd of Ghaznī who desecrated and plundered them early in the 11th century; and also from the temples built in the middle of the 10th century in the feudatory Rājput states by artists who had found a refuge there after the sack of Kanauj by the Rāshtrakūtas.

The sculpture of Bhīnmāl was a carefully copied import of late Gupta models. At Osiān we find an odd medley of tolerable late Gupta and stiff, lifeless barbarian figures and ornaments; later, however, the characteristic high Pratīhāra taste of the reign of Bhoja I: well-modelled figures, heavy and strong, of a rustic earthiness. But the late Pratīhāra style had already been developed under Mahendrapāla: light, elegant, erotic, superficial in the details, elaborate and involved in the composition. That painting had been an essential form of artistic expression, we know, but there is nothing preserved. Of applied art we have a number of ivory reliefs in London, and an ivory chess man, once the property of Charlemagne, in the *Cabinet des Médailles* in Paris.

*Rajput successor states* The first to break away from the Pratīhāra Empire were the Paramāras (c. 948—1260) who, during the struggle with the Rāshtrakūtas, had migrated to the contested province of Mālva, had helped to overthrow the Rāshtrakūtas and had then threatened their successors, the Western Chālukyas of the Deccan, in alliance with the Śilāhāras (8th—12th century) of the western coast. Under Bhoja of Dhāra (c. 1010—1055) they became the paramount power in India. Bhoja's power, however, was broken by a coalition of the Western Chālukyas, the Kalachūrīs and the Chaulukya-Solankīs of Gujarāt (942—1242) who, under Kumārapāla, conquered Southern Rājputāna and defeated the Chālukyas. After Muslim raids had weakened the Solankīs, their ministers, the Vāghelās (1244—1304) at last succeeded in uniting the central provinces of Gujarāt, until the country was annexed by Sultān A'lā-ud-dīn Khiljī of Delhi. The Chandrātreyas (Chandellas, c. 831—1202—1308) of Bundelkhand were the major domos of the emperors of Kanauj, since Harsha had re-installed Mahīpāla after the Rāshtra-kūta capture of Kanauj. Dhanga (954—1002) and Ganda (1002—1019) took over the eastern Pratīhāra provinces, but were seduced to indulging in erotic-mystic rituals and a voluptuous life by their vassals, the Kalachūrīs or Haihayas of Chedi (Eastern Central India, c. 9th—12th century), who, after the disappearance of the Pratīhāras and a defeat of Vidyādhara Chandella by Mahmūd of Ghaznī, finally eliminated the Chandellas. Under Gangeyadeva (1030—41) and Karna (1041—1070) the Kalachūrīs were the leading power of Northern India, but were at last defeated by a great coalition which restored Kīrtivarman Chandella, until northern Central India was conquered by the Muslims between 1202 and 1288. The next powers in Northern India were the Gāhadavālas (c. 1075—1200) at Kanauj and the Chāhamānas of Śakambharī (near Ājmer) in Rājasthān (8th century) who, under Prithvīrāj III, conquered Delhi, but were decisively defeated by the Muslims in 1192/3, after which they retired to Ranasthambhapura (Ran-

Kandāriya-Mahādeva temple, built by King Ganda Chandella in 1002 at Khajurāho.

tambhor) in north-eastern Rājasthān and in the 14th century started the line of mahārājās of Būndī and Kotah. Other branches of the dynasty played an important role in southern Rājputāna during the 13th—16th century and even later. In Orissa, finally, the Buddhist Bhauma or Kara kings were superseded in the later 8th century by the Śivaite Keśarīs, the builders of the great Bhuvaneśvara temples, in the 11th century by the Gangas, the builders of the famous Konārka and Purī temples, and finally by the Sūryavamśīs (15th—16th century). During this period Orissā transferred its cultural allegiance from Buddhist Bengal to the Pratīhāra-Rājputs and finally to the Deccan.

*Building mania* All these dynasties produced great builders who, after their rise to power, also wanted to have their own temple cathedrals by the side of those great temples which were all-Indian or regional centres of pilgrimage, and the more modest sanctuaries in the residences of the feudatories. Thus there developed ten different dynastic styles which, however, can be reduced to five groups: the Chandella-Haihaya, based on the late Pratīhāra style; the Chāhamāna-Gāhadavāla-Kachhwāha-Trigarta group, developed mainly from 9th century Pratīhāra art, though later also adopting some of the late Pratīhāra style; the Paramāra-Śilāhāra group in the South, mixing 9th century Pratīhāra with Rāshtrakūta features; the Solankī-Vāghelā group, developed from early Pratīhāra art under Paramāra influence; and Orissā, basically early Pratīhāra with an admixture of Pāla-Sena and Chandella-Haihaya characteristics.

Most important of all these are the temples (Kandāriya Mahādeva, Viśvanātha, Ambājī, Lakshmana, etc.) of Kharjurāhaka (Khajurāho), the first capital of the Chandellas of Jejakabhukti (the present Bundelkhand). Erected between 954 and 1002 by the kings Dhanga and Ganda, they have become famous for the exquisite perfection of their architecture and the elegance of their sculpture, and notorious for the gross eroticism of some of their most conspicuous reliefs. The first was due to the transfer of the best Pratīhāra masters from declining Kanauj, the latter to the introduction of a Tāntrik Śaiva cult, by means of which the Haihaya feudatories of the Chandellas corrupted and at last overthrew their overlords. A similar group of small but exquisite temples further west is that in the small fort of Surwaya (south of Gwālior). The Vaishnava temples of the later Chandella capitals of Mahobā and Kālanjar are much more modest. Haihaya-Kalachūrī temples are still standing in the ruins of Chandrehe, Bilhari, Tewarī (Tripurī) and Sohāgpur in southern Bāghelkhand; the best monu-

The Mukteśvara temple at Bhuvaneśvara in Orissā, the most beautiful of all Orissā temples, c. end of the 9th century. In front a holy pool. The temple is on a platform decorated with miniature chapels. In the centre of the picture the shrine proper with its tower (*śikhara*); on the left the ceremonial hall.

ments of this style, however, at Karna's capital of Banāras, have long since disappeared.

*Orissā* The older monuments of Mediaeval Orissā, the Paraśurāmeśvara (7th century), the hall of the Rājarānī temple, and the Vaitāl Deul (early 9th century) at Bhuvaneśvara, are, like the Mahāyāna-Buddhist sculptures of Nalatigiri, representatives of the late Gupta style. The Keśarī kings first introduced 9th century Pratīhāra architecture. The earliest example is the fine small Mukteśvara temple, the sculpture of which still links up with that of the Vaitāl Deul. Yayāti Keśarī (c. 970—1000) was the founder of the huge Lingarāja temple (Krittivāsa) on the embankment of an artificial lake at Bhuvaneśvara, a shrine 1280 feet (55 m) high, with three successive cult halls (added by Anantavarman Chodaganga 1076—1147 and Anangabhīma III, 1211—1238). The numerous smaller temples within the enclosure of this state sanctuary were donated by later kings, queens, and ministers. Anantavarman Chodaganga built the Jagannātha (Vishnu) temple at Purī, world famous as the "Juggernaut", under the wheels of whose procession car so many fanatical victims were once crushed; he also added another sanctuary and *sikhara* to the Rājarānī whose sculptures reveal a strong dependence on Haihaya art (through his queen). Last of all there is the Sūrya temple of Konārka, the third skyscraper sanctuary of Orissā, a creation of King Narasimhadeva I Ganga (1239—64) and of his queen Sītā-Devī. It is designed as the chariot of the sun, the wheels of which are reproduced on the plinth, while stone horses flank the stairs leading up to the cult hall. The plinth has become notorious for its very outspoken sexual sculptures, in this case not inspired by any secret ritual, but connected with the many dancing girls once dedicated to the sun temples; their rich repertoire of dance is depicted on the walls of the dance hall in front of the temple. The master artists responsible for the many beautiful reliefs and statues, however, do not seem to have carried out these objectionable erotic scenes which are from the hand of crude apprentices. Orissā architecture differs considerably from the other North Indian styles. It preserved the beehive — shaped early Pratīhāra *sikhara* — in contrast to the more common pointed type. Its walls show a simpler organization: the plinth never became more than a supporting terrace, the walls reveal a greater uniformity of the projecting *pagas*, the sculpture is spread more uniformly over them. The ceilings of the halls in the biggest of these temples, too large to be covered in the traditional Hindu trabeate technique, are supported by long girders of hand-wrought iron.

Part of the plinth of the great sun temple of Konārka in Orissā (13th century). At the bottom, a frieze of elephants, then a wheel of the 'sun chariot', with a frieze of minor deities (yakshas, snakes, etc.) and a frieze of erotic groups (old fertility deities) behind. On top a frieze with scenes from social life. Mannered, over-elaborate, and erotically decadent in manner.

The influence of Orissā art made itself felt in the temple ornamentation of both Java and Cambodia (Bantéay Srei; Angkor).

*The Chāhamāna princes*
To the west of the Chandellas the Chāhamāna princes, loyal to the last to the emperors of Kanauj, were the most conservative champions of the pure Pratīhāra style. The Harshanātha temple of Sīkar (mid 10th century) of which only fragments are left, must likewise have been an example of the best late Pratīhāra art. Chāhamāna art of the 11th century, however, was rather rustic, but powerful, becoming more elegant again in the 12th. Its principal monuments at Ājmer and Delhi have been transformed into mosques; but at Vīsalpur in the Banās Gorge, at Barolli, Menāl, Nāgdā and Bijoliā in Mewār, etc., there still stand fine temples. The last phase of Chāhamāna architecture (13th century) at Osiān, Kirādu, Jālor, Sānchor, Nādol, Sādrī, etc., is more or less an elegant and over-elaborate, rather lifeless repetition of late Pratīhāra formulas. A variety of the Chāhamāna style with an interesting admixture of Central-Asian nomadic ornamental motifs and concepts of style, is found in the temples of the early Kachchhapaghātas (Kachhwāhas) of Gwālior, especially the so-called "Sās-Bahu" (Padmanābha) group of Gwālior Fort (1093, by Mahīpāla Bhuvanekamalla). Other variants are those of the Gāhadavāla kings of Kanauj (1075—1200) of which little is known, except some small temples near Banāras and in Kumāon, and the most impressive Buddhist monastery (with an underground chapel reached by a tunnel) built by Govindachandra (1114—55) at Sārnāth; and that of the Trigarta kings of Kāngrā, in the Western Himālaya, a crossbreeding of Chauhān and Kashmīr art.

The monuments of the Solankī capital of Anahilavāda have completely disappeared except for the partly re-excavated Sahasralinga Talāo, an artificial lake dug and surrounded with temples by Jayasimha Siddharājā (1094—1144). Many generations have worked, from the 10th to the 13th century, at the famous Śiva temple at Siddhpur (Rudramahālaya) and the sun temple of Modherā — the most beautiful ruin in Gujarat. And similarly the Somanātha temple in Saurāshtra was several times destroyed by the Muslims (1026 by Mahmūd of Ghaznī), and rebuilt at least three times. The Rishabhanātha (1031),
*Rishabhanātha*
erected at Dilwāra on Mt. Ābū by Vimala Sāh, a minister of Bhīma I, inaugurated the long series of temples in white marble which the rich Jain community, big merchants, bankers, ministers and generals, built in Gujarāt, Saurāshtra and South Rājputāna. Though Dilwāra is best known, situated as it is in a much frequented summer

resort on the great tourist route, there are other temples of the same quality, at Āchalgarh (also on Mt. Ābū), Kumbharia, Jālor, Nāgdā, Chitorgarh, Tarangā Hill, Girnār, Palitāna, on Mt. Śatrunjaya and in a number of other places (often on mountain tops). Many go back to the reign of Kumārapāla (1143—73) who had ascended the throne with Jain support. Under the Vāghelā dynasty which was put into power by the Jains Vastupāla and Tejahpāla, Jain architecture flourished (e.g. Tejahpāla's Neminātha temple at Dilwāra, under King Vīradhavala, 1232—42). The fortifications, city gates with ceilings supported by several levels of brackets alternating with sculptures, and the Kālī temple at Dabhoi (Darbhāvatī) in Gujarat are of the reign of his successor Vīsaladeva (1244—62). But the majority of Jain temples were erected in Muslim times. They differ from ordinary Hindu temples in that the principal shrine occupies the centre of a closed court surrounded by chapels of the 24 Tīrthankaras (with or without a small *sikhara* on each of them). Sometimes the central shrine houses four images grouped around a small microcosm of the world (*samavasārana*), open to the four winds (Chaturmukh Mandir, and another at Dilwāra, of the 16th century).

The last group of Mediaeval North Indian temples is that of the Paramāra emperors of Dhāra and Māndū in Mālwa, almost as massive as those of Orissā and very densely decorated. Best known is the temple of Nīlkantheśvar at Udaypur in Mālwa (1059—80); less important are those of Ūn, Nemāwar, Bhīlsā, Jamli, etc. The immense artificial lake of Bhojpur in Bhopāl (now dry) and the iron column at Dhāra also deserve mention; however, old Dhāra has completely disappeared since it was made a Muslim capital in the 14th century. A branch of Paramāra architecture is shown in the temples of their allies in the Konkān, the Śilāharas, of which the Ambarnātha (1060) near Bombay (railway station of the same name), the very impressive Gondeśvar at Sinnār (south of Nāsik) and the Balsane temples, may be regarded as the best.

*The Paramāra emperors*

There is hardly any need to emphasise that an extensive secular architecture had once also existed; but all that can be traced now is fortification walls, without bastions, in cyclopic or polygonal work, on many hill forts. Yet the theoretical texts give us descriptions not only of palaces, but also of theatres, and of highly developed town planning.

The sculpture of these temples represents a highly efficient mass production. Scenes in even complicated compositions are repeated from

Part of the shrine façade of the Kandāriya Mahādeva temple, Khajurāho, erected by King Ganda Chandella in 1002. The extraordinary erotic scenes are connected with the ritual of the Matta-Mayūras, a Kaula-

Kāpālika sect which, between c. 960 and 1002, were very influential at the Chandella court. According to their teachings the erotic relations between men and women mirrored those between Bahādeva and the Great Goddess and thus showed the way to salvation.

temple to temple, often identically, more often with slight variations. Variations in quality are mainly accounted for by the masters who did the planning and their assistants and apprentices who were responsible for the minor work; and can be seen in the idols and the most conspicuous statues on the temple walls. The master sculptors (silpin) were, like the architects (sūtradhara), highly cultured people, often of priestly rank and bearing high-sounding titles. The names of many of them are known to us from official inscriptions as well as by signatures on their work, though for the time being their personalities remain shadowy to us, as no systematic research has hitherto been undertaken on this subject. And indeed, a vast knowledge must have been required in order to execute, without error, the innumerable figures distinguished by so many different forms of the body, proportions, crowns, gestures and symbols, and to fulfil the many rituals connected with this work. However, there is no indication that all this symbolism still meant much to them. The very refraction of the Divine into so many visual forms appealed more to the intellect than to emotion. Many of the Khajurāho sculptures were carelessly executed, are anatomically utterly impossible, but prove convincing because of a sweeping rhythm and a seductive sensuality. When, in the 10th century, the former feudatory dynasties became independent, the influence of the provincial artists brought a temporary return to religious and artistic seriousness. The deities regained majesty, sometimes even tragic greatness, the figures show careful modelling, though at the cost of musicality. However, by the middle of the 11th century, the fashionable sleekness and sensuality, in fact often frivolity, again got the upper hand. The human figure was increasingly reduced to a conventional, lifeless doll. Instead, the ornament became richer and richer, and the composition gained effects of depth unknown since Gupta times, achieved, on the one hand, by a building up of groups projecting on successive levels from the wall, on the other by chiaroscuro through working away the background of the figures until they were, in fact, treated in the round, though held together by close interlinking (12th century). In the same way, all wall surfaces were broken up into a fine filigree of ornamentation. It is impossible to describe the transformation of the stone in the

*Mediaeval Rajput sculpture and painting*

13th—14th centuries into a lacework of the most intricate and beautiful geometrical motifs of flowers, rosettes, figure friezes, etc., so delicate that one wonders how the stone was not broken a thousand times. The "bronze" (i.e. *ashtadhātu* = 8 metal-alloy) images reveal a similar development, from almost life-size, elegant statues like the Gaurī-Śankara group at Chambā, to the numerous Jain idols of Gujarāt, inlaid with gold, silver and copper, transformed more and more into intricate filigree compositions of which the figures of the Tīrthankaras or Yakshīs (especially Ambikā) merely form the centre. Of painting we know very little: some Paramāra ceiling frescoes in the Kailāsa at Elūrā and at Madanpur (Lalitpur District) and a few Jain illustrated palm-leaf manuscripts (mainly from the once almost inaccessible vaults of the Jain temples in Jaisālmer Fort, in the heart of the Thar Desert). Their subjects are very various, their narration is lively, their colours bright, their composition very decorative, but the figures are much more mannered and expressionless than those of the Pāla-Buddhist manuscripts, and the scenes are without depth. The Tibetans saw in these features a characteristic of the "School of the Ancient West", the foundation of which they attributed to Śringadhara, a master of he 7th century.

*Last renaissance*
The Muslim invasion in the 13th century annihilated the aristocratic-theocratic Hindu civilization of the Middle Ages. Worse than the systematic iconoclasm of the conquerors was the political chaos created by the Rājput aristocracy retreating to and fighting for the possession of such countries as had escaped direct Muslim administration. For a long time the only monuments were clumsy adaptations of ruins and funeral stelas of local chieftains. Only the Jain merchants, who now co-operated with the new masters of the country, could afford to build temples in lonely places, in the desert or on mountain tops. The most opulent renovations, e.g. at Dilwāra go back to the early 14th century, apparently because numerous trained arists were available at cheap rates. But slowly their skill declined. Instead, new opportunities arose in the new Rājput states growing up in the late 14th century. And when, in the 15th century, a powerful Rājput federation withstood all Muslim onslaughts on Rājasthān, when in Orissā Kapilendra, Purushottama and Pratāparudra took the offensive, when, even in the Himālayas, the small Mediaeval states recovered, Hindu and Jain architecture, sculpture and painting experienced a renaissance which, under the tolerant rule of the first Mogual emperors, lasted until the first quarter of the 17th century. At the start artists

The Jain Tīrthankara Pārśvanātha protected by a king cobra. On both sides a protective yaksha and yakshinī. 'Ashtadhātu' bronze, partly inlaid with silver. From the Akotā hoard, 7th—8th centuries. 7″ high. *Baroda Museum.*

Mahāvira, the 'founder' of the Jain sect, carried by the gods in a palanquin out of the town, intending to renounce the world. 15th century. Miniature on paper. About double height of original. *Baroda Museum.*

had to be summoned from Nepāl, Orissā, Hoysala Maisūr, the Tamil South. The theoretical texts were studied, the still existing ruins copied. In particular eighty forts and numerous temples were erected under Mahārānā Kumbha of Mewār (1433—68) which, superficially seen, could vie with the monuments of pre-Muslim times (Chitorgarh; Kumbha-Meru = "Tower of Victory" 1459, Kumbha-Śyāma; Kumbhalner, Rānakpur 1440, Bhilodā, etc.). In the 16th and 17th centuries the Jains not only rebuilt all their old ruins, but founded numerous new temples at Mt. Ābū, Palitāna, Girnār, etc. Even during the period of Mughal persecution and temple destruction in the later 17th century new temples were built in defiance, at Udaipur (Jagannātha, 1651—52), Jaisālmer, Kulū, etc.

But it was no more than a scholarly, antiquarian fashion, favoured for a time by the political revival. The architecture often lacks understanding for the functional role of its individual parts, the sculptures, though lively, bear no relation at all to the human body, the iconography oscillates between a naïve pride in the vast learning of the artists (especially Kumbha's chief architect Mandana) and the grossest misunderstandings. Painting was for a long time reduced to one Jain standard text, the Kalpasūtra, whose decorative compositions are, however, nearer to pure ornament than to representation of natural objects.

*Religious reform*

This renaissance style died not so much from Mughal oppression as from a reform of Hindu religion which again made an appeal to the human heart and, in the cults of Krishna and Rāma, made new demands on the religious imagery which the Mediaeval tradition could not fulfil. The revival of Hindu orthodoxy in the 18th century by the Marāthas, however, inaugurated another wave of temple restoration (Banāras, Dwārka, Trimbak, Dākor, etc.) and another revival of Mediaeval Hindu architecture and sculpture, yet in a style mixed with Deccanī-Hindu and Mughal elements which is alive even today in Mahārāshtra, as is that of the Jains in Gujarāt and Rājputāna. However, its role was, and is not more than that of, for example, neo-Gothic church art in Europe.

THE DECCAN AND THE SOUTH

The South Indian Renaissance arrived about two hundred years after Gupta civilization. It thus had more creative originality left, and crystalized into Mediaeval Indian civilization two centuries later. The 8th—10th centuries, dominated by the Rāshtrakūta Empire, thus formed a transition period, similar to that in Pāla-Bihār and Bengal, or in Kashmīr.

The Rāshtrakūtas (753—974), after the invasion of Lalitāditya of Kashmīr (736—47), had overthrown their overlords, the Chālukyas of Bādāmī. Their empire comprised the whole Deccan, Mālva and Gujarāt; in the south the Gangas of Maisūr, and in the east the Chālukyas of Vengi were their vassals, while in the north they temporarily occupied all the countries up to Chitorgarh, Kanauj and Kālanjar. However, this immense empire built up by Dantidurga (735—57), Krishnarāja I (757—72), Dhruva (780—934) and Govinda III (793/4—814) was always threatened by disruption. Under Amoghavarsha I (814—80) Maisūr, Vengi and Gujarat revolted, and Mālva was overrun by the Paramāras. Krishna II (880—914) and Indra III (914—17) extended their power to the Ganges and conquered the Pratīhāra capital of Kanauj. After two decades of easy-going reigns Krishna III (939—68) again reasserted his rule up to the Himalayas and the Nīlgiris. But then the resources of the state were exhausted. Amoghavarsha IV (968—72) was slain when Sīyaka Paramāra sacked the capital Mānyakheta (Mālkher, on the Wādi-Hyderabad railway). In 974 Karka II (III) was overthrown by Taila II, the founder of the "Western" Chālukya dynasty of Kalyāni.

*The art of the Rāshtrakūtas*
Our knowledge of the monuments of this powerful dynasty is curiously one-sided. On the one hand, the last group of the famous cave temples of Elūrā, especially the Kailāsa, was their creation; on the other, we can hardly assign to them a single temple constructed in dressed stone; and the ruins of Mālkhed are unexplored to the present day. Yet, it must be here and not at Elūrā that the decisive new developments of the time must be sought. For, seen in the general perspective of the time, Elūrā was no more than an aftermath of the 7th century. The cave temples were growing unfashionable, and the famous Rāshtrakūta temple at Elūrā is an imitation of a stone temple, hewn from the rock, not a cave.

Elāpura (Elūrā, Ellora) was the capital of the first Rāshtrakūta emperors. In the cliffs at the foot of the ancient town, at the Tīrtha sacred to brahmans, Buddhists and Jains, Dantidurga dug the Dasāvatāra cave temple, similar in plan to the neighbouring Buddhist Tin-Thal, with the difference, however, that it ends in a linga chapel, that its walls are covered with relief scenes from Hindu mythology and that in the centre of its front court there stands a sacrificial hall (*yajna-sālā*) cut into the rock.

*The Kailāsa*
The next monument to the north is the famous Kailāsa, consecrated by Krishnarājā I and therefore generally believed to have been of his

creation. In reality this biggest and richest of all temples cut into the rock (164' × 109', in a court 276' × 154', 100' deep on the back wall) has had a very complicated history. Already in Dantidurga's time a small, but very holy cave temple of Svayambhū-Śiva had stood there, half-way up the cliffs, harbouring a natural linga. Dantidurga began to enlarge its court, adding, in front, a hall for Śiva's bull-companion Nandi. Krishnarājā got a court cut round the original cave shrine and had it elaborated into a "ratha" of the Māmallapura type, but on the model of the Kailāsanātha at Kānchī and the temples of Pattadakal, whose architects, masons and sculptors he could employ after the destruction of the Chālukyas. But as for the excavation of an entrance building in the later Kānchī manner, the hill-side left no room: the front court was excavated a storey deeper so that the actual temple had now to be reached via two staircases. Though the capital was transferred to Mānyakheta, the Kailāsa became, as it were, the religious centre of the empire. Dhruva, Govinda III and Amoghavarsha surrounded its courts with chapels of the river goddesses and mother goddesses, with the vast cave temple of Śiva-Lankeśvara and a big unfinished shrine opposite it. And when, through the conquest of Kanauj, the Pratīhāra conception of the temple-cathedral became familiar, Krishna III started to transform the Kailāsa to conform with this, by expanding the lower front court around the whole building, thus doubling its height. This work was only completed much later when the Paramāras had conquered the northern half of the Rāshtrakūta empire. The Kailāsa has been as much admired as criticized. But a fair appreciation has to keep in mind that, being the shrine of a Svayambhū-lingam, its situation within an artificial cleft is as it should be (natural lingas being found, as products of erosion, mainly in glens and clefts), and that the building, such as we know it, with its excessively high plinth and too low roof, is the product of a transition period, the cathedral being no more than an afterthought to a well-planned Chālukyan temple.

The Kailāsa does not stand quite alone. At Elūrā the Jain "Small Kailāsa" represents a rather modest imitation, while the Indrasabhā cave has cross-bred with the halls of the Daśāvatāra cave. Finally, in Mālwa, near the old Buddhist caves of Dhamnār, the Dharmanātha temple was carved out in a narrow court accessible by means of a corridor, just as the great Śiva temple at Elephanta was completed in early Rāshtrakūta times. However, the real new development in architecture followed the line from the earlier Chālukyan (6th—8th century)

*The small Kailāsa*

163

to the "Western" Chālukyan (10th—12th century) temple, and in all probability some of the monuments still attributed to the latter dynasty, e.g. those of Dichpalli and Bodhān, may possibly prove to have been erected by the Rāshtrakūtas. The only temple of dressed stone of which we know for certain stands at Sandūr, and has portrait statues of Indra III and of one of his ministers.

*Rāshtrakūta*
*sculpture*

Rāshtrakūta sculpture represents the final peak of Hindu art, because it was still the product of intense religious and human experience. The earliest, rather simple creations of the time of Dantidurga possess a wild ferocity and overwhelming vitality (e.g. the Dasāvatāra cave,

śiva as Tripurāntaka, 'the destroyer of the three fortresses'. Relief on the Kailāsa rock-temple, Elūrā, middle of the 8th century. According to an old myth told in the Vedas, Brāhmanas, Purānas and Āgamas, the Asuras (giants) defied the gods in three inpregnable fortresses built by the Asura architect, Māyā. After Indra and Brahmā had been ignominiously defeated, śiva at last triumphed, attacking the demons in his chariot driven by Brahmā, while Vishnu, Agni, Yama and Soma gave their power to the arrow which alone could overcome those fortresses and their inhabitants.

164

and the Bhairava reliefs at Kailāsa). Those of the reigns of Krishna-rājā (the entrance and upper storey of Kailāsa) and Dhruva (river goddesses, in an elegant, semi-Pallava taste) are very unequal because both the Chālukyan and the Pallava traditions had to be absorbed; there is a remarkable susceptibility to new ideas and experimentation with new effects. Under Govinda III a new classical harmony is re-gained, reflecting the grand Chālukya style of the later 7th century, though in a more realistic and optimistic spirit. Under Amoghavar-sha I (the Lankeśvara cave) Rāshtrakūta sculpture turned baroque, nervous and pessimistic, full of chiaroscuro effects. By the 10th cen-tury, especially under Krishnarājā III (the big relief of Śita and Pār-vatī on Kailāsa), the light, fashionable elegance and also the super-ficiality of late Pratīhāra sculpture had been reached.

And the few fragments of painting (the first level of ceiling frescoes in the Rang-Mahal, i.e. in the cult hall of the Kailāsa; or paintings in late Buddhist and Jain caves) tell the same story.

*The Western Chālukyas*

Taila II, who annihiliated the Rāshtrakūtas, claimed to renew the line of the Chālukyas of Bādāmī. A rebel feudatory, he had to compete with other rebels, the Paramāras, who occupied all the Rāshtrakūta provinces in the north, their allies on the western coast, the Śilāhāras, and, most dangerous of all, the rising Chola power in the Tamil South. The Western Chālukyas (973—1200), therefore, had a much smaller empire and much less control over their vassals. In the 11th century the Hoysalas of Maisūr became increasingly independent, and in the 12th century the empire broke up into the Hoysala king-dom (1022—1342) in the south, that of the Kākatīyas (1000—1199—1326) in its eastern, and that of the Yādavas (1189—1321) in its north-ern provinces. Social and political conditions now became very sim-ilar to those in Northern India during the last centuries before the Muslim conquest, though popular activity, expressing itself in the religious movements of the Śaiva Lingayats and the Vaishnava reform of Rāmānuja, Mādhva and Nimbārka, remained much more active.

The temples (*gudi, basti*), now always consisting of an open porch (*bali-mandapa*) or pillared front hall (*sukhanāsi*), closed cult hall (*navaranga*) and massive shrine (*sannidhi*), and in addition a gateway (*nahādvāra*) surmounted by a *gopura,* a hall of sacrifices (*yagaśālā*), *vāhana mandapa* (for the statue of Nandi, Garuda, etc.), stores (*kot-tāra* and *ugrana*) and kitchen (*pākaśālā*), were decorated with an in-creasing wealth of architectural motifs, ornaments and sculptures of gods and goddesses. And ritual dances played an important role in

*Mediaeval art of the Deccan*

which even queens (e.g. Śāntale, the senior wife of Vishnuvardhana Hoysala, 1100—1152) participated.

The starting point of this architecture was the temples of the early Chālukyas at Bādāmī, Pattadakal, etc. But the open front hall was now often expanded into a rectangle or cross of up to ten rows of pillars, and the interval between the parapet (*jagati*) and the roof was closed by perforated stone screens (*pinjrā*), while the entrance to the temple from outside as well as to the sanctuary was often framed by a perforated screen frieze of scrolls filled with flowers or figures. The Navaranga, on the other hand, rarely had more than four pillars (not including the wall pilasters), but it often communicated with several, generally three shrines (*trikūtāchala*). The plinth never became so high as in Northern India. The walls were decorated with alternating sets of overslim pilasters and wall niches surmounted by a small śikhara. The pillars of the open hall as well as of the navaranga are very heavy, either round, turned on a lathe, or of polygonal ground-plan. Their capitals are huge "cushions" or "flower cups". The roof, rising in *pancharams* on a row of eaves (*chhajja*), is flat, except on top of the sanctuary, where it rises in a number of pancharam storeys to a big cupola (*śringa*). This tower, much broader and shorter than in Northern India, also developed into the polygon by means of repeated projections of the sides, until at last a genuine polygon crowned by a short cone was constructed by the intersection of three squares.

*New emphasis*    The accent lies not on the verticals — as in Northern India — but on the horizontals which are emphasized by pronounced plinth mouldings, lintels, deep incisions in the columns, a horizontal co-ordination of all vertical motifs, pilasters, niches, *śikharas*, etc., repeated rows of caves, not only along the walls, but also along the tower. And also all contrasts are accentuated — in antithesis to the smooth transitions and figures of North Indian art: projections and recessions, light and deep shadows, deeply drilled-out ornaments, bizarre, exaggerated curves and arches, figures with marked, angular movements. The same contrasts that determine the character of South Indian music and dance! From the 10th to the 13th century this constructive and decorative system became richer and richer and more and more involved, to end at last in the exuberant Rococo of Hoysala art where hardly a corner exists that is not replete with a surging exuberance of figures and ornaments of every possible size and description.

There are hundreds of similar temples of Western Chālukyan times in the upper valley of the Krishnā, the Tungabhadrā and Bhīmā. Unfortunately the dates and history of only a few buildings are known. The best of them are the Kallesvar at Kukkanūr and the great Jain temple at Lakkundi, both probably rather early, the Siddheśvar (1087) at Haveri, the Tārakeśvara at Hangāl, the Arvattukhambada (1091—1138) at Bankapur, the Mahādeva (1112) at Ittagi, the Dodda Basappā at Dambāl, and especially the splendid Kāśīviśveśvara (1171) at Lakkundi, the Mallikārjuna at Kuruvattī and the Someśvara at Gadag (12th century). A further 88 temples of the Hoysalas, generally well documented, are known. Those visited by most tourists are the Chennakeśava, erected in 1117 at the first capital, Velāpura (Belūr), in commemoration of Vishnuvardhana's conversion by the great Vaishnava reformer Rāmānuja; the quadruple Lakshmīdevī (1113) at Dodda Goddavallī; the majestic Hoysaleśvara at the later capital of Dorasamudra (Halebīd, "old capital"), built by Narasimha I in 1141, and the small Keśava at Somnāthpur built in 1268, by a minister of Narasimha III.

The sculpture of this period is consciously decorative. Most of the divine figures, merely intended as part of a comprehensive rhythmical composition, are lifeless and without expression. Those of minor deities, human beings and animals, are lively, but likewise highly stylized, inspired rather by scenes from dance and theatre than by ordinary life. The earlier statues of heavenly nymphs, e.g. at Kedrapur, reflect fashionable court life. Those at Kuruvattī are of a sultry sexuality; those in the great Hoysala temples are of a cool, elegant sexiness. Everywhere ornamentation predominates: jewellery and crowns on the figures, trees as backgrounds, scrolls, flowers and arabesques on the mouldings, all of them executed in a fine filigree work comparable to that of the late Chāhamāna and Vāghela ceilings of Northern India. The most important sculptors have signed their works, the artists parading arrogant titles such as "the smiter of the crowd of titled sculptors", "the knife to the necks of titled sculptors", etc.

*Sculpture*

In the Kākatīya and Yādava kingdoms, on the other hand, art became simpler. The sculptures were increasingly stylized until they looked, for example, like primitive Greek or Etruscan bronzes. Yet they have the same quaint charm of pure rhythm and abstract form. The ornament was also reduced, until, half a century before the Muslim conquest, an almost plain temple style had evolved, called Hemādpanthi, after Hemādri, minister of the Yādava king Krishna (1247—60). The most important Kākatīya temples are those of Warangal, Pālampet (1213 sculptures!), Śrīśailam, Hanamkonda and Ittagi. Yā-

Chenna-Keśava temple, Belūr, erected in 1117 by King Vishnuvardhana in commemoration of his conversion to Vishnuism at Velāpura or Beluhūr. 'Chenna' means 'frog' after a defect in the idol's stone.

dava temples are found mainly in the Khāndesh, Ahmadnagar, Nāsik, Sholāpur and Sātārā districts and in Berār. Both dynasties constructed a number of fortresses of which Warangal, Raichūr and Deogiri (the later Daulatābād) are the most important. The latter, today a much frequented sightseeing spot, was the impregnable capital of the Yādavas, a wonder of mediaeval military engineering. Its citadel occupied the top of an isolated rock cone rising 600 feet above the surrounding plain. All around, the sides of the rock were scarped vertically for a height of 150 feet so smoothly that any escalade was impossible. One had to pass over the deep wet moat thus excavated, by means of a drawbridge, and had then to climb a mighty bastion and a narrow, steep and tortuous tunnel which could be filled with the deadly hot gases of an iron brazier connected with it by a special tunnel. The entrance to this passage is ornamented like that of a temple shrine; the stones of the other Yādava buildings there were later used by the Muslims for several additional fortification lines and two mosques.

*South India*

The civil war of 731 which had brought Nandivarman II on the throne, had weakened the Pallava Empire. After his death in 795 it began to disintegrate under the attacks of the Pāndyas in the south, the Eastern Chālukyas in the north, and the Rāshtrakūtas in the west. While the Eastern Chālukyas and Rāshtrakūtas were interlocked in a bitter war, the Cholas recovered their old capital Tanjāvū (Tanjore) as federates of Nandivarman III about 846, and soon became independent. In 897 Āditya I overthrew the Pallavas, and while the Rāshtrakūtas were occupied in the north by their wars with the Pratīhāras and Paramāras, Parāntaka I, Rājarājā I and Rājendra I subdued the Pāndyas. The Eastern Chālukyas were at this time linked through marriage, and when, in 1070, the Eastern Chālukya, Kulottunga I, a Chola on mother's and grandmother's side, ascended the throne of Tanjore, all the South Indian lowlands were united under one crown. Under Rājarājā I (985—1016), Rājendra I (1012—44), Rājādhirājā (1018—54), and again under Kulottunga I (1070—1118) and Kulottunga II (1133—1150), the Chola Empire was the leading power in India, controlling northern Ceylon and temporarily parts of Bengal, Burma, Malaya and Sumatra. But already under Kulottunga II the Pāndyas had recovered, and Rājarājā III (1218—56) could hold his own against Māravarman Sundara Pāndya only with Hoysala support. While the Cholas faded out with Rājendra III (1246—79), the Pāndyas became the sovereign power of the South under Jātavarman Sundara (1238—68) and Māravarman Kulaśekhara (1268—1308/9), only to be overthrown by the Muslims a few years later, in 1323.

*Chola period*

The Chola period was the golden age of Mediaeval times, putting its stamp especially on civilization and art in South India, so that they have remained the same, in principle, up to our time. The aristocratic-theocratic rule was tempered in considerable measure by village

and municipal self-government. The temples (e.g. Madurai 847′ ×
729′ = 258 × 222 m), growing into holy (śrī, tiru) temple-towns
found nowhere else in India, were not only the religious, but also the
social and economic centres, involving the individual citizen in a
number of committees and honorary functions. Social stratification
meant not merely rulers and subjects, but a social order of divine
origin allotting to everybody his special function in society. The pride
of the priests was, therefore, kept in check by a religiousness which
concerned itself also with the poor and the outcast. Literature, in the
Tamil language, was intelligible also to the masses, with only the
construction and a high flown Sanskrit vocabulary marking the difference between the sophisticated poetry of the court and the devotional hymns and legends of the people.

*Drāvida*
*Architecture*
The Pallava period had witnessed the rise of a new type of temples,
superseding the earlier brick or marble shrines of semi-Buddhist style
which had flourished under the Ikshvākus, as well as more primitive
sanctuaries, sacred trees, hero tombs, etc. Under the Cholas and Pāndyas such temples (*kovil, koil*) were built in almost every village,
most of them of rather modest dimensions. But since Parāntaka I
(907–55) also larger ones became common, and when the dynasty
was at its zenith (11th–12th centuries), five huge imperial temples
were erected. Simultaneously also the earlier, by now very famous
and sacred sanctuaries were expanded, though with the difference
that the innermost sanctum was no more altered, except by being
covered with gold sheets. Instead, vast courts and enclosures (*prākāra*)
were added, with galleries and higher and higher *gopuras* (gateways),
further cult-halls of many pillars, dance halls (*nat-mandapa*) for the
devadāsīs, halls for swinging the idols (*uyyala mandapa*) and for the
annual wedding of the divine couple (*kalyāna mandapa*), and subsidiary temples for the consort (*amman*) and children of the god (in
most cases Pārvatī-Umā, Subrahmaniar-Kārttikeya and Ganesā) as
well as for famous saints, and finally holy ponds (*teppe kulam*). With
the progress of time, the number of these enclosures increased (on the
average up to four) in order to house the growing host of priests, pan-
dits and other brāhmins, of dancing girls and temple musicians, and
likewise other high-caste people who had settled round the temple.
With every wider *prākāra* also the *gopuras* in their four axes became
higher and higher (up to 150 feet, in the 17th century). As this progress of expansion has continued until our own time, with special
intensity under the emperors of Vijayanagar (15th–17th centuries), al-

The Brihadīśvara temple at Gangaikondasolapuram. Erected by Rājendra I Chola in 1025 to commemorate his advance up to the Ganges. Like the Mahābodhi temple, a pyramid of storeys consisting of small cells (*panchārām*), culminating in a dome.

most all South Indian temples are a complicated jumble of buildings, columns, sculptures, bronzes, etc. of the most diverging age, whose history is rather difficult to disentangle, notwithstanding innumerable, generally well-dated inscriptions.

Generally speaking, the Chola style continued the Pallava and Eastern Chālukyan tradition (the latter represented mainly at Vijayavāda *Chola style*

171

(=Bezwāda), Bichchavola, Mādugulu, Bhīmavaram and Śrīkākulam).
The earliest temples (Panangudi, Tirukkattalai: Sundareśvara, Enādi,
Tiruppūr, Talkād: Pātāleśvara Maraleśvara, 9th century; Erumbūr
935, Kodumbālūr: Mūvar Koil, Nārthamalai, Virālūr, Viśalūr, Kumbakonam: Nāgeśvara, 10th century) take up the type of the later
Pallava and Chālukya sanctuaries, however in a chastened, classic
simplicity: a one-storeyed cult hall, a two-storeyed *vimāna* crowned
by a central third storey and a dome. The lion friezes, reduced to small
dimensions, now are a common feature along the plinth and the cornice. The finest examples of this type are the beautiful Vettuvan Koil
at Kalugamalai (a rock temple) and the Tiruvalīśvaram temple at
Brahmadeśa near Tirunelveli, already of the first years of Rājarājā I.
In a varied form, with a circular *vimāna*, a complicated transition to
the crowning *śringa* by means of corner *pancharams* and arched window
niches, and with a much richer sculptural decoration, it was continued
through the whole Chola period for independent temples like the
innermost cella of the Ranganātha at Śrīrangam, Ālagar Koil, the
Jvarahareśvara and Pāndavaperumāl at Kānchī, and many subsidiary
shrines.
However, with the Koranganātha (940) at Śrīnivāsanālūr (near Tanjūr) and the Bhīmeśvara at Drāksharam a new development set in,
mainly by means of a reduplication of the storeys of the *vimāna*, of
the cult hall and even of the galleries surrounding the court, which
ended in the huge imperial temples, the Brihadīśvara or Rājarājeśvara
at Tanjūr, built by Rājarājā I the Great in 1000—1012 (consecrated
1009), the Brihadīśvara at Gangaikondaśolapuram (1025), the Kampa-
hareśvara at Tirubhuvanam built by Rājendra I (1012—1054) (all
around Kumbakonam), and the temple of Bāhūr not far from Pondicherry, all of them closely connected with various imperial residences. The plinth became higher, the walls of the *vimāna* were
strongly articulated by rows of pillar-framed projections enclosing
image niches, the tower led up, in a more or less steep pyramid
of many storeys of *pancharams*, to the crowning cupola (at Tanjūr
190′ = 58 m high). These high *vimānas*, of course, demanded hardly less monumental *gopuras* with the result that where the origi- *Gopuras*
nal small sanctuary was not altered, the *gopura* became much more

---

The goddess Sarasvatī. Relief on the walls of the Brihadīśvara temple at Gangaikondasolapuram near
Tanjūr, built 1025.

173

The Great Temple at Madurai, seen from the eastern *gopuram*. In the foreground, the Golden Lily Pond. Left, the principal *gopura* in the second enclosure of the Sundaresvar Temple. Right, the Tiruvāchi *gopura* (entrance to the Mīnākshī Temple). Behind, the principal eastern *gopura* of the third enclosure. Mainly 18th century.

śiva Natarājā, lord of Chidambaram. Processional bronze image of śiva's cosmic Tāndava dance on the demon Muyulaga-Kali in a circle of fire. C. 11th century. *Museum van Aziatische Kunst, Amsterdam.*

prominent than the first, a relationship characteristic for all South Indian temples since the later Chola period. The plan of the high *gopuras* is the same as that of the high *vimānas*, with this difference that, as gateways, they are oblong and, therefore, crowned by a wagonroof (cp. Baitāl Deul at Bhuvaneśvara, Telī-kā Mandir at Gwālior, Bhīma and Sahadeva Rathas at Māmallapuram), ending in half-round arches distorted to grotesque flaming "fans" topped by demon masks. The *gopuras* of Chola times were rather broad, with rather high storeys (e.g. at Chidambaram, or the Padmanābhasvāmin at Trivandrum).

Only the temple of Dārāśuram forms an exception to some degree. But it had been erected to house an idol looted by prince Vijayarājendra, after the victory of Rājādhirāja I over Someśvara I Āhavamalla, from the Western Chālukyan capital Kalyānapuram (Kalyāni), and it was, therefore, decorated with reliefs in the Western Chālukyan style, and even with some original dvārapāla statues from the destroyed enemy temple.

Suchlike Chola temple buildings are found dispersed over more than 70 temple towns, from Cape Comorin to the lower course of the Krishnā. The most important ones are those at Tiruvorreyūr, Tirukkalukkunram (the "Kite Hill"), Tiruvannamalai, Chidambaram (sacred to Śiva Natarāja), Kumbakonam (Kumbheśvara), Tiruvālūr, Tiruchirāpalli (Śrī Mātrubusheśvara), Jambukeśvaram, Śrīrangam (Ranganāthasvāmin), Sūchīndram, Udipi (Krishna temple), Trivandrum (Padmanābhasvāmin), Tirumayam, etc. Most of them belong to late Chola times, especially the reign of Kulottunga II and III. The Pāndya temples represent but an elegant variant of the Chola style, more gracious and richer. Their principal monument, the great Sundareśvara-Mīnākshī temple at Madurai, was badly damaged during the Muslim occupation in the early 14th century, and later superseded by the huge reconstruction of Tirumalai Nāyak (early 17th century). Some good examples are the Ranganātha Perumāl at Tirubhuvanam, *gopuras* at Śrīrangam and Jambukeśvaram, and number of small temples all over the utmost south, e.g. at Tirumayam, Kudumiyāmalai, etc.

Of the secular architecture of this period we know very little. Near Uraiyūr, Gangaikondaśolapuram and Kumbakonam there are vast

Śiva Natarāja, lord of Chidambaram. Close-up of a bronze figure. 12th century. ▶

areas of mounds covering the former imperial palaces which should deserve early excavation. The inscriptions mention "Golden Palaces" in various towns. On the analogy of the remnants of Parākrama Bāhu's palaces at Polonnāruva and of those of the emperors of Vijaya-

Śiva as Vīnadhara-Dakshinamūti. Gilt bronze, 11th—12th century. Dakshinamūrti is the patron of the South Indian brahmans, Vīnā-Dhara (the lyre-player) the patron of music and art. The sitting god rests his foot on the demon Muyulaga; the *vina* is lost. The great mane of matted ascetic's hair is bound back. About original size. *Musée Guimet, Paris.*

nagar, it seems that they consisted of gold-plated wooden buildings on richly decorated stone platforms.

The walls of the temples were covered with sculptures, first very sparingly, but increasing in number from century to century. Those of early Chola times have the same quaint charm of a transition period as the "Korai" of the Acropolis of Athens, a decadent fragility combined with a naive youthfulness. They represent rather the last phase of Pallava art, related to the Chālukyan temples of Pattadakal which had been planned and decorated by artists deported from the Pallava capital Kānchī. But also the art of the last Chālukyas of Bādāmī seems to have contributed directly to their formation. The acme of this sculpture is found in the temples of Kodumbālūr and Kalugamalai. But at Tiruvalīsvaram its decline is evident; the individual figures have become petty and pretty, but their composition the richer. For with the reign of Rājarājā I the Great a revolution had set in. The divine statues on the temples of Tanjūr and Gangaikondaśolapuram are gigantic and powerful, but also coarse and often enough dull. The refined tradition inherited from Gupta times was dead for ever, replaced by a lifeless repetition of the hieratic formulas prescribed by the Śilpaśāstras. Instead, a new folk style turned up in the subsidiary reliefs, expressing an ideal of beauty diametrically opposite to the classical canon, especially in female figures reminding rather of Gauguin's Tahiti women. In the later 11th and the 12th century this ideal began to pervade also a good deal of hieratic sculpture, endowing it with a somewhat maladroit grace (e.g. in the Rishi women from Dārāsuram, now in the Tanjūr Art Gallery). Misproportioned and effeminate under the last Cholas, sculpture recovered under the Pāndyas, slim and elegant, but without the warmth that distinguished the Chola style. This period witnessed a renaissance of cave sculpture, e.g. at Tiruparankunran (near Madurai), Nārthamalai and in the Rāmnād district.

Better known in Europe and America than the stone sculptures are the numerous bronzes, especially portable procession images which, discarded because of some damage or other, have found their way into museums and private collections, amongst them some really grand masterpieces like the Madras Natarājā. Other then favoured forms of Śiva were Chandraśekhara, (Vīnādhara-) Dakshināmūrti, Umā-Sahita, Kalyānasundara, Gajasamharamūrti. Vishnu images were much rarer, generally in the company of his two consorts Bhū and Śrī. Also statues of the great Śaiva and Vaishnava saints, especially of Appar, Manikkavāchakar, Sundara and Tirujnānasambandar, and many Dīpalakshmīs (i.e. oil lamps in the shape of a girl holding a lamp) were donated to the temples. Their style development, from Pallava to Pāndya times, follows more or less that of the work in stone.

*Chola and Pāndya Painting* The most comprehensive set of Chola murals were discovered, three decades ago, in the circumambulation passages of the Brihadīsvara at Tanjūr, beneath a renovation of the 17th century. These paintings which describe the inauguration of the temple by Rājarājā I, the legend of Sundaramūrti, etc. are of a tremendous vitality; but they reveal the same trend away from the idealized Gupta "naturalism" so characteristic also of North Indian mediaeval pictures. The swiftly moving, very summary outline is everything; colour, though bright, is supplementary; details are neglected. Other Chola murals still survive at Tirumalaipuram and in the Vijayālaya Cholīsvaram temple at Nārthamalai (Pudukkottai).

One of the great arts of the time was the dance, sacred to the Lord of Chidambaram, Śiva Natarājā. The Koyilpurānam of Umāpathi Sivāchārya (13th century) presents the legend of the god's mighty Tāndava dance, the origin of the creation and of all dancing. And the reliefs on the walls of the Chidambaram temple (but also in those of Dārāśuram and Tirubhuvanam) depict all its postures and movements. In fact, Bhārat Nātyam such as it is danced today, was then more or less formulated. That the *of art theory literature* of this period was considerable and still is authoritative, hardly needs elaboration.

*Influence of Chola-Pāndya Art* Because of the political supremacy first of the Cholas, then of the Pāndyas, their art exercised considerable influence. With the conquest, Drāvida temples spread up to Kerala (Travancore, Cochin and Malabar) where the shrines of Pārthivaśekharapuram (9th century), Trikatithānam, the Guhanāthasvāmin at Cape Comorin, Sūchīndram, Kidangūr (11th century), Trivikramangalam (12th century), Tirunandikkari (13th century), their sculptures and murals, all, are based on the Chola-Pāndya tradition. A local speciality, perhaps connected with the round *garbhagrihas* of Tamilnād, is the circular temples. In Ceylon which between 1001 and 1017 had been subdued by the Cholas, the impact of South Indian art had to be immense, even after the liberation of the country between 1055 and 1073. Polonnāruva (since the 8th century the capital) was, therefore, rebuilt by Parākrama Bāhu I the Great (1158—86) more or less in a variant of Drāvida architecture. The Śiva Devāle no. 2 is a provincial Chola temple, conserving the 10th century type, the Śiva Devāle no. 1 a Pāndya shrine. The Watadāge, on the other hand, is a round temple of the Kerala type. In the Lankātilaka, the Tivanka-Pilimā-ge (Image House), the Thūpārāma and Podgal Vihāra, finally, the Tamil forms are intermixed with Gupta and Pallava elements of the older Anurādhapura tradition. Naturally, also the sculptures of these monuments follow the Drāvida style, not to mention the South Indian bronze images found in the various Śaiva temples in this Buddhist stronghold. Less pronounced was the Chola influence in Indonesia, especially on sculptures in Malaya which early in the 11th century had been made dependent. Further in the east, in Java, many bronzes testify to an intensive contact with South India. At Negapatam (near Kumbakonam) even a Javanese Buddhist monastery (Chūdāmani Vihāra) was erected under Rājarājā I; and the sculptures of the Vettuvan Koil at Kalugamalai look like a more virile variety of the famous relief friezes of the Borobudur.

The Muslim conquest had made an end to the Yādava, Kākatīya, Hoysala and Pāndya kingdoms between 1296 and 1326. Yet during the subsequent crisis the countries south of the Krishnā and along the eastern coast regained, under Vijayanagar, their independence. The empire of Vijayanagar withstood, under three successive dynasties, all Muslim onslaught from 1336 until 1565 when Rāma Rājā, the regent for the last Tūluva emperor Sadāśiva (1542—76), was disastrously defeated south of Talikota by the allied sultans of the Deccan. Under the Aravīdu dynasty the empire still lingered on until 1649, dissolving into a federation of states of which those of Jinjī, Tanjūr, Madurai and Maisūr (Mysore) were the most important and could, as vassals of their Muslim neighbours, continue at least the cultural tradition up to British times.

These events had far-reaching consequences for South Indian art; the tradition was interrupted, though not so disastrously as in the North. The Deccan, Tamilnād and Kerala came under the same rule. With the Telugu emperors of Vijayanagar a race came to the throne to whom the Mediaeval tradition was a sacred national trust but no more a genuine form of self-expression. And this gulf was both bridged and widened by the Hindu reform movements which had been the reaction against Muslim rule and the spiritual source of the liberation.

Traditional mediaeval art experienced a glorious renaissance. Of no other period of India's past we know so many, so impressive and so

Reliefs in the folk style on the throne terrace, Vījayanagar (Hampi), early 16th century.

richly decorated temples, halls, enclosures, gateways, votive images in stone and bronze, murals, etc. But it was a onesided, religious art, more and more dissociated from the people, and thus in the long run permeated by the real folk art of the time, until merely a framework of types survived, transformed almost beyond recognition. In their new capital (founded 1336) the rulers of Vijayanagar had first revived the late Yādava-Kākatīya style of architecture in a very plain form (Ganigitti temple 1385; Jain temples on Hemakūta, near Achyuta Rāya's temple, etc.). But in the early 16th century an intensive building activity set in, both at Vijayanagar (throne platform 1513, Vitthalasvāmin 1513—65, Hazāra-Rāma and Krishna temples 1515, royal palaces, etc., by Krishnadeva Rāya 1509—29; Achyutarāya's, Pattabhirāmasvāmin and Pampapati temples, by Achyutadeva 1529—42; the Zenāna Enclosure with the Lotus Mahal, etc., the Dannāik's Enclosure, under Sadāśiva 1542—76) as well as in the provinces (e.g. Tirupati, Lepākshī, Śriśailam: Mallikarjuna; Kānchī: south *gopura* of the Ekambareśvara, 1509—30; Tadpatri: Śrī Rāma, 1550—60; Vellūr: *Kalyāna Mandapa*, 1560; Chidambaram: north *gopuram*, ca. 1520, etc.). Muslim architects and stucco workers were employed for the imperial palaces, South Indian masters for the imperial temples. Thus the Drāvida *vimāna, kalyāna mandapa* and *gopura* became the fashion also in the Deccan and along the north-eastern coast. But the decoration of these buildings remained very simple, and for their sculpture the local folk style was used.

Thus, there developed a new type of architecture: very simple halls (*mandapa*), the horizontal ceilings of which rested on plain beams supported by pillars of alternatingly square and octagonal cross-section, decorated with small reliefs in the folk style and ending in a simplified *pushpabodigai* abacus the *pancharams* along the edge of the roof were replaced by shallow brick chapels containing stucco reliefs of deities and mythological scenes. This type spread also to Southern India and became very common when the genuine Drāvida style went into decline. It could easily be adapted also to European architecture and today such roof chapels adorn modern small temples, houses, even cinemas.

In the Tamil country the ancient tradition was better preserved, but likewise underwent great changes. The popularization of the cult led to the construction of vast halls, generally in the second enclosure, and along the principal axis also in the outer enclosures. Here pilgrims could rest, or look at the processions, or buy house-idols, lamps, rosaries, or various souvenirs. These *mandapas* (or *chāvadī*, "choultry") are of two types: Long corridors flanked by raised platforms, connecting the sanctuary with the principal *gopuras* or winding round the innermost *prākāra* (inaccessible to the public); and "Thousand Pillar-Halls" (*Sahasrastambha mandapa*), a sort of expanded *kalyāna mandapa*, like those latter with a stage for special ceremonies, dances and theatrical performances.

The ceilings of these halls and broad corridors could, of course, not be supported by the traditional pillars. Instead, complicated pilasters (generally carved from one gigantic stone block) were used, decorated, like the late mediaeval pillars of Northern India, with successive figural panels, or with bundles of columns, in front of which groups of Pallava-Chola miniature columns were placed, or groups of prancing horses, elephants, lions, etc., or gods and goddesses, donors and devotees. Later the animal groups were transformed into battle scenes, horsemen triumphing over defeated enemies, or led in procession by grooms and foot soldiers. On these pilasters a second storey or colonnade (*karnakudū*) of far-projecting brackets (*palagai*) was set, thus extending the span of the ceilings of long stone slabs covering the corridors.

Correspondingly, also the *gopuras* became higher and higher. The gateways proper became two to four storeys high and so broad that several chariots can pass through them side by side. Their many upper brick storeys, covered with numerous stucco sculptures, rose in an elegant sweep, ending in an overhanging baroque wagon-roof which projects in a mighty curve (set with a row of pointed *kalasas*) in two "fans" topped by grim demon masks. In contrast, the temples proper remained small, rather adjuncts of the vast *mandapas*, reinterpreting the traditional Pallava-Chola type in a baroque, or finally Rococo spirit.

*Nāyak Style* When at last the empire disintegrated, the Nāyaks of Jinjī, Tanjūr, Madurai and Maisūr again spent vast amounts in order to win over the influential priesthood of the great temples. Most prominent amongst them were Raghunāth of Tanjūr, one of the party leaders in the last struggle for the imperial crown, and Tirumala of Mandurai (1623—59), the actual engineer of the downfall of the empire. To the first we owe most of the Chidambaram and Jumbukeśvaram temples, and the beautiful *mandapas* of the Varadarājaperumāl at Kānchī and of the Rāmasvāmin at Kumbakonam; to the latter most of the stunning Sundareśvara-Mīnākshī temple at Madurai, completely reconstructed after the Muslim devastation, the "Thousand Pillar-Halls" of Śrīrangam and Chidambaram, and many other temples and halls. The gigantic "Rāya *gopuras*", begun by him in most of the prominent temples and intended to reach a height of c. 300 feet (= more than 90 m) were, however, never completed. However, building activities continued all over Southern India until our own time. But the monuments have not yet been surveyed.

The most famous of all, the Madurai temple, reconstructed between the 16th and the 19th century, has already been mentioned. It consists of three adjoining inner enclosures, containing, within minor enclosures, the chapel of Mīnākshī (a goddess already known to the Greeks and Romans as the "daughter of Pandyon", later identified with Umā), the much greater but still modest shrine of her later husband, god Śiva, and the "Golden Lily Pord" (*suvarnapushpakarinī*) and outer enclosure comprising several huge corridors and Tirumala Nāyak's Thousand Pillar-Hall. Everywhere there are dark corridors on which numerous chapels, dance halls, colleges, etc. are opening, eleven *gopuras*, administrative buildings, in front of the principal entrance the marvellous *Pudū* or *Vasanta* (Spring) *Mandapa*, with the statues of the royal donors, and the unfinished Rāya *gopura*. Very similar are the temples of Chidambaram (with four inner courts), of Jambukeśvaram, and of Rāmeśvaram at Rāmnād, on the "Setu", i.e. the bridge of islands which Hanuman's loyal monkeys had constructed for Rāma, the divine hero of the national epic, the Rāmāyana, in order to reach Lankā (Ceylon) and to save his abducted wife Sītā. This most famous place of pilgrimage, said to have been founded by Rāma himself, was in the 17th and 18th centuries completely rebuilt by the local feudatories of Madurai, the Setupatis. Of smaller monuments the delicate Subrahmanya temple in the court of the Brihadīśvara at Tanjūr, and the *mandapas* of Raghunāth Nāyak at Kānchī and Kumbakonam deserve special mention because of their exquisite sculptures.

In these late temple buildings there spreads a gloom formerly unknown to Hindu religion and art. The early sanctuaries had stood in intimate relation to nature, on the banks of lakes and rivers, in gorges and on mountain peaks, almost an integral part of nature like the Svayambhū lingas and the trees sacred to the gracious-terrible mountain goddess (Pārvatī). Since the Middle Ages, however, the sanctuary was hidden behind a dark *vimāna* or *mandapa*. In late Pallava and Chola times the vast enclosures began to develop. Under the emperors of Vijayanagar they were more and more filled with huge pillar halls when in the 17th century Islam was victorious and Hinduism on the defence, the enclosure walls became higher and higher, and the temple courts were systematically transformed into almost pitchdark halls, often of black stone, in which grotesque statues in stone, wood and bronze could be more felt than seen in the vague light of oil lamps reflected on the gold sheets of the shrine doors. The mysticism of nature had given way to a mysticism inspired by the mysterious darkness of the temples!

*Secular architecture*

Secular architecture has been preserved in the ruins of Vijayanagar (Hampi-Hospet), Chandragiri, Jinjī (Gingee), Tanjūr and Madurai. The palaces of Vijayanagar, as far as they were not built in a semi-Islamic (Golkonda-Bījāpur) style, had been wooden structures, several storeys high and once covered with gold sheets and costly clothes, standing on stone platforms within high enclosures. The throne platform (Mahānavamī Dibba) is such an exceptionally high terrace erected by Krishna Deva Rāya in commemoration of his victories over Orissa 1513, embellished with reliefs depicting court receptions, processions, foreign embassies, dancing girls, etc., in a delightful simple folk style. The Zenāna enclosure, with its guardrooms and high watch towers, on the other hand, was the gilded prison of Krishna Deva's successors, tools in the hands of their ruthless prime ministers. The other palace buildings comprise the Lotus Mahal, the Dannāik (Commander General)'s palace, several baths, elephant stables, barracks. Of other buildings we have the huge fortifications, only in their last stage provided with bastions, double gates, a river bridge on granite pillars, and the arcades of the bāzārs along the procession avenues of the great temples. The palaces of Chandragiri (1539–40) and Jinjī (Kalyān Mahal), in a semi-Islamic style, consist of several arcaded storeys crowned by Hindu step-pyramid roofs ending in a *sringa*. The palaces of the Nāyaks of Madurai and of the Nāyaks and Marātha Rājās of Tanjūr are of Islamic design, though tempered by stucco friezes and innumerable stucco figures of pure Hindu character.

*Sculpture of Vijayanagar*

The indigenous sculpture of Vijayanagar developed from the style of the funeral stelas (Vīrakkal and Satikkal) and snake stones of Western Chālukyan times. Their representation is naive, in flat stripes, without foreshortening or perspective, but immensely vital. Under Krishnadeva Rāya it became an integral part of official art (throne platform; Śrīsailam), but lost much of its freshness under the discipline of the learned priesthood (Hazāra-Rāma temple, renovations of the throne platform, minor friezes of the Vitthalasvāmin and Achyuta Rāya's temples).

The same switch-over to folk art is visible also in the paintings of which still a fairly good number has been preserved. The earliest ceiling paintings at Tiruparuttikunram differ hardly from the Chola type. In the extensive murals of the Virabhadrasvāmin temple at Lepākshī (1538) and in the less satisfactory ones at Somapālayam the expression of the artist frees itself from the traditional bonds. In the later ceiling friezes at Tiruparuttikunram a simple style is reached, very similar to early Rājput and Assamese painting of the 16th century.

After the collapse of Vijayanagar 1565 this last style was brought by refugees also to the Muslim courts of the Deccan, to Bījāpur, Golkonda and Ahmadnagar. Likewise the art crafts of Vijayanagar, once famous for their luxury, seem to have influenced later Islamic architecture and applied art in the Deccan. At Vijayanagar, finally, South Indian music ("Kanarese style") and dance (Bhārat Nātyam) were cast into the form in which we know them today.

In the Tamil country, however, tradition was not broken. But having lost contact with real life, it suffered the same degeneration as already, some centuries earlier, that of the Deccan under the Kādatīyas and Yādavas. In the 16th century, e.g. the votive bronze statues of Krishna-Deva Rāya of Vijayanagar and his queens in the Tirupati temple, though lacking the elegant ease of Chola-Pāndya works, at least have dignity and decorative beauty; 17th century sculptures and paintings are barbaric, but possess rhythm and heroic vitality, while in the 18th century figures grew grotesquely fat and histrionic. The best examples of this late style are the murals in the Trichakrapuram palace and the Padmanābha temple in Travancore, and also in the Mattancheri Palace at Cochin; and the same qualities have determined the character of Kathākalī ballet. At the first impression almost ridiculously grotesque, this art still has an immense capacity to move the onlooker, as soon as he has become accustomed to its conventions. But in the 19th century even this power was lost, a philistine dullness sinking down on all creations, distorting their traditional gestures into improbable histrionics. Temples are still being constructed and covered with innumerable sculptures and paintings, but their art is no better than the decoration of a provincial fair booth. Bronze images are still cast, mainly as fakes for fashionable collectors and for tourists. This art no longer exercised any influence ouside South India. Indian cultural influence overseas was already on the wane at the turn of the second millennium. After the Muslim invasion it collapsed and was superseded by the reawakening indigenous traditions. Not that it was completely wiped out; but what was left became so much transformed as to be almost unrecognizable.

*The Last Phase*

Only one unfavourable influence was left: that on Europe, which created the prejudice against Indian art as a whole as the abstruse nightmare of a fanatical, priest-ridden world interested only in the beyond. This judgment had been justified to some degree, but merely with regard to the final decadence of a once great civilization and a once remarkable tradition of art.

# VI. THE ART OF THE ISLAMIC PERIOD

The conquest of India by the Muslims in the 11th—14th centuries THE PROBLEM inaugurated a new and very interesting chapter in the history of Indian art. Islamic art was a total stranger, and some prominent scholars, therefore, have excluded it from their field of studies, with the result, however, that their interpretation of later Hindu art, and also of Indian art as a whole is defective and muddled. As the Muslims were merely a ruling minority, it was inevitable that their art should in many respects fall under the spell of indigenous Hindu art, to such an extent that important local styles prove to be no more than adaptations of Hindu techniques, forms and ornaments, and that the psychological attitude of its last phases is almost identical with that of the Hindus. As a result, later Hindu art borrowed so extensively as well as intensively from Indo-Islamic art that it is quite unintelligible without a knowledge of its sister. Nor can this late form of Hindu art simply be rejected as a bastard. For it became the carrier of the great movements of reform which rescued Hindu cultural life from the stagnation into which it had relapsed during the centuries preceding the Muslim conquest, and which endowed it with powerful ethical and creative impulses, with the energies that feed it up to the present day. The Muslim conquest proves to have been not only the destroyer of the exterior forms of traditional Hindu civilization and art, but also a challenge, the stimulus to a renewal of its roots. Indo-Islamic art has thus been both a branch of Islamic, and an integral aspect of Indian art. Its history has been the struggle between both associations, the accent alternating from century to century.

Islamic art is the very antithesis of Hindu art. Its background is not THE NATURE OF ISLAMIC ART the fields or the jungle, but the desert and the oasis. Its spatial sense expresses itself not in the continual aggregation of small local units, but in infinity systematically subdivided into continents, countries, districts, towns, etc. The Hindu sense of time is determined by the seasons of agricultural life, the birth and death of generations, the pace of the foot-soldier and of the elephant rider; that of the Muslim by the swiftness of the horse and the endlessness of God. Hindu life has the traditionalism of growth; Muslim life, that of abstract law. Hindu life is within nature; Muslim life has to shelter from the climate of the desert. It is a harem, secret, protected, sacred, like the garden, like love and women. Hindu architecture is part of nature; Islamic architecture isolated from it. Hindu buildings neglect and hide construction; Islamic buildings are masterpieces of bold engineering. Hindu sculpture is vegetative or figurate; Islamic, abstract. Hindu painting is depiction of nature (in the widest sense); Islamic painting is calligraphy, or nature transformed by calligraphy. Hindu colour tends to be broken, subdued; Islamic colour to be bright. Hindu ornament is irregular, individualistic, symbolical; Islamic is mathematical, continuous, abstract. Hindu art uses script only as a subordinate medium of supplementary information; Islamic art treats it as one of its principal means of expression, as the carrier of the word of God, and of the greatness of its kings.

FORMS OF ISLAMIC ART
Islamic art emerged from the selective fusion of Arab, Syrian, Byzantine, Sasanian-Persian, later also Turkish and Mongol-Chinese traditions. Its basic forms are the pillar hall and the dome resting on pillars, predominating around the Mediterranean, and the brick vault and cupola common in Iraq, Īrān, Turkestān and India. The most characteristic building types are as follows: the mosque (*masjid*), consisting of a court (*sahn*) surrounded by an arcade (*līwān*) with several entrances from outside; a vast pillar nave with a central vaulted or domed hall (*maqsūra*); prayer niches (*mihrab*) and a pulpit (*mimbar*) on the back wall; slim towers (*minār, manāra*) or lower platforms (*ma'zīna*) for the mu'ezzin calling the faithful to prayer. In the central mosques (*jāmi'masjid*) there is often a screened section for women; the *īdgāh*, for the mass prayers at the Īd festival, however, is merely a long wall with prayer niches and perhaps also a pulpit. The theological college (*madrasa*) is very similar to the mosque, with the difference that the central hall of the big nave and most entrances have been replaced by lecture halls, and the arcades and naves by cells for the professors and students. The tomb (*maqbara, gumbad*) is generally a cube crowned by a dome (*gumbad*); the tomb proper (*qabr, rauza*) is often relegated to an underground chamber (*hazra, astāna, tākhāna*), while a cenotaph (*zarīh*) stands under the dome. There are innumerable tombs of saints (*ziārat*) generally surrounded by mosques, pilgrim halls, other tombs, etc. forming a place of pilgrimage (*dargāh*). The house (*khāna*) is generally laid out round a court, with halls (*aiwān*) and verandahs (*dālān*). There is always a strict division between men's quarters (*mardāna*) and women's rooms (*zanāna, harām*). Mansions (*mahal*) and palaces (*sarāī*) combine several courts of

this kind with gardens and garden houses. The festival rooms were richly painted (*rang mahal*) or decorated with mirrors (*shīshmahal*). For the hot dry season underground rooms (*sardāb, tākhāna*) round wells (*baoli*) were provided; for sultry months, airy upper storey halls and terraces (*hawā-mahal*). Royal representation added audience-halls (*darbār, dīwān-i'ām and khāss*), special sleeping rooms of the ruler (*khwābgāh*), a police court (*kachahra*), offices (*daftar*), stables, workshops, bazaars and barracks. The gardens (*bāgh*) were generally arranged on a rectangular plan (*chār-bāgh*) with one or several water channels radiating from central pools, with lighted waterfalls and fountains, the space in between planted with tulips, narcissi, hyacinths, etc. In the centre there stood a garden palace with a vast open hall (*kūshk*) or consisting of several pillar rooms (*bārādārī*); at the end of the water channels there were airy halls (*bhavan*) with or without sleeping rooms, and at the corners of the high enclosure, towers (*burj*) with colonnaded and domed pavilions (*chhattrī*). The Muslim towns were generally strongly fortified; and in India even the gardens and hunting boxes (*shikār kūshk*).

*Gardens*

Islamic sculpture is almost exclusively ornamental, evolving an amazing wealth of geometrical, floral (arabesques) and calligraphic motifs, of the most various origins and combined with excellent taste, in endless combinations. Figurate sculpture was permitted in private rooms, baths, etc., but under Sāsānian and Turkish influence it developed rather in the direction of a heraldic stylization. Painting, as far as it was not purely ornamental, was restricted to murals in baths and harems, or to book illustrations of rather calligraphic character, first based on Syrian and Sāsānian, then on Chinese models. Industrial art was amongst the finest achievements of Islamic culture; functional, and of absolutely sure taste. The ceramic wares in particular possess designs and colours surpassed not even by Chinese pottery and porcelain.

*Sculpture*

The Muslims had already got a foothold in India under the Umayyad caliphs, when Muhammad bin Qāsim, marching through the deserts of Mekrān, conquered the lower Indus Valley in 711—12. The invasions of the next Arab governors into Gujarāt, Rājasthān and the Panjāb were beaten off by the Hindus. Late in the 10th century, however, the Turkish governors of the Sāmānid sultans of Bukhārā made themselves independent and founded the vast empire of Ghazna in Afghānistān. Sultān Mahmūd (998—1030) devastated north-western India and annexed the Panjāb; but his successors had to defend themselves against the Saljuq nomads, the Ghuzz, and later the Ghorids, who expelled and finally overthrew them in 1186. With the conquest of Northern India by Sultan Mu'izz-ud-dīn and his slave governor Qutb-ud-dīn Aibak in 1192—1206, the Islamic period of Indian history really started. For in 1206 Aibak founded the first (Mamlūk) dynasty of the sultāns of Delhi, which was soon cut off from the other Islamic countries by the Mongol invasion under Chinghīz Khān and Hulagū. The highly efficient army formed in the defence against the Mongols was used by the Khiljī (Ghilzāi) and Tughluq sultāns to overrun the whole of India down to Madurai between 1292 and 1326. However, this loosely knit empire was soon racked by rebellions; between 1337 and 1347 Bengal and the Deccan were lost; and after the sack of Delhī by the conqueror Tamerlane of Samarkand in 1398, the other provinces also broke away. In the 15th and early 16th centuries India was divided into a number of warring sultanates (Kashmīr, Sind, Delhī, Jaunpur, Bengal, Mālwa, Gujarāt, and the Bahmanī empire of the northern Deccan) and Hindu states (the great Rājput federation under the leadership of Mewār; Orissā; Vijayanagar). In the later 16th century Northern and Central India were conquered by the Mughal emperors, descendants of Tamerlane, while Vijayanagar and the Bahmanī Empire disintegrated, the latter into the sultanates of Berār, Bīdar Bījāpur and Golkonda. In the 17th century the Mughal Empire expanded to the southern tip of India, but simultaneously

*Sack of Delhi*  began to disintegrate. The sack of Delhi by Nādir Shāh of Persia and Ahmad Shāh Durrānī in 1738 sealed the fall of the empire, though nominally the emperors ruled until 1803—57. For some time the Hindu Marāthas of the Western Deccan, who had risen against the Mughals in the second half of the 17th century, controlled and looted India. But after the disastrous defeat by the Afghāns at Pānipat in 1761 the country became a chaos of states and principalities of which the Sikhs in the Panjāb, the Jāts south of Delhī, the nawābs of Oudh, Bengal and Gujarāt, the Rājput mahārājās, the Nizām of Haidarābād and the nawāb of the Karnātik, the Marātha principalities of Ujjain-Gwālior, Indore, Barodā, Nāgpur, Poona and Kolhāpur, and the sultanate of Maisūr (Mysore) were the most important. Not long before the battle of Pānipat the British began, as "vassals" of the Mughal emperors, to subdue one state after the other, until, between 1818 and 1847, they were ruling the whole of India. And with them the modernization of the country set in.

Excavations in the ruins of Brahmanābād-Mansūra in lower Sind have yielded remains of some small mosques of the Sāmarrā type, with rows of thick brick pilasters. However, echoes of 'Abbāsid ornamentation have survived in the Hindu art of north-western India, e.g. in the "Ghaznī" throne of the rājās of Pūgal (Bīkāner) or the Hirmā Temple at Manāli in Kulū. The monuments of the Yamīnid sultāns of Ghazna, in their turn, represent the Buwayhid-Samānid style of Īrān (inspired mainly by Sāsānian Īrān), though with a certain infiltration of Hindu motifs. Unfortunately little is left, as Ghazna and other Afghān towns were destroyed in 1155 by the Ghorid Husain "Jahān-soz" (the World Burner), and Lahore, with other places in the Panjāb was destroyed in 1241 by the Mongols. At Ghazna the victory towers of Mahmūd and Mas'ūd III are still standing, with their star-shaped ground-plan, their twelve sides covered with ornaments and inscription bands. The doors of Mahmūd's mausoleum, brought to Āgra as the alleged gates of the Hindu temple of Somnāth which was sacked in 1026, are masterpieces of Sāmānid wood carving. In the palace ruins of Lashkarī Bāzār, on the other hand, murals in a semi-Hindu style have been found. And the cenotaph of the Ghorid governor, Muhammad ibn Sām at Ghazna (1192), is the work of Hindu masons from Gujarāt.

After the battle of Tarāin near Bhatinda in 1192, Delhi, the northern capital of the Chauhān Rājputs, was taken and made the capital of Qutb-ud-dīn Aibak, destined to become, some years later, the first sultān of India. In its strong fortress of Lālkot, Aibak built the first mosque, Quwwat-ul-Islām in 1193, using the colonnade around a destroyed Jain temple, expanding it with columns from other Hindu temples, and adding a façade in front, and mihrabs on the back of the principal nave. Though the designs for these were by Muslim hands, the execution had to be left to Indian masons who gave to the Arabic inscription friezes a purely Hindu background of flower scrolls. But soon more Muslim artisans became available, and in the gigantic minaret the Qutb-Minār (238 feet = 73 m high), begun in 1199 by the side of the Quwwat-ul-Islām and intended to be both a watch tower and a memorial of victory, and in the Arhaidin-kā-Jhomprā mosque at Ājmer (1200), also built of Hindu spoils, Islamic forms and ornaments of great beauty predominate. This is the case also in the buildings of Sultān Īltutmish (1211–36) who first put the new sultanate on a sound administrative basis. In his extension of the Delhi mosque, in the completion of the Qutb-Minār, in his own richly decorated mausoleum behind the mosque, and especially in that of his son ("Sultān Ghārī") at Mahīpālpur (1231/2), and in a mosque at

Budāun (1223), the fusion of Islamic and Hindu forms and ornaments is perfect, without however impairing the purely Islamic general impression. The imposing mausoleums of the saints Bahā-ud-dīn Zaqariā (1262) and Shams-uddīn Tabrīzi (1276) at Multān have unfortunately been reconstructed so much that hardly more than the core of the original buidings survives.

The conquest of Gujarāt and of the Deccan under the Khiljī sultāns introduced new tendencies. A'lā-ud-dīn's (1296—1316) extension of the Quwwat-ul-Islām mosque was planned on such a megalomaniac scale that only the foundations of the new naves and arcades were finished while the A'lāī Minār (intended to reach double the height of the Qutb-Minār) never progressed beyond the first turn of the staircase; and the southern entrance alone, the A'lāī Darwāza, was completed. It is a gigantic cube crowned by a very low dome, but the walls are richly decorated with trellis windows and niches covered with a great variety of ornaments in red and yellow sandstone, white and black marble and blue schist. These colour effects, as well as about half of the ornamental motifs, were innovations from the Hindu art of Gujarāt. A characteristic permanent addition to Indo-Islamic architecture was the ogival arch fringed with small scallops which end in flower buds. Very similar to this gateway was the mausoleum of the saint Nizām-ud-dīn, which was expanded into a hall for devotional meetings (jam'at-khāna, a sort of mosque) under the next dynasty.

*Break with Islamic tradition* Under the Tughluqs the break with the Islamic tradition as it had hitherto existed became complete. The hold over the immense empire proved very precarious, and the ruling minority was everywhere on the defensive. Ghiyās-ud-dīn-Tughluq (1320—25), in bad relations with the populace of the capital, founded Tughlaqābād, 6 miles east of Lālkot, with one of the greatest citadels of India and his own mausoleum on an island in an adjoining artificial lake, while his successor Muhammad added the fort 'Adīlābād at the other end of the fortified dyke of this lake. Behind the moat there rise high sloping walls faced with granite, with several tiers of defence ways, innumerable loopholes, and huge bastions projecting at regular intervals. But

The Qutb-Minār, 1199—1230, with upper storeys of 1368 and 1503, seen from the *madrasa* of Sultān A'lā-ud-dīn Khiljī (1296—1316). In the middle distance, the back of the screen of Sultān Īltutmish (1211—1236) ▸ and part of the colonnade of the original Quwwat-ul-Islām mosque (1193). Lālkot, Delhi.

195

it is crude ashlar work around a core of rubble, hastily constructed, and the palace too is of poor workmanship, formerly hidden behind painted and gilt stucco decorations (first traceable in the ruined tomb of Sultān Balban, 1266—87). The mausoleum, standing on a fortified island, also has sloping walls covered with big slabs of red sandstone and white marble; while, in contrast to the preceding dynasties, ornamentation is sparsely used, the main effect relying on the size, proportions and colours of the stones used. The same massiveness is characteristic of the Hazār-Sūtūn (Bijai-Mandal) Palace of Muhammad bin Tughluq (1325—51) at Sirī, the Delhī suburb founded by A'lā-ud-dīn; only the foundations of the wooden pillar hall are left, but the palace south of it is massive, like a hollowed mountain, with sloping exterior walls, low zenāna halls inside, whose vaults rest on short Hindu columns, and with slowly rising ramps for palanquins. The numerous palaces of Fīroz Shāh (1351—88), especially Kotila-i Fīroz Shāh, Hauz-i Khāss, the dargāh of Qadam Sharīf, the Kalān and Begampur mosques of his ministers Khānjahān senior and junior, in and around Delhi still preserve this general heavy character, but reveal a richer variety of detail and were once brightly painted. Kotila comprised an audience hall, a *hawā mahal*, a sardāb around a well, a great mosque and comprehensive women's quarters. Hauz-i Khāss was a private palace on the banks of an artificial lake, consisting of alternating open pillar halls and domed pavilions, the most important of which, with beautiful friezes of carved stucco, became the sultān's

*Disintegration*    mausoleum. After his death the empire which had already begun to disintegrate under Muhammad, quickly went to pieces. The many monuments of the last period, mainly in the provinces, were erected by nobles who had become more powerful than the sultans. Innovations of the Tughluq style are shown in the mausoleums of octagonal ground-plan, surrounded by a lower arcade (first: the tomb of Khān-Jahān Telingānī), the central pylon of the mosque façade (first in the Begampur mosque), the pyramidal roof, (rare) decoration in encaustic tiles, simple Hindu pillars, lintels eaves and lotus balconies. Fīroz Shāh Tughluq had the portraits of the sultans and other paintings in the Hazār Sūtūn and other palaces destroyed; however, fragments of an Amīr Khusrau MS. in a heavy Central Asian taste (Injū school), but with Indian details, must have been illustrated at his court, probably under the patronage of Khān-Jahān. Copies of similar pictures form part of many Jain MSS. of the Kālakāchāryakathā.

Between 1346 and 1412, especially in 1392, the empire disintegrated into a number of provincial sultanates. The Sayyid sultāns of Delhī (1414–51) who had only a precarious hold over the neighbourhood of the capital and the Panjāb, have left us merely the mausoleums of Mubārak (1421–34) in Mubārakpur, and of Muhammad (1434–44) at Khairpur (now Lodī Gardens) in the northern outskirts of ancient Delhi, with an arcade surrounding the octagonal domed hall over the tombs proper. The Lodī sultans (1451–1526) who recovered the North Indian plains up to the frontiers of Bengal and northern Central India, have left many fine buildings in the Delhi area: at Mehraulī (south of Lālkot), Khirkī, Sirī, and Khairpur, but also at Sarhind, Āgra, Sikandra, Dholpur, Kālpī, Bayāna, etc.; tombs of the cubic type (feudal mausoleums near Mubārakpur, Chhotā Gumbad at Khairpur) and of the octagonal type (the mausoleum of Sikandar, 1517); mosques (at Mehraulī, Moth kā-Masjid 1489 and Nīla Masjid 1505/6 at Sirī, and the beautiful "Lodī Mosque" of Abū Amjad, 1494, at Khairpur); Īdgāhs and palaces (Jahāz Mahal and Rājon-kī Bāin at Mehraulī, Bārā Khamba at Khirkī). Many of them are constructed of rubble and plaster; but quite a number are again executed in red and cream-coloured sandstone. The building types represent an elaboration of Tughluq architecture, enriched by new ornamental motifs from Tīmūrid Persia and Turkestān. Characteristic are the tapering buttresses on otherwise vertical walls, first ogival, then slim, later broad depressed keel-arches, small fluted cupolas, turrets and columns, pavilions (*chhattrī*) on the roofs, high drums and high, keel-shaped domes, later with a lantern, rich, once colourful stucco-carvings (most famous being those in the "Lodī Mosque"), encaustic tiles used sparsely outside, more freely inside.

The Lodī style survived the first Mughal conquest of 1526, and had a last, glorious renaissance under the Afghān Sūr dynasty (1540–56) which temporarily succeeded in expelling the Mughals. To the transition period belong the beautiful Jamālī Masjid (1536) with the tiny, exquisite mausoleum of Maulānā Jamāl Khān (1528/9) at Mehraulī, whose well-preserved stucco carvings still glow in their original colours, and the small marble shrine of Imām-Zamān (1537) outside the A'lāī-Darwāza. Sher Shāh Sūr (1540–45) was a prodigious builder of forts and towns. Best known are his Delhī citadel (Purāna Killa), with the beautiful Killa-Kohna Mosque, and his mausoleum at Sāsarām in Bihār. The fortress which faces the Lāl Darwāza, the entrance to Delhi, forms a parallelogram of mighty bastions and gateways decorated with the imperial emblem, the sigillum Salomonis. On its

*Provincial*
*Sultanates*

197

former river-side stands the mosque, a rather ponderous, large-scale repetition of the Moth-kā-Masjid and Jamālī Mosque, decorated with an amazing wealth of ornament. Hindu columns, bases, brackets, lintels, balconies, lotus roundels and ceilings; ogival, keel, pointed horseshoe and scalloped arches, squinches of seried Tughluq arches or stalactites (*muqarnas*), or of successive rows of small niches; Lodī stucco and marble friezes; encaustic tiles, Mamlūk-Egyptian marble mosaic; and mihrabs of multicoloured marbles. No less magnificent is Sher Shāh's mausoleum, a gigantic cupola on an octagonal substructure surrounded by an arcade once richly decorated with encaustic tiles, on a fortified island in the centre of a lake. The unfinished mausoleum of Islam (Salīm) Shāh (1545—53) nearby and the family tombs at Chainpur are much less impressive. The best tombs of those later years are that of Īsā Khān (1547) outside Humāyūn's mausoleum at Delhī, and that of Fath-Jang at Ālwar (1547).

*Three styles*   The art of the provincial Sultanates may be divided into three distinct groups: styles connected with the Delhi tradition: Jaunpur, Nāgaur, Mālwa; styles based on the Hindu tradition: Kashmīr, Gujarāt, Bengal; styles of the Deccan.

The buildings of the Sharqī sultāns of Jaunpur (Ātala Masjid 1408, Khalīs-Mukhlīs and Jhanjhrī Masjids, Jāmi' Masjid 1438—1478, Lāl-Darwāza Masjid, c. 1457) make more use of Hindu remains, but also of the Khiljī arch, of mosaic, of small encaustic tile pieces and of the Tīmūrid central niche in front of the domed central hall of the principal mosque nave. At Nāgaur in Rājasthān (a dependency of Gujarāt) the Tarkīn-kā Darwāza is a gateway constructed of Hindu remains, while the Shams Masjid (1403—51) combines a Tughluq façade with tapering corner buttresses, with a nave of Hindu columns.

The best monuments of the Mālwa style are at Māndū, Dhār and Chanderi. The Lāt Mosque (1405) and that of Kamāl Maulā at Dhār, like Dilāvar Khān's Mosque (1405) at Māndū were also built from Hindu remains. Māndū, the capital since 1405, was built on a plateau above the Narmadā Valley, accessible only via a narrow neck of land. Most of its buildings were built by Sultān Hoshang (1405—35): the Jāmi' Masjid and the sultān's tomb of white marble, and by Mahmūd I Khiljī (1436—69): the Ashrafī Mahal (tomb, madrasa and tower of victory) opposite the Jāmi' Masjid, the latter (completed) being the finest of the royal palaces in the north-west corner of the fort, especially the Hindola Mahal (durbar hall) and the Jahāz Mahal (women's palace) between the Munja and Kapūr Talāo (lakes). Most of the fine tombs near the Sāgar Talāo are also of his reign, whereas the palaces near the southern circumvallation, connected with the romance between Sultān Bāz Bahādur (1555—61) and the beautiful singer Rūpmatī, go back to Nāsir-ud-dīn (1500—1510), and "Gadā Shāh's Shop" (a huge durbār hall) was erected by Medinī Rāi, the Rājput dictator over Maḥmūd II in 1512—17. At Chanderi the big Kūshak Mahal (1445), a garden palace of Mahmud I, is especially worth mentioning. Generally speaking Mālwa architecture is a transformation of the Tughluq style, slim and elegant, and executed in beautifully dressed limestone. The domes, at first low, were soon raised on very high drums. From Gujarāt, free ogival arches and fine *jālī* (stone grill) work came into fashion, and in Mahmud I's buildings around the Munja Talāo even Mamlūk-Egyptian and European Gothic influences seem to be traceable.

In the second group, Hindu influence is very diversely visible. The mosques and *ziārats* (tombs of saints) of Kashmīr, converted to Islam since 1346, seem to be an adaptation of the preceding wooden architecture of the last Mediaeval period: cubic block houses with a low pyramidal grass roof and a *ma'zīna* on top, the spire of which is obviously an adaptation of the Buddhist *chattrāvalī* and Hindu *sikhara*. The Jāmi' Masjid of Sikandar Būtshikān (1393/4—1416) adapts this block house type to the Persian mosque with four aiwāns arranged crosswise and interconnected by naves of huge wooden pillars. The mausoleum built by Sultān Zain-ul-'Ābidīn (1420—70) for his mother is a brick structure of five domes on Hindu foundations of cross-shaped ground-plan. The mausoleums of Madīn Shāh and Bumzu are transformed Hindu stone temples.

The architecture of Bengal, mainly at Gaur (Dakhil Darwāza, 1459—74, Tantipārā, Daras Bārī, Nattan, Chamkan, the Gunmant mosques 1474—81, Chhotā Sonā Masjid, the mausoleum of Makhdūm Ākhī Sirāj-uddīn 1493—1518, Barā Sonā Masjid 1526), Pāndua (Adīna Masjid 1358—89, Eklākhī Masjid and the tomb of the sultān Jalāl-uddīn Muhammad 1414—31), Mālda, Tribenī, Bāsirhāt, Satgāon, Bāgerhāt, Vikrampur, Kusumbha, Masjidkur, etc., is based on the indigenous brick style of the vast alluvial plain, with sparse decorations in black marble and schist. The buildings are all very massive, with convex (*bangaldār*) roofs and delicate decorations (mainly Hindu patterns) carved into the bricks.

In contrast, the architecture of Gujarāt is, with rare exceptions (the brick tombs of 'Azam and Mu'azzam, and of Daryā Khān at Ahma-

*Hindu influence*

*Bengal*

dābād, and minor tombs at Champaner) of beautifully carved lime-stone. For here the Hindu tradition of temple architecture and sculpture was still alive and had already been adapted for Islamic purposes in Khiljī and Tughluq times (the mosques of Broach, An-hilwāda 1305, Cambay 1325, Dholkā 1333, Mangrol 1401). Hindu shrines, superimposed, became a minaret, the shrine door a mihrab, a series of mandapas the nave of a mosque, and the ornamentation was also taken over after the "idolatrous" figures had been replaced by flower motifs; to these were added Islamic ogival arches, arabesques and geometrical designs. Curiously enough, the Islamic tradition proved strongest in the secular monuments, in palaces and mansions. The earliest buildings (especially in the reign of Ahmad I, 1411–42) are rather heavy and their decoration is not yet properly integrated; the classic period of perfect balance was the reign of Mahmūd Begadā (1458–1511); under Muzaffar II (1511–26) the late phase of some-what feminine elegance and exuberant decoration set in. The chief centres were the capital, Ahmadābād (founded 1411: Bhadr citadel, Tripolia Gate, mausoleums of Ahmad Shāh and his queens, Jāmi' Masjid 1423/4, mosques and tombs of Dastūr Khān 1486, Muhāfiz Khān 1492, Rānī Rūpvatī 1500, Bībī Rānī, Rānī Siparī 1514, Sidī Sa'īd 1572 — with famous trellis windows — dargāhs of Shāh 'Ālam and Burhān-ud-dīn, Kānkarīya Lake, etc.), Sarkhej (6 miles to the south-west: pool, dargāh of Shaikh Ahmad Khattū 1451, royal palaces), Meh-medābād (mausoleum of Mubārak Sayyid 1484, palace of Mahmūd III 1538–54), the second capital, Champaner (1484–1535/6: Jahānpanāh citadel, with ruins of the royal palaces, Jāmi 'Masjid 1508/9, Nagīna Masjid, tombs of Sultan Sikandar and his brother Latīf Khān at Halol 1526), etc.

*Bahmanī sultāns of the Deccan*

The Bahmanī sultāns of the Deccan (1347–1538), involved in almost uninterrupted wars with the Hindus of Vijayanagar, Telingāna and Orissā, strengthened the ranks of their nobles and soldiers by immi-grants from overseas. Their architecture, therefore, came more and more under the spell of Persian art. However, Hindu elements are not absent, and during the last phase the influence of the Mālwa sultanate was also felt. Their first capital was Gulbarga (Bāla-Hissār-citadel by A'lā-ud-dīn Bahman 1347–58, Jāmi' Masjid 1367 by an architect from Qazwīn, royal tombs up to Fīroz Shāh 1397–1422, most of them in the Īlkhānī-Persian taste). Fīroz Shāh built a summer residence, Fīrozābād, on the Bhīmā. Ahmad Shāh Wālī (1422–36) moved the capital to Bīdar in 1428–32 (in the fort, the Takhtkhāna =

Chār-Minār at Haidarābād, Deccan, built 1591 by Sultān Muhammad Qulī who founded the town in 1589. Similar central halls, serving as police station, market, etc. (mandī, mandvī) are found in most Indian towns.

throne hall, Shāhburj = royal palace, Sola Khamba Masjid, the Gagan-, Tarkash-, Chīnī- and Nagīna-palaces by Ahmad III 1461–63 and Muhammad III 1463–82, in the town the Shī'ite Takht-i Kirmānī by Ahmad II, 1436–58, and the madrasa of the minister Mahmūd Gāwān, 1472, once completely covered with encaustic tiles; in the suburb Ashtūr, the royal tombs). The Chānd Minār at Daulatābād (1436) reminds one of Gujarātī and Turkish minarets. Most of the fortresses of the Deccan were constructed by the Bahmanīs, making use of experience made during the crusades.

*Changing styles* Between 1490 and 1512 the empire broke up into the sultanates of Bīdar (Barīd-Shāhs), Ahmadnagar (Nizāmshāhs), Berār (Imād Shāhs, not very important), Bījāpur ('Ādil Shāhs) and Golkonda (Qutb Shāhs), each called after its capital. The art of these sultanates first continued in the late Bahmanī tradition: Ahmadnagar (Fort, Dāmarī Masjid); Bīdar (tombs and mosques of 'Alī Baūd, Amīr Barīd, Khān-Jahān Barīd, etc.); Bījāpur (Shaikh-Rauza at Gulbarga; and the huge Gagan- and 'Adālat-Mahal, Jāmi' Masjid, 'Alī's tomb); Golkonda (Jāmi' Masjid, tomb of Ibrāhīm I). But it completely changed its character after the decisive victory over the Hindus at Talikota in 1565, and the sack of their capital, Vijayanagar. After a first irruption of the undiluted Vijayanagar style into the minor arts about 1570, architecture became semi-Hindu in form (Hindu columns and column bases, "metal rings", round pillars, lintels, brackets, eaves, balconies, heraldic lions and peacocks) and in sentiment, dissolving clear, constructive forms into baroque, sculptured vegetal motifs (lotus domes, lotus-bud minaret — cupolas, lotus — petal drums, etc.): Bīdar (Rangīn Mahal, with wooden Hindu columns, but Persian encaustic tiles; tombs and mosques of Ibrāhīm, Qāsim II Barīd, Kālī Masjid, etc.); Bījāpur (Jal-Mandir, Ibrāhīm Rauza = the mausoleum of Sultān Ibrāhīm II 1581–1626, Mihtar-Mahal 1620, Andū Masjid 1608, Torwa-Nauraspur for Ibrāhīm's Hindu dancers and singing girls, gateway of the Gol-Gumbad); Golkonda (royal tombs); Haidarābād (Chār Minār 1591, Jāmi' Masjid 1598, Mushīrābād Mosque, Tolī Masjid 1671). In the 17th century there followed, finally, a wave of Ottomān-Turkish influence: Bījāpur (wall decoration of Ibrāhīm-Rauza, the Gol-Gumbad = the mausoleum of Sultān Muhammad 1526–56, an imitation

'The spiritual form of the 10th aspect of the Earth'. Illustration in a manuscript of *Nujūm-al-'Ulūm*, executed for 'Ali I 'Adilshāh in 1570. An example of the irruption of the Hindu style of Vijayanagar into ▶ the Islamic art of the Deccan. *Chester Beatty Collection, Dublin.*

A Sultan of Bijāpūr, probably 'Ali I 'Adilshāh (1557–1580). Deccani miniature, about 1600. *Bibliothèque Nationale, Paris.*

of the Aya Sofia in Stambul); Haidarābād (Bādshāhī Āshūrkhāna, 1593—97, decorated with Turkish encaustic tiles).

In the 15th century remains of more perishable works of art also become more common. A very interesting MS. of Laur-Chandā (a Hindu romance in Āwadhī-Hindī, in 1379, dedicated by Maulānā Dāūd to Fīroz Shāh's minister Khān-Jahān The Younger) in the Bombay Museum, combining early Persian and "Rājput" features, seems to be from Jaunpur, in the reign of Husain Sharqī (1458—79). We know of early Gujarāt painting, dependent first on the "'Abbāsid" miniatures of 'Irāq, then on the Tughluq style of Delhi, and finally on the Tīmūrid School of Herāt, from a Panchatantra fragment, copies in Jain MSS. of the Kālikāchārya-Kathā, echoes in a Rājput album from Jālor (?), etc. Of the Mālwa school we possess the Ni'mat-Nāma of Sultān Ghiyās-ud-dīn (c. 1500), in the India Office Library, and the murals in Gadā Shāh's House at Māndū. From Bengal there comes the portrait of Sultān Fīroz Shāh (1533). Late Bahmanī MSS. in a preponderantly Persian style have also been traced. The material from the later Deccanī sultanates is much richer: the Tarif-i Husain-Shāhī MS. from Ahmadnagar in Poona, and Rāgmālā miniatures at Bīkāner (mixed Turkish-Vijayanagar); from Bījāpur, first the Persian-Hindu murals of Kumatgi, then the Nujūm-ul-'Ulūm MS. at Dublin (1570) and Rāgmālā pictures, in a semi-Hindu style, later miniatures in a variation of the Akbarī-Mughal and early Safavid-Persian styles, belonging to the reign of Ibrāhīm II (1581—1626); miniatures in an increasingly Mughal, and late Safavī-Persian manner of the time of the last rulers; while a curious product of the reign of Muhammad (1526—56) are the "Italian" (imitation of Paolo Veronese) murals in the Āthār-Mahal. From Golkonda we have the Tīmūrid-Persian Hātifī MS. at Patna (1550), the mixed Khawar-Nāma (1645) in Bombay, and miniatures as well as large-size-canvas pictures in the Deccanī style proper from the reign of Sultān 'Abdullāh (1626—72) onwards. The latter is a variation of the Mughal style, of flatter treatment, more sweeping lines, with much gilding and many Hindu female costumes.

The applied arts are less explored. Glazed pottery, partly dependent on Persian models, partly with Indian designs, has been found at 'Adīlābād (Tughlaqābād), Sirī (Hazār Sūtun), in Gujarāt and at Māndū. The "Kanauj" Throne at Bīkāner is mainly 15th century work, reminiscent of Mamlūk-Egyptian carvings. A lion tapestry in the Calico Museum in Ahmadabad may be of the 15th, perhaps even the 13th or 14th century. Among the crown insignia of some Rājput

Gunkarī Rāginī, a Rājput lady sitting on a palace terrace at night awaiting her husband. Early Rājput miniature, probably from Orchhā, second half of the 16th century. 5½″ × 7½″. ▶

princes there are sword blades said to be of the 15th century, unfortunately with late hilts.

EARLY
RAJPUT ART

As already mentioned in the previous chapter, a revival of Hindu art set in at the end of the 14th century. This revival was at first purely antiquarian. But the catastrophe of the Muslim conquest had given an immense impetus to reforms already demanded in the late Middle Ages, i.e. the equality of all men before one God, accessible in his boundless love and mercy to every genuine devotee without regard to social status and learning, and thus also the social equality of men. Such ideas were, in principle, very old. They had been taught in the Bhagavadgītā, and had been championed by the Śaiva Nāyanār and the Vaishnava Ālvār. In the 12th century they were elaborated by the Śaiva Lingayats and the Vaishnava leaders, Rāmānuja and Mādhvachārya. In the 14th century they were preached throughout Northern India, in the language of the people, by the Vaishnava reformer, Rāmānanda. In the 15th and early 16th centuries a wave of mystic emotion, carried by saints like Chaitanya (1486—1533), Vallabhāchārya (1478—1531) and Mīrā Bāī (1498—1560), filled the people with love of Vishnu in his incarnation as Krishna, the cowherd god of Mathurā and Brindāban. This cult had been developed by Nimbārka in the early 12th century, had as its classic poem the Gītāgovinda of Jayadeva (1178—1206) and as its popular form, the songs of Vidyāpati (1398—1458), Narsingh Mehta, later of Mīrā Bāī, Haridās, Sūrdās, etc. All the gods were reduced to insignificance, if not wholly denied (e.g. by Kabīr and Nānak), and most of the Hindu rites were ignored. Only the eternal game of love between Krishna and Rādhā, God and the saintly soul, was allowed, which the cowherds (gopas) and milkmaids (gopīs), i.e. the less advanced souls, were permitted to witness. In the language of human love the mysteries of divine bliss were sung. Although as a social movement the Vaishnava reform was at last broken by the combined forces of feudalism and orthodoxy, it gave a tremendous impetus to independent artistic creation. And it found a less extreme successor in the Rāma cult propagated by Tūlsī Dās (1532—1623), which extolled the just rule of ideal Hindu kingship within the framework of orthodox Hindu dharma, in the image of Rāma, another incarnation of Vishnu.

Krishna mysticism made the traditional Hindu temple, with all its

*Museum of Fine Arts, Boston*

Rājput miniature in amber, about 1600, 1½ times original size. *Baroda Museum.*

The maid brings a message to her mistress from her lover. An illustration to the Rasikpriyā (The Moods of the Beloved) by Keśavadās Sanādhya Miśra, a very famous poet of Orchhā in Bundelkhand in the late 16th century. In the 15th and 16th centuries Rājput princesses often selected their own lovers and husbands. Moreover, the princes had illicit relations not only with courtesans and concubines, but also with married women; and some were slain by the husbands. The emotions of such women (nāyikā) are the subject of innumerable Hindī poems.

symbolism and imagery, superfluous; on the other hand, it demanded ed a new iconography which the Mediaeval śilpa-śāstras could not supply.

Moreover, the whole style of life had changed. The Hindus had been compelled either to absorb much of Indo-Islamic civilization in order to be tolerated as subjects, or to make a stand against the military technique of the conquerors. Islamic gateways, vaults, domes, battlements invaded Hindu architecture, differing only in a vaster use of Hindu columns, brackets, lintels, balconies and figurate sculpture. Muslim dress, though in a more conservative fashion, became common among the upper classes. Islamic paintings were copied into Jain and Hindu miniatures, increasingly independent of their mediaeval prototypes. At last a new style emerged: an architecture using Islamic forms for the heavy substructures and highly simplified Hindu forms for the lighter upper storeys. The traditional temple (*mandir, deval*) was superseded by a mansion with an inner court, an open (cult) hall and a simple sanctuary room. The palaces (*chakī, garh, kothī*) differed from those of the Muslims mainly in an irregular, picturesque planning. Sculpture was enormously simplified, the figures adorned in modern dresses. Cult images generally became very small and thus easily removable in case of danger; but they were placed on brass, silver or gold stands carried by the serving animal (*vāhana*) of the deity, and protected by a chapel-like shrine and a metal umbrella. Paintings were executed in a very primitive, but highly expressive style: flat, in glowing colours, the figures built up like those in ancient Egypt, grouped in rows, the features expressionless but for almost hypnotic eyes, and all expression concentrated in speaking postures and poses. Decorative art was very plain: simple creeper borders on spherical or cylindrical boxes, heraldic or divine figures on sword hilts, heraldic animals on textiles in bright colours.

In the earliest attempts at a renaissance of the mediaeval tradition there is a curious admixture of Indo-Islamic, as well as of indigenous folk art. In the 15th century the antiquarian style dominated in

*Change in style*

Rājasthān. However, in the Gujarātī MSS. of the Vasantavilāsa and Bālagopālastuti, and later of the Devī Māhātmya, the ossified iconography of the 14th century Jain Kalpasūtra MSS. is freely varied in order to depict any new subject. In the palace of Rāja Mān Singh Tomār (1486–1516) on Gwālior Fort, North-Indian as well as South-Indian architectural motifs are also freely developed and combined with friezes in Islamic encaustic tile work, and in the dancer and musician scenes of the fretwork windows scenes in the "Rājput" style (described above) turn up for the first time. Early in the 16th century the "Rājput" style type appeared also in Jaunpur (Laur-Chandā and Chaurapanchāśikā MSS.). When, in the second half of the 16th century, the Rājputs became rich as vassal-generals and governors of the Mughal emperors, an extensive art activity began all over Rājasthan, at Āmber, Bīkāner, Jaisālmer, Jodhpur, Būndī, etc., and also in the religious centres of Hinduism, at and around Mathurā, at Banāras, etc. After about 1620 Rājput art had completely ousted the Mediaeval renaissance, merely to be superseded by Mughal art in the course of the 17th century.

In the Himālaya this art revolution came later, the renaissance dominated the 16th and early 17th century, the Rājput style, imported from Rājasthān, coming to the fore only in the 17th century.

In Bengal and Assam the Mediaeval brick architecture had never quite disappeared, though the Hindu shrine with its circumambulatory passage adjusted itself to the Islamic *bārādārī*, the garden pavilion enclosed by an open gallery. The oldest known MS. (Bhāgavata-Purāna), illustrated in a style related to that of Rājasthān, had been painted in 1538. About 1600, when the rāja Mān Singh of Āmber was governor, Rājput architecture and painting were also introduced. The later temples excel in beautiful brick reliefs narrating all the famous Hindu myths and epics.

MUGHAL ART   In 1526 Bābur, originally Tīmūrid ruler of Ferghāna, then of Samarqand, and finally of Kābul, invaded India and smashed the two grand powers of the North, the Lodī sultāns and the Rājput rānās of Mewar. His son Humāyūn (1530–56), conquered Bengal, Mālwa and Gujarāt, but was expelled in 1540 by Sher Shāh Sūr, was only able to return in 1554, and died just after his first victories. The reason for this instability was that the Mughals were total strangers without roots in India. And so was their art. Both Bābur and Humāyūn were highly cultured art lovers, but the architecture they liked consisted of the octagonal pavilions, the vast open halls and lofty bays, the bulbous

gardens of tulips, hyacinths and narcissi, the semi-Chinese calligraphic
domes covered with brightly coloured encaustic tiles, the geometrical

A Hindu widow seeks permission
from Akbar's son, Prince Dāniyāl, to
burn herself on the price of her dead
husband. Illustration to Nauʿī's romance *Soz-u-Gudāz*, by Āqā Rizā. A
Persian illustration for Prince Salīm
of a poem on a Hindu subject, composed at the instigation of his younger brother. End of the 16th century.
*Bibliothèque Nationale, Paris.*

miniatures, the big-flowered, heavy brocades which were then the fashion in the Tīmūrid capitals of Samarqand, Bukhārā, Herāt. Both lived too much in the saddle to leave behind more than a few buildings (a mosque and garden at Āgra, the Sher Mandal in Purāna Killa, and some tombs at Delhi, Sarhind, Bhatner, etc.). At first, during the early years of Akbar the Great (1556–1605), especially during the residence of the court at Delhi 1560–62, a more intensive building activity set in. The residence there was Sher Shāh's Purāna Killa. Around it were built the mosque of 'Abd un-Nabī, the Khair-ul-Manāzil *madrasa*, the tomb of Bū Halīma, Nīla Gumbad, Nīlī Chhattrī, the vast garden of Humāūn's tomb, the 'Arab Sarāī, and after 1562 the small but exquisite mausoleum of the assassinated minister, Ātga Khān at Nizām-ud-dīn, the Afsarwalla Maqbara, the Sabz Burj and finally the gigantic mausoleum of Humāyūn, erected by his widow Hājī Begam 1568–80. In all these buildings a progressive Indianising is evident, in the replacement of the encaustic tile mosaic by mosaic in variously coloured sandstone, marble and schist, then by the intrusion of Hindu *chhattrīs*, balconies, eaves, columns and lintels. The same happened with painting. The large-size illustrations to the Hamza-Nāma — a fantastic adventure story, describing the first conquest of the heathens by Amīr Hamza, an uncle of the prophet Muhammad — begun probably under Humāyūn for the edification of the young

Rejoicing at the birth of Prince Salīm in 1569. Illustration of an Akbar-Nāma. In 1562 Akbar had married a Rajput princess of Amber, a pupil of the Vaishnava saint-singer Mīrā-Bāi, whom he called Maryam-az-Zamānī (the St Mary of her time). He expected her to bear a son who would be the Messiah of the Age, uniting the hostile Muslims and Hindus under one peaceful rule. Salīm however was born only seven years later, under a most auspicious horoscope, thanks to the intercession of the Muslim saint, Salīm Chishtī. At his hermitage Akbar founded the beautiful town of Fathpur Sikrī. Though a not unimportant emperor, ▸
Jahāngīr (Salīm) never fulfilled the high hopes which his father had set on him.
In the background the astrologers read the prince's horoscope; in the centre, Hindu dancing girls dance to the music of the imperial *naubat-khāna*; in the foreground food is distributed to the poor.
*Chester Beatty Collection, Dublin.*

Akbar, are purely Persian; but in time Indian costumes, Hindu idols, scenes of Indian village life were incorporated into them. *Eclectic phase* The definitive subjection of Northern India and the expansion of the empire into Mālwa, Gujarāt, Rājputāna and Bengal, were accompanied by a political and cultural revolution. Akbar employed in his service officers from all over the empire, Muslims as well as Hindus, and latterly relied mainly on the support of the Rājput princes who had first obstinately opposed him, but who afterwards became his relatives and most loyal followers. Like the earlier sultans, he married Hindu princesses, but did not interfere with their religion, and the style of life at his court became a mixture of Mughal, Indo-Islamic and Rājput features. In art, the Indo-Islamic style (Lodī-Sūr) was first employed in the mausoleum of Adham Khān (1562) at Mehraulī, the mosque and entrance to the dargāh of Shaikh Mui 'īn-ud-dīn Chistī at Ājmer (1562), a tomb on the Golf Links at New Delhi, the shrine of Shaikh Makhdūm Yahyā at Māner near Patna (pure Gujarātī style), the gigantic mausoleum of Shaikh Muhammad Ghaus (1563) at Gwālior (Mālwa-Gujarātī style) and lastly that of Shaikh Salīm Chishtī (1573) at Fathpur Sikri (Mālwa-Gujarātī style).

The Rājput (simplified Hindu) style first came to the fore in Āgra Fort (rebuilt 1565–73) and Fathpur Sikrī (23 miles south-west of Āgra, 1573–80). The palaces of Fathpur Sikrī, situated on a ridge of cliffs where Salīm Chishtī's hermitage had been, in particular proved to be an amazing experimental centre in creating a new imperial architecture. The Great Mosque enclosing the saint's tomb has Hindu pillars, but a *maqsūra* of the Jaunpur type is decorated with Mamlūk-Egyptian mosaic like the Purāna-Killa mosque, and nearer the town it has a gigantic entrance (Buland Darwāza) in the purest early Mughal fashion. Most of the palaces are kept in a very simplified Hindu style, that of Empress Jodhbāī even in pronounced Hindu taste. In contrast, the sleeping rooms of the emperor and "Raja Bīrbal's House" assume the Lodī style, fused with Mughal and Rājput motifs. Finally, the "Turkish Sultāna's House" is a Rājput pavilion, covered with flower decorations and animal scenes such as were then the fashion in book illumination at Bukhārā.

The emperor Jahāngīr receiving his ambassador Khān 'Ālam after the latter's return from the court of Shāh 'Abbās I of Persia. Jahāngīr sits on a throne of part European workmanship. The scene in the background is probably Lake Pushkar near Ājmer, where the emperor built a garden palace in 1615. *Berlin Museum.*

When Fathpur Sikrī had to be abandoned because of water shortage (notwithstanding an amazing water-lift), a standard style developed, in which Mughal, Indo-Islamic and Rājput forms and ornaments were kept in a very pleasing balance. It is characteristic of the earlier architecture of the palace-fortress at Lahore (1580–1618, and 1632), Allahābād Fort (1583–84), the palace of Ājmer (1572) and many sarāis and minor forts. It was continued during most of the reign of his successor, Jahāngīr (1605–27): Chālīs Sūtūn at Allahābād, Jahāngīrī Mahal at Āgra, Akbar's Tomb at Sikandra (1614), the Shālimār Garden palace in Kashmīr, etc. These later buildings are more elegant, their forms slimmer and more involved, their decoration richer. The best monument of the later style is Akbar's mausoleum, a pyramid of arcades, screens and pavilions rising in the centre of a vast Persian garden, the upper storeys of white marble, ending in a quiet court where the emperor's cenotaph, once bearing a rare diamond, rests lonely under the hot Indian sun.

A similar style of painting was also evolved by Mīr Sayyid 'Alī and 'Abd-as-Samad, two painters whom Humāyūn had brought from the Persian court of Shāh Tahmāsp I, and whom Akbar ordered to train a large studio of Indo-Muslim as well as Hindu artists. The result was the illustration of a great number of historical works, epics, romances and didactic books (most famous is the Akbar-Nāma in the South Kensington Museum in London, and the Razm-Nāma at Jaipur) in a style basically Safavid-Persian, but Indian (mainly Rājput) in most of its detail. Jesuit missionaries from Goa at the court, imported Christian paintings and prints, introducing not only whole copies or detail transpositions of Christian figures and scenes, but also a delicate naturalism much recommended by the emperor. Under Jahāngīr the naturalistic tendency gained the upper hand, though the Persian bird's eye perspective was superseded by a Rājput approach (strict side view, stripe composition) only slightly tempered by apparently naturalistic details. The careful studies of animals, birds, flowers, trees, etc. executed by Jahāngīr's orders are some of the most exquisite masterpieces of Mughal art.

*Classical phase* With Shāhjahān (1628–58) — in fact in the last years of Jahāngīr — the orthodox Muslim party returned to power. The semi-Hindu eclectic style was therefore abandoned, and in the Panjāb, and to some extent also in the capitals Delhī and Āgra, Safavid-Persian architecture again came in fashion. Its brick core was covered first with a mosaic of specially cut monochrome tiles in bright blue, white, yellow and

Studies of various birds by Miskīna, a painter of the Akbar and Jahāngīr period. An example of the intelligent observation of nature by Mughal artists. *Musée Guimet.*

green encaustic colours, later with square tiles on which a much richer decoration, predominantly green, sometimes also pink or marine blue, had been painted; the design of this tile decoration, of course, was not strictly Persian, but comprised many Indian elements (most pronounced on the north and west walls of the Lahore Fort). Features of the contemporaneous Mughal court style also infiltrated into the architectural forms. The best known buildings of this type are the tombs of Āsaf Khān (1641), 'Alī Mardān Khān (1657), Zebinda Begam (1669) and of Sharaf-un-Nisā Begam (18th century, "Sarūrwalla Maqbara") at Lahore and of Afzal Khān (1639, "Chīnī-kā-Rauza") at Āgra, the mosques of Wazīr Khān (1634, with a bazaar for its maintenance), Dāi Ānga (1671) and Zaqariā Khān (in Begampur) at Lahore, the gardens of Roshānārā (died 1671) and the Shālimār (1632) at Delhī, the Shālimār (1637) and the Shāhdāra gardens at Lahore, and especially the famous Shālimār and Nishāt gardens in Kashmīr.

However, because of the political tension with Persia, the Safavid style was in the event not accepted by the imperial court. And even some "Persian" buildings, like the mausoleums of Khānkhānān at Delhī (1626) and of Jahāngīr's mother Maryam-az-Zamānī at Sikandra (1623) were, as in the early part of Akbar's reign, constructed in red sandstone with marble panels or, like the Patthar Masjid (1623) and the mosque of Mullā Akhūn (1649) at Srīnagar, in grey limestone, or in the white marble of the new imperial style, like the Tāj-Mahal at Āgra (1630—48). The Tāj-Mahal, mausoleum of Shāhjahān's dearly beloved empress Mumtāz-Mahal — and later also of the emperor — though the most famous monument of India, can thus be called Indian only with considerable qualifications. Its swivel dome on top of an octagonal structure of arched recesses and balconies, flanked by four minarets, on a terrace between a mosque and a hall for pilgrims and lying between the Jamnā river and a geometrical garden, is of the purest Persian design, the creation of two Persian architects, Ustād Ahmad and Ustād Hamīd; and yet it is utterly un-Persian, thoroughly Indian in its spirit, chaste and pure, subdued and dreamy, the very antithesis to the gaudy vitality of genuine Persian works.

*New imperial style* The new imperial style developed from three sources: the white marble architecture of Gujarāt (Sarkhej) and Mālwa (Hoshang's tomb at Māndū), the Indo-Muslim architecture of Bengal (scalloped arches, lotus columns, convex *bangaldār* roofs) and — later — of the Deccan (bulbous minaret bases, square towers with broad balconies, lotus domes) and the flower decoration of Kashmīr (under Jahāngīr and

Muslim poet-scholar. Mughal miniature, c. 1630. The poet is sitting in a Kashmīr garden during an early summer night. Flowers on almost leafless trees are a peculiarity of the Indian summer. The nights are hot at first, but later the temperature falls sharply so that warm clothes become necessary. About 4″ × 4″. *Museum of Fine Arts, Boston.*

Shāhjahān the imperial summer residence). It was probably the invention of the empress Nūr-Jahān, herself a well-known artist, famous for her embroidery. White marble had already been used for some specially costly buildings under Akbar and Jahāngīr (the mausoleum of Shaikh Salīm Chishtī at Fathpur Sikrī, the central court of Akbar's tomb at Sikandra). Now the accent shifted; red sandstone continued to be used for substructures and subsidiary buildings, white marble dominated the imperial palaces and tombs. Later, in the 17th century, when the empire went bankrupt, painted marble stucco became the general substitute, and in the early 18th century even red sandstone became an exceptional building material. The first buildings were still in the eclectic early Mughal style, e.g. Chausat Khamba at Nizām-ud-dīn, Delhi (1624), the palaces on the Āna Sāgar at Ajmer (1637), even the mausoleum of Nūr-Jahān's father I'timād-ud-daula (1628) at Āgra, in which in other respects the new style first appeared in all its glory. The Bengalī elements became common first in Shāhjahān's famous palaces in Āgra Fort (1637), the Shāh-Burj in Lahore Fort (1631—34) and especially in the palaces of his new capital of Shāhjahā-nābād (1639—48) at Delhī. These palaces, together with their palace mosques (Moti Masjid Āgra, 1646—53) and town mosques (Jāmi' Masjids in Āgra 1648 and Delhī 1644—58) represent the peak of

*Peak of Mughal art*

Mughal art. The palaces are excellently planned: from the entrance a bazaar leads to a music pavilion and to the great audience hall (*dīwān-i 'āmm*) in a vast court surrounded by offices; along the river front there are the private palace rooms, on the south side the zenāna, in the centre the emperor's living and reception rooms (*dīwān-i khāss, musamman burj*), on the north side the palace mosque, hot baths and gardens. In contrast to the early Indo-Muslim and Deccanī palaces all the buildings are only one-storeyed; but their splendour and perfect taste are indescribable: there are marble arches, pilasters and screens, water channels, waterfalls, fountains, and swimming pools with their water seats, little roof pavilions and domes, perforated screens, embossed brass and silver doors; there are decorations of arabesques, inscriptions and flowers, partly in delicate relief, partly inlaid in agate, carneol, etc., partly painted in gold, turquoise blue and purple; there are gilt ceilings covered with delicate flowers, and mirror rooms where thousands of small mirror glasses are mounted between stucco ledges and slabs forming the most wonderful mosaics.

And the same perfection can be observed in the other arts. The style of the paintings became fixed. No more experiments, but a harmoni-

Mausoleum of Ghiyās Beg I'timād-ud-daula at Āgra, erected by his daughter, the powerful Mughal empress Nūrjahān, in 1628. This detail shows the exquisite decoration, mostly mosaic of fine stones in white marble.

ous and sometimes even gorgeous depiction of court ceremonies, of social parties and zenāna life, noble, representative, refined, but without the vitality of Akbar's or the keen interest in life of Jahāngīr's time. The costumes, reserved in both cut and colour, are of transparent white muslin or soft green or wine red wool, embroidered with gold or with small flowers. There are none of the dashing coats, bright-coloured materials and big flowers of the preceding decades. There are swords with hilts of jade, or gold or silver intarsia on steel or enamel, fine cups of jade, crystal inlaid with gold wire and rubies, etc.

But the peak was passed. The intensification of the orthodox Muslim policy by the bigoted emperor Aurangzeb (1658—1707) generated a widespread religious tension, rebellions all over the empire, an endless ineffective war in the Deccan, secret disaffection of princes and nobles, military rule and general bankruptcy. Under Muhammad Shāh (1719—48) the provinces asserted their independence from a frivolous, intrigue-ridden court; after his death the emperors were no more than puppets in the hands of the nobles, until, in 1803, they had to accept British tutelage. Art changed. During Aurangzeb's early reign (Moti Masjid, Shāh Burj and Hayātbakhsh Garden in Delhi Fort; Bādshāhī Masjid 1673 at Lahore) architecture became nervous, baroque, with strong composition- and chiaroscuro-accents, bellied columns, arhythmical flower decorations and excessively complicated ornaments with almost gaudy colour effects. The monumental mosques erected at Mathurā, Banāras, Mertā, etc. on the ruins of famous Hindu temples, are of an unimaginative dullness. Thereafter (especially in the Killa-i Arh = imperial palace, and the Bībī-kā Rauza 1678, the mausoleum of the empress Rabi'a Daurānī, at the war capital Aurangābād in the Deccan), buildings became cheap (bricks covered with marble stucco), petty in composition, strongly tainted with form motifs from the newly conquered sultanates of Bījāpur (1686) and Golkonda (1687). And during the last two decades building activities practically stopped. The small and petty Moti Masjid at Mehraulī near Delhī (1709) was the last monument in white marble; the Zīnat-ul-Masājid at Delhī (1710), the last representative mosque in red sand-

*Last phase*

Prince Parvīz, brother of Khurram, later the emperor Shāhjahan, on a garden terrace, attended by several maidservants. Signed by Govardhan, one of the best of Jahāngīr's painters. On the edges, Kashmīr flowers. Mughal miniature. *Chester Beatty Collection, Dublin.*

stone. All subsequent buildings were the creations of nobles, and of these only two, the mausoleum of the grand wazīrs Ghāzī-ud-dīn the older and younger, and the mausoleum of nawāb Safdar Jang of Oudh (1753) at Delhi — a lame imitation of Humāyūn's tomb though with beautiful ornaments — were erected in red sandstone with marble slabs. Under British rule the emperor Bahādur Shāh II (1837–57) attempted a last renaissance of red sandstone architecture (Zafar and Hīra Mahal in Delhī Fort, Zafar Mahal at Mehraulī 1847–48). Otherwise, brick and painted marble stucco became the rule, evolving a fantastic "Rococo" of repeated, involved and fused, predominantly rounded and often naturalistic "vegetative" forms in gaudy colours.

*Qudsia Bāgh*    The key monument of this late architecture was the Qudsia Bāgh (c. 1748–50) outside the Kashmīr Gate of Delhī, almost destroyed in 1857. Other Delhi monuments worth mentioning are the Tripolia Gates at Sabzī Mandī (1728–29), and the two Sonehrī Masjids (1721 and 1751), both with gilt domes. Most of these late buildings, however, are found in the residences of the provincial governors at Lahore (Sonehrī Masjid of Bikhārī Khān, 1753), Faizābād (palace ruins, tombs of Shujā'ud-daula and of the Bahu Begam), Lakhnau (= Lucknow: Great Imāmbāra and palaces of Āsaf-ud-daula, palaces and tombs of the kings of Oudh), Murshīdābad (Moti Jhīl Palace, Jafargani Deorhi, Khūsh Bāgh), Bhopāl, Haiderābād (Moti Mahal, Purānī Hāvelī), Ārkot, and Seringapatam (Daryā-Daulat Bāgh, Lāl Bāgh tombs) in Mysore.

Painting was discouraged by Aurangzeb except for political purposes; but the artists dismissed from the imperial studio found employment with the princes and great nobles. Under Farrukhsiyar (1713—18) and Muhammad Shāh (1719—48) painting again became a favourite art at the court but the sack of Delhi by Nādir Shāh 1739 and the later occupation by the Marāthas and Afghāns induced more and more artists to find a more secure existence in the service of some nawāb or rājā. Mughal painting at Delhī, grown almost extinct during the last quarter of the 18th century, was revived by the last two emperors, Akbar II and Bahādur II, and thereafter survived as a bazaar craft.

The pictures of the period, about 1680—1720, represented war scenes or religious subjects, with Muslim as well as Hindu saints and rituals, profoundly devotional and often with a touching melancholia. Between c. 1710—60 court revelries, zenāna scenes and sentimental romances were the fashion, together with Hindu music motifs. In the second half of the 18th century the centre of Mughal painting shifted to the court of the nawābs of Oudh at Faizābād, later at Lakhnau, becoming superficially a most brilliant art of rich composition and warm colours, but in fact no more than clever jig-saw puzzles, fabricated by means of stencils, and enriched with landscapes inspired by contemporaneous British paintings and prints. The late Delhī school too achieved no more than clumsy copying, figures without stance, structure, proportions, expression, in dull colours; the ivory miniatures, similarly inspired by European models, were better, but today they too have degenerated into a dull, lifeless convention. Other local schools were those of Murshīdābad, Banāras, Patna and Haiderābād; the last especially producing fine work in the early 18th century under the impact of late Deccanī painting.

Applied art in this last period was very opulent; new techniques were introduced, especially heavy gold and tinsel embroidery; the ornaments became elaborate, figure scenes romantic and sentimental, and amongst the flower motifs were new kinds imported from Persia, China and Europe. The great art of the time, however, was the dance in the North Indian Kathak style, with twirling, flying wheel-skirts and most complicated footwork. It was an age of courtesans and dancing girls, the *bayadères,* and many of them made a career as princely mistresses, even queens. Some princes kept up to 10,000 dancing girls, and the last king of Oudh, Wājid 'Alī Shāh, experimented even with an Indian opera (Indrasabhā, by Amānat).

In the course of the 17th century the Hindu princes of Rājasthān adopted first the eclectic art banished from the Mughal court (after 1620), then the classic imperial style, first Āmber (Jaipur) c. 1625–27, then Bīkāner, Jodhpur and Būndī, last of all Mewār (Udaipur) about 1700. Mughal architecture, dying out at Delhi, flourished all over Rājasthān, in its Baroque stage at Jaipur (founded 1728), in other *Late Hindu art*  places mainly in its Rococo phase. Indeed, the finest "late Mughal" creations are found there, e.g. the Hawā Mahal at Jaipur, the Anūp Mahal and Gaj Mandir at Bīkāner, the palaces of Mān Singh and the Mahā Mandir at Jodhpur, the Amar Vilās at Udaipur. However, in this transition the Mughal style was adapted to the Rājput taste, becoming arhythmical and picturesque, and mixed with figure sculptures and religious or erotic murals. In the second quarter of the 17th century Mughal painting was also imitated, but with the characteristic transposition into a flat, brightly coloured, romantic style. Due to the continuous immigration of Mughal painters between c. 1680

Knuckle-pad cover from a shield, cotton embroidered with silk. Lovers in a garden palace: Girl with a peacock. Rājputāna, end of the 18th century. 5" × 5". *Indian Museum, South Kensington, London.*

Shish-Mahal at Āmber near Jaipur. Built in the middle of the 17th century and redecorated in the late 18th century.

and 1760 Rājasthānī painting became almost Mughal, but later regained its independence in a very decorative style of sweeping curves and strong colour contrasts. The subjects were taken mainly from Hindu religion. But the spirit had changed, and the Vaishnava mystic revival had ended in some more orthodox sects. The stories of young Krishna's pranks with the cowherd boys of Gokul, which so charmingly describe genuine village life, were almost forgotten. Instead, the love of Rādhā and Krishna became the pretext for a sophisticated court poetry describing the erotic experiences of the princes and nobles with their wives, concubines and mistresses. These were illustrated with various sets of "Nāyikās" (mistresses), Seasons (Varsha), Months (Bārāmāsā), Musical Moods (Rāgmālā), where nature and music mirror the sentiments of the lovers (pedantically classified). In the later 18th century many "religious" pictures actually depict "mys-

Rādhā-Krishna at the Rasa dance. Rājasthānī miniature, end of the 18th century. The picture actually represents the young mahārājā Sawāi Pratāp Singh of Jaipur acting in a Vaishnava mystery play the role of god Krishna, while a concubine acts that of Rādhā. During the whole of his reign Pratāp Singh II was under the domination of his mother who encouraged his dissolute life. The famous Raslīlā cartoons published by A. K. Coomaraswamy are similar representations of Pratāp Singh in the company of professional dancing girls. *Baroda Museum.*

tery" plays, which offered to the young princes a pretext for indulging in the charms of their many concubines and courtesans. Of course, illustrations to the classic epics continued to be in fashion by the side of portraits and court ceremonies.

In the small Rājput states of the Western Himālaya Mughal influence made itself first felt at Baśohlī and Nūrpur (late 17th century), but became important for the first time after the invasion of Nādir Shāh, when a semi-Mughal architecture and a Rājputized Mughal pictorial art developed at Guler (Kāngrā Valley) and Jammū. Later, the court of Sansār Chand II (1775–1823), "Kāngrā" (the fortress capital of his family, long in Mughal, but later in Sikh hands) at Tira-Sujānpur became a splendid centre of Oudh-Mughal architecture (Tira castle, Sansārchandeśvar and Narbadeśvar temples, 'Ālampur and Nadāun gardens) and of the "Kāngrā" school of painting, one of the culmination points of Indian art. For it combined the dashing sweep and colour of Rājasthānī painting with the delicate grace of the Guler school, and the sophistication of the court of an ambitious, Macchiavellian ruler with a genuine romanticism and mysticism to which the myth of the cowherd god and his beloved was still a living symbol of divine love. Kāngrā art spread over the whole Himālayas from Kashmīr to Garhwāl, but degenerated into lifeless dullness when, after 1796, these tiny states had to submit to the Nepālese, Sikhs and British in turn.

The Kāngrā heritage was taken over by the Sikhs, a Hindu reform sect which, in the Panjāb, had successfully rebelled against the Mughals and Afghans and who, in 1800–1847, became, under the mahārājā Ranjīt Singh (1799–1839), a considerable power in North-Western India. They were rough peasants and freebooters of rather vulgar tastes, and under their patronage the refined Kāngrā style became pompous and gaudy (Lahore; Golden Temple at Amritsār, etc.). However, their pictorial art makes up for this by a keen observation and sense of humour.

*The Sikhs*

A similar transformation came over Rājput art of the Rājasthān type under Marātha patronage. Though the dominating power in 18th century India, the Marāthas were a nation of rough peasants and conservative orthodox brāhmans who had to borrow the paraphernalia of power and luxury from their more refined neighbours, first from the sultanate of Bījāpur, then from the Mughals, and lastly from the Rājputs. In the middle of the 18th century they evolved an art of their own, of rather boorish taste, but important because innumerable

*Rājasthān*

Rādhā visits Krishna in the night, offering betel to him. Rājput miniature (Baṣohli, Panjāb Himālaya), early 18th century. The mystic theme of Divine Love, as described in Jayadeva's *Gītāgovinda*, was later a

temples, religious bathing ghāts, pilgrim houses, etc. destroyed by the Muslims were rebuilt by them, especially by Queen Ahilyā Bāī of Indore, (1767—97). Moreover, they founded new capitals at Sātārā, Kolhāpur, Pūna (Poona), Nāgpur, Indore, Barodā, Ujjain and Gwālior, and embellished practically every town in the Marātha country.

The Marātha house consists of bricks in a wooden framework, on trap-stone platforms around several courts, decorated with Mughal wall niches (and windows), rather crude murals, and rich wood carvings (under Gujarātī and Chinese influence). The Marātha temple — generally provided with a huge lamp stand (*dīpmālā*) — represents a renaissance of the mediaeval Western Chālukyan or Śilāhāra sanctuary, often combined with Mughal arches and cupolas; its spire is a curious transposition of the ancient *sikhara* into Deccanī-Mughal forms, a bulbous lotus dome (in place of the *āmalaka*) rising on top of several storeys of domed *chhattris*. Marātha sculpture imitates mediaeval iconography, but often in contemporaneous costumes. Marātha painting is generally an adaptation of Mughal or Rājput (Jaipur) miniatures, with sturdy figures and gaudy, warm colours. A special fashion was underglass painting, originally imported by Chinese artisans, but later developed into a national art.

*Tanjūr*

A local variety of the Marātha style developed in the 18th—19th century in Tanjūr, a cross-breed with late South Indian art of the Madurai type, baroque and fantastic and utterly strange to all our European ideals, but rich and cultured in its own way.

Another Hindu style flourished in Bengal under early British rule, patronized by the big landlords such as Rānī Bhavānī of Natore (1716—1795) who alone built more than 400 temples. Generally these temples are of the *bārādārī* type, high, with vaulted *bangaldār* roofs, now with Mughal arches and other semi-Mughal decorations, and very beautiful (though little known) brick reliefs (religious scenes), such as at Murshīdābād (Bārnagar), Khaliā (Farīdpur), Vishnupur (Bankūra), Kenduli, Handiāl, Bhandirban, Comilla, Girigovardhan, etc. Most of them are devoted to the cult of Krishna or of Kālī, the terrible but also gentle (Gaurī) black goddess, after whom Calcutta (= Kālī Ghāt) has been named. At Calcutta there also developed a

pretext for erotic poetry. Rādhā appears here as an Abhisārikā, a heroine who in the night goes to her lover; she has happily met him at the rendez-vous in Vrindā grove. 5" × 8". *Museum of Fine Arts, Boston.*

Rānī of Kulū in the Himālaya.
Rājput miniature (Panjab Hima-
laya), early 19th century (?).
*Baroda Museum.*

local type of religious pictures (*pata*), representing its subjects in a simple, but very rhythmical and expressive style (reminiscent of the English engraver William Blake); another type features small scenes on sheets of mica, mainly scenes of daily life.

However, by the end of the 18th century Mughal art and its Hindu contemporaries began to be ousted by new fashions introduced from Europe. Manners changed, chairs and tables replaced carpets and cushions, and old houses and palaces became inconvenient. Old-style miniatures could not withstand the competition of fashionable European oil paintings. The old handicrafts were ruined by the import of modern factory products wherever railways opened up the interior of the country. The agony dragged on over the whole 19th century, advancing from the administrative and mercantile centres into the less accessible districts, and the old art finally died out early in this century, but handed on its heritage to the pioneers of a modern national art.

Krishna returns to the lovely Rādhā in the Vrindā grove, announced by the messenger maid (dūtikā). Rajput miniature (Guler, Panjab), middle of the 18th century. The scenery is characteristic of the foothills of the Himālaya near Guler. *Museum of Fine Arts, Boston.* (See fig. on page 3).

The dancer Mrinalini Sarabhai in two Bhārat-Nātya poses. On the right, a story through the medium of hand language.

# VII. EPILOGUE: MODERN INDIAN ART

By the end of the 18th century Indian art of the Islamic period had also completed its cycle of life. What was good in the foreign Islamic culture had been completely absorbed into the Indian tradition. Islamic art in India had become thoroughly Indian, formally as well as emotionally, and Hindu art had become almost indistinguishable from its Islamic sister. But, with the tension between them, the creative stimulus had also disappeared. The Mughal style, now effeminate and over-ornate, had passed the peak of its evolutionary possibilities. There was even a contraction, a fusion of too complicated motifs into new standard patterns subordinated to a simple composition. And here a new experimentation set in, a search for new creative opportunities: the late Marātha temples, for example, with their simple fluted śikhara cones, or the late Rājput palaces planned in simple storeys covered with a rich covering of intricate, but uniform ornamentation. The time was ripe for another cultural and artistic synthesis. This emerged from the contact with Europe. But it was a slow and painful process lasting more than a century. And it is not finished even today, because European art was also at that time in a critical stage and, under the impact of a long series of revolutionary discoveries, has not yet overcome it. Thus, out of the conflict between East and West there has grown a new and technical world civilization, overthrowing all older ways of life, whether Eastern or Western, but without finding its own form. And as all genuine art has to be the expression of the spirit of its time, modern Indian art has become no less experimental than that of Europe or America, though in a somewhat different way. **THE NEW SITUATION**

The few Europeans living amidst the teeming millions of the Mughal Empire or of the South had no alternative but to adjust themselves to the foreign milieu. They lived, in Indian dress, in Indian style, with Indian wives, in Indian houses; and European articles, especially cult objects, were highly valued rarities. Many were buried in Mughal mausoleums (at Āgra there was even a miniature imitation of the Tāj Mahal), or beneath tomb stones decorated in the Mughal taste (Āgra cemetery, in the 16th century). In the interior of India this practice continued well into the early 19th century when it was sternly sup- **EUROPEAN COLONIAL ART** pressed by the British East India Company. Even then, European tombs remained semi-Indian; an obelisque type was but a tranformation of the *sikhara* of the Hindu funeral shrine, and a sarcophagus type an adaptation of the Tūls'ī shrine customary for deceased Hindu women. In the coastal settlements ("factories"), however, rich merchants had their "Baroque" mausoleums, amateurishly designed and clumsily executed (e.g. Balasore, Ahmadābād, and especially Surat).

*Portuguese art* The Portuguese first introduced the late Renaissance and Baroque art of their country into their independent towns at Goa, Bassein, Damān, Dīu, and also into smaller mission stations in the interior (e.g. Haiderābād, or San Tomé at Mylapore). They had good architects and painters especially amongst the Jesuits, and they imported Christian paintings and prints (mainly from Antwerp). The churches and monasteries of Velha (Old) Goa, the viceregal palace, Sta. Fé, the Misericordia, San Francisco d'Assisi, above all of Bom Jesus with the silver shrine of St. Francis Xavier, or those at Bassein (the Matriz, the Franciscan, Dominican, Jesuit and Augustinian churches, St. Paul, governor's palace, senate, etc.) are very impressive. However, they are purely European, and only in the many wood sculptures is the hand of the Indian artist to be felt. The paintings and prints were also brought to the Mughal capital, and Jahāngīr had his Lahore palace decorated with copies of the Madonna, Christ, etc. Under Shāhjahān, when "Firengī" mercenaries served in the Mughal artillery, Tuscan and French mosaic workers were employed in the decoration of the Delhi palaces and of the Tāj Mahal, while Italian paintings (in the manner of Veronese) decorated the Āthār Mahal at Bījāpur. Again, under Bahādur Shāh, when Donna Juliana Dias de Costa had much influence in the imperial zenānā, European paintings were in fashion. But taken all in all, European art was, outside the Portuguese possessions, no more than a whim, like the Chinoiserie of Rococo Europe.

*Louis XVI style* By and by other European nations obtained their share in the colonial competition, and built forts and settlements along the Indian coast; the Dutch at Surat, Cochin, Ceylon, Chinsūra, the British at Surat, Bombay, Madras and Calcutta, the Danish at Tranquebar, and the French at Pondicherry and Chandernagore. This had no influence on the interior of India, except for the curious rooms decorated with Portuguese blue and Dutch blue-and-white Delft tiles in the palace of the mahārānās of Udaipur; but the great struggle for supremacy between the French and British first began to exercise some tangible influence on Indian art. The French, beaten, continued to control much of India through their officers in the armies of the Mughal nawābs, the Marātha rājās and the sultans of Maisūr. Then the French Revolution, and later the Restoration forced a number of aristocrats, then Jacobines and Bonapartist officers, to try their luck at the courts of Haiderābād, Lakhnau, Indore, Gwālior, Sārdhanā and Lahore. In consequence, palaces in the French taste of the later 18th century, or at least similar decorations on Indian houses, turned up all over India, often indiscriminately mixed with elements of Mughal style, at Seringapatam, Tanjūr, Vellore, Sātārā, Haiderabad, Bhopal, Nāgpur, Gwālior, Barodā, Jaipur, Delhī (in the Red Fort, now destroyed), but especially at Lakhnau (La Martinière, Dilkushā Palace, Sikandar-Bāgh, Chhattar-Manzil, Hazrat-Ganj, Kaisar-Bāgh, even with Chinoiserie features!). They continued in this style until c. 1850—70.

With the British conquest of the country English architecture of the period was also introduced, first in the "Presidency towns", in Calcutta( Old Mission Church 1770, St John's Cathedral 1787, Roman Catholic Cathedral 1797, Warren Hastings' Belvedere House, Government House 1802, Ochterlony Monument 1823, etc.), in Bombay (St. Thomas Cathedral 1672—1718, Town Hall 1835, Mint, etc.) and in Madras (Fort St. George, St. Mary's 1680, St. Andrews' 1820). They fit into the tropical scenery like the classical mansions on the vast plantations of the American South. They were imitated by the last nawābs of Bengal at Murshīdābād (Barā Kothī 1829), the Kings of Oudh at Lakhnau (Motī Mahal, Tārāwalī Kothī, etc.), the Nizām of Haiderābād (Falaknumā Palace, etc.). Sculptures and paitings, of course, were entrusted to British artists: Chantrey, J. H. Foley, Woolner, Flaxman, Sir Joshua Reynolds, Tilly Kettle, Zoffany, Dance, Thos. Daniell, Lemuel Abbott, William Hodges, etc. whose representations of contemporary personalities and of palaces, many of which have since then disappeared, are of great interest. The prints determined the larger size of late Oudh miniatures and the landscapes therein; the painter Mihr Chand in particular executed many careful copies after Zoffany and Kettle.

*English influence*

Thereafter, all the "historical" architectural styles of the 19th century found their way into India: neo-Gothic (Bombay government offices, the university and the Victoria Terminus; St. Paul's Cathedral and High Court in Calcutta, etc.), looking utterly out of place in the Indian scenery; Norman (e.g. Lahore railway station, bridge heads over the Jumnā and Indus); neo-Italian (mahārājās' palaces in Gwālior,

*Art of the late nineteenth century*

Indore, Barodā, and the Victoria Memorial in Calcutta, etc.). The so-called "Babu" (= Hindu clerk) Gothic architecture of utilitarian offices and barrack buildings with badly proportioned, too narrow Gothic windows and gables, became especially common, but also a byword for lack of taste. Many mansions of rich Hindu merchants, overburdened with bad sculptures and clumsy paintings, trick mirrors, figured chiming clocks, etc., are veritable horrors. European painting was now taught in the government Schools of Arts, generally provoking an aversion against Occidental "materialistic" art. The only Indian painter of reputation was Rājā Ravivarman of Travancore, a tolerable portrait painter, but known all over India because of his mythological pictures in very histrionic taste, sold in millions of bad oil prints.

REVIVAL OF
NATIVE ART

In the last quarter of the 19th century a reaction finally set in, first amongst a handful of Englishmen who had learnt to appreciate the beauties of Indian art and deplored its disappearance, then amongst Indians who first timidly tried to copy and imitate old masterpieces of art, but at last broke away completely to new inspirations.

By and by an increasing number of genuine masterpieces of ancient Indian art became known. In 1862–87 Sir Alexander Cunningham surveyed most of the surviving monuments of Northern and Central India, Jas. Burgess undertook a similar job in Western India, H. Cousens in the South and in 1879 Jas. Fergusson brought out his History of Indian and Eastern Architecture. In 1896 J. Griffith created a mighty wave of enthusiasm by the publication of the Ajantā murals, in 1902 the newly founded Archaeological Survey of India started its Annual Reports, and in 1905 the Law for the Protection of Ancient Monuments was passed. Museums of archaeology and industrial art were founded, especially at Lahore, Jaipur, Calcutta, Madras, under the initiative of G. C. Birdwood, J. L. Kipling (father of the poet), Th. H. Hendley, F. S. Growse, B. H. Baden-Powell and E. B. Havell. The still surviving crafts were surveyed and encouraged. The traditional late Mughal-Rājput architecture was used for new buildings: the town of Bulandshahr in Uttar Pradesh, the Lord Curzon Museum at Mathurā, the government buildings at Jaipur, Jodhpur and Bīkāner (by Sir Swinton Jacob), Barodā Palace (by Mant and Chisholm), Lahore (by Sardār Rām Singh), the India Gate, General Post Office and Prince of Wales Museum at Bombay (by G. Wittet). The last stage of this rather artificial revival was the building of New Delhi (1911–30) by Sir Edwin Lutyens and Sir Edward Baker in a mixed Indo-European the masses. International modern trends more and more got the upper hand. Notwithstanding official efforts to boost a "national" architecture inspired by Gupta models (Birla Temple at New Delhi, neo-Buddhist shrines at Calcutta, Sārnāth, etc., "chaitya" arches, chhattrīs, Hindu columns, in recent government buildings, etc.), modern functional architecture has now become the rule, and Le Corbusier has been responsible not only for the planning of Chandīgarh, the new capital of the East Panjāb, but also for administrative buildings and villas at Ahmadābād and other towns; Otto Koenigsberger at Bangalore; and quite a generation of younger India artists is working in the same spirit. In sculpture, the impressionism of Rodin and Epstein is represented by Prodosh Dāsgupta, Khastgīr, Rāmkinkar Baij, S. K. Bakre, etc. A very simplified and strong style is found in the works of Shanko Chaudhurī, Dhānrāj Bhagat and Bakre. In painting, Manishī Dey, Sailoz Mookherjee, Jaminī Roy, K. Sreenivāsalu have tried to revive traditionalism by falling back on other, not yet exploited aspects of ancient or of folk art. The leaders of Impressionist painting are N. S. Bendre, Kalyān Sen, D. J. Joshi, Kanwāl Krishna, K. C. S. Paniker. S. D. Chavda, K. H. Hebbar, B. Sanyāl, K. S. Kulkarni, Lakshman Pāi, and Rathin Moitra have evolved a modern style via a study of folk art. The extreme modern wing is represented by K. H. Ārā, H. A. Gade, S. B. Palsikar, Samant, George Keyt ("the Indian Picasso"), Rāsik D. Rāval (comparable to Matisse), M. F. Husain and Amīna Ahmad (symbolic, and decorative abstraction). The poet Rabīndranāth Tagore has become known by very personal pen-drawings reminiscent of Odilon Redon. The best and most individual painter has probably been Amrita Sher-Gil, a girl of Sikh-Hungarian mixed descent who, trained in Italy and Paris, after her return to India evolved an increasingly Indian style via Gauguin, Modigliani and Japanese masters such as Korin and Koetsu; a style very simple and decorative, yet most sensitive and moving. She died young in a village, soon after her marriage, in 1942.

But the struggle over modern Indian art is not yet ended; it will probably continue as long as this subcontinent passes through the labours of modernization, as long as the integration of past and present is still uncompleted. Only then will the Indian art of the future reveal itself. But it cannot be a mere renaissance of the past; it will be something new, like all former styles emerging from a revolutionary crisis.

# APPENDIX

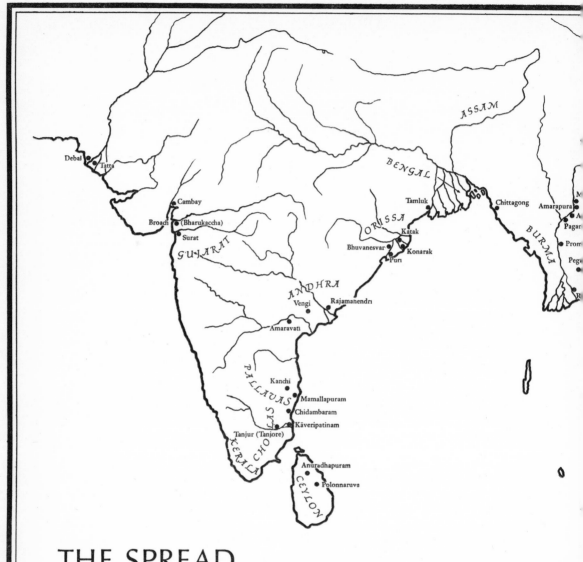

Debal
Tatta
Cambay
Broach ● (Bharukaccha)
Surat
GUJARAT

ASSAM

BENGAL
Tamluk
Chittagong        Amarapura
ORISSA
Katak                    BURMA
Bhuvanesvar        Pagar
Puri ● Konarak              Prom
ANDHRA                              Peg
Vengi ● Rajamahendri
Amaravati                              R

PALLAVAS
Kanchi
Mamallapuram
Chidambaram
Kāveripatinam
Tanjur (Tanjore)
KERALA CHOLAS

Anuradhapuram
● Polonnaruva
CEYLON

# THE SPREAD
# OF INDIAN ART

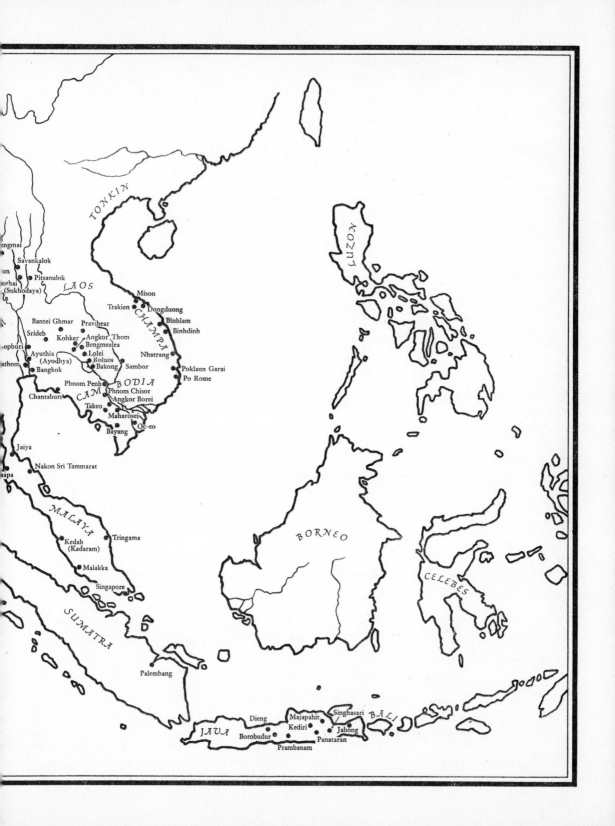

| | MEDITERRANEAN AND SOUTH WESTERN ASIA | INDIA |
|---|---|---|
| **2900** and earlier | Lagash Dynasty (*Old Chronology*) in Mesopotamia. Old Kingdom in Egypt: Pyramids (*Old Chronology*) | Indus Civilization (*Old Chronology*) |
| **2800** | Sargon of Akkad (*Old Chronology*) in Mesopotamia | |
| **2700** | | Amri Culture (*New Chronology*) |
| **2600** | Gudea of Lagash (*Old Chronology*) | |
| **2500** | | Indus Civilization (*New Chronology*)<br>Mohenjo-Dāro, Harappā I (*Old Chronology*) |
| **2400** | Old Kingdom in Egypt<br>(*New Chronology*) | Mohenjo-Dāro, Harappā II etc. (*New Chronology*) |
| **2300** | Sargon of Akkad (*New Chronology*) | |
| **2200** | | |
| | Hammurabi (*Old Chronology*),<br>Luristan Bronzes I | |
| **2100** | | |
| **2000** | Gudea of Lagash (*New Chronology*) | |
| **1900** | | End of Indus Civilization: Jhukar Culture<br>(*Old Chronology*) |
| **1800** | | |
| | Hammurabi (*New Chronology*) Hyksos Invasion of Egypt (*Old Chronology*) | |
| **1700** | Hyksos Invasion in Egypt<br>(*New Chronology*) | |
| **1600** | | |
| | New Kingdom in Egypt | |
| **1500** | Kassites in Babylonia. Queen Hatshepsut in Egypt: Red Sea Expedition. Knossos in Crete | |

246

| | | |
|---|---|---|
| | | *2900 and earlier* |
| | | *2800* |
| | | *2700* |
| | | *2600* |
| | | *2500* |
| | | *2400* |
| | | *2300* |
| | | *2200* |
| | | *2100* |
| | | *2000* |
| | Polychromous Pottery | *1900* |
| | Yang-Shao Pottery in China | *1800* |
| | | *1700* |
| | | *1600* |
| | | *1500* |

| | CENTRAL- AND EAST ASIA | INDIA |
|---|---|---|
| *1400* | Mittannis in Upper Mesopotamia. Amenhotep III & IV in negotiations with them. Tell El-Amarna | End of Indus Civilization (*New Chronology*). Aryan Immigration into India |
| *1300* | Temples of Karnak & Luksor in Egypt | Rigvedic Period (Tribal) |
| *1200* | Decline of Hittite Kingdom. Trojan War? | |
| *1100* | Invasion of Sea Peoples into Egypt: Medinet Habu | |
| *1000* | David and Solomon in Palestine: Expedition to Ophir (Sopara north of Bombay). Rise of Assyria. | Background of Mahābhārata |
| *900* | | |
| *800* | | |
| *700* | | |
| | Destruction of Assur & Nineveh. Neo-Babylonian Empire | |
| *600* | | Bimbisāra of Magadha (544—493): Buddha. |
| | Achaemenian Empire. Early Greek Art | Foundation of Old Rājgir |
| | | Darius conquers N.W. India |
| *500* | | Buddha's Death (486). Ajātaśatru (493—462): New Rājgir, Pātaliputra founded. Early Ujjain. |
| | Parthenon, Phidias in Greece | |
| *400* | | |
| | Praxiteles in Greece | |
| | Alexander the Great, Seleukids in Asia | Chandragupta Maurya (323—300): Pātaliputra Capital of Mauryas (323—187) |

|  |  |  |
|---|---|---|
|  |  | *1400* |
|  | Shang Dynasty in China: White Pottery. Early Bronzes. Anyang. | *1300* |
|  |  | *1200* |
|  |  | *1100* |
|  | Western Chou Dynasty in China | *1000* |
|  | Middle Chou Style (c. 900—600) | *900* |
|  |  | *800* |
|  |  | *700* |
| Anurādhapura in Ceylon founded |  | *600* |
|  | Huai or Chan-kuo Style |  |
|  |  | *500* |
|  |  | *400* |
|  | Tombs of Chin-ts'un Tombs of Chang-sha, Hsin-yang Li-yu Bronzes, lacquer, sculpture |  |

| | MEDITERRANEAN AND SOUTH WESTERN ASIA | INDIA |
|---|---|---|
| *300* | Parthian Empire (247) | Basarh-Bakhīra Column. Aśoka (273—236): Stūpas, Columns, Barābar and Nāgārjuni Caves, Dhauli Elephant. |
| *200* | | Maurya Statues, śunga Dynasty (187—75). Bhārhūt Stūpa (170—160). Coins of Indo-Greek Kings, śiśupālgarh in Kalinga founded. Stūpas of Sānchī enlarged. |
| *100* | Augustus | Kānvas (75—30): Bodhgayā Railing. Khāravela of Kalinga: Udaigiri Caves. śātavāhanas of Deccan: Bhājā, Kanheri, Ajantā 9—10, Sānchī Toranas, Early Mathurā School. Indo-Scythians: Hāritī of Skarah-Dheri, Bimarān Reliquiary. |
| *0* | Baalbek | śātavāhanas: Bedsā, Aurangābād, Kanheri, Kārle, Pithalkhorā, early Stūpas on Andhra Coast, Begram Ivories, Pompeii Lakshmī. Mathurā: Amohinī, "Holi" Reliefs. Indo-Parthians: Taxila (Sirkap), Beginnings of Gandhāra Sculpture. |
| *100* | Pantheon in Rome Hatra in Iraq<br><br>Baalbek in Syria | Nāsik: Pandu Lena, Kārle, Junnār, Jūnagadh, Amarāvatī, Nāgārjunikonda, Arikamedu. Mathurā School of Sculpture, Kushāna Statues of Mat. Kushāna Art: Gandhāra Stūpas (Kanishka's at Shāhjī-ki-Dheri) & Sculptures, Surkh-Kotāl Fire Temple, Mīrān Frescoes. |
| *200* | Doura-Europos & Palmyra in Syria. Ardeshīr founds Sāsānian Empire (224), Fīrozābād, Tāq-i Kesrā (Ktesiphon) | Decline of Kushānas: Gandhāra School. Mathurā: Late Style. Nāgārjunikonda & Jaggayyapetta Stūpas (Ikshvāku Style). |
| *300* | Theodosius I. Suppression of Non-Christians | Afghanistan: Gandhāra Sculpture, Khairkhāna (Kābul). Gupta Era (320): Samudragupta (328—76). Gupta Empire. Pāwāya, Mankuwār Buddha. Mandor Stela. Chandragupta II (376—414) Udaypur Temple, Udaigiri (Mālva) Caves (402—06). Deccan: Ter, Chezārla. |

| GREATER INDIA | CENTRAL- AND EAST ASIA | |
|---|---|---|
| | Ch'in Dynasty (221) & Early Han Dynasty (207) in China Stūpas in Nepal. | *300* |
| Aśoka's Mission to Ceylon (243) | | |
| Early Stūpas of Mihintale & Anurādhapura in Ceylon, especially of Dutthagamani (161—137) | | *200* |
| Funan Kingdom in Cambodia, Ruanweli Pagoda at Anurādhapura, Abhayagiri Dāgaba | | *100* |
| | Later Han Dynasty (25—220) First Contact with Buddhism Tombs of Shantung | *0* |
| Amarāvati Sculptures in Ceylon, Java, Cambodia. Dvāravatī in Siam | Graves of Wu Pan, & c. | *100* |
| | Six Dynasties (220—589) Tomb of Kao-I | *200* |
| Zenith of Anurādhapura; Mahāsana (334—361): Īetavana Dāgaba, enlargement of the older dāgabas | Eastern Chin Dynasty: Kuk'ai-Chi (321—79) Mīrān in Eastern Turkistan | *300* |
| | Northern Wei Dynasty (389): Yun-Kang cave-temples | |

| | MEDITERRANEAN AND SOUTH WESTERN ASIA | INDIA |
|---|---|---|
| *400* | | Gandhāra Art: Hadda, Akhnūr, Ushkur. Kashmīr: Hārvan. Gupta Art: Conquest of Ujjain by Chandra-gupta II (400–409), High Gupta Style, Kumāra-gupta II (415–55) & Successors: Temples of Nāchnā Kuthārā, Bhumara, Tigowā, Deogarh, Mukunddarra, Nagarī. Stūpas of Mīrpur Khāss & Thul Mir Rukan. Bāgh Caves Sārnāth Buddhas, Māniyar Math, Dah Pārbatīya & c. Deccan: Ajantā Caves 16–17 (Harishena) |
| *500* | Justinian at Byzantium, Hagia Sophia Ravenna<br><br>Khusrau I & II in Persia, Sarvistān, Tāq-i Bostān | Gandhāra Art: Bāmiyān, Tarim Basin. Gupta Art: Bodhgayā, Bhītārgāon, Sirpur, Maitraka Temples. Ajantā, Ghatokacha, Elūrā, Jogeśvarī, Aurangābād Caves, Sāmlajī Mātrikās. Mandasor Stelas, Nālandā. Deccan: Aihole (Lād Khān, Kontgudi, Durga, 7, 11) Mahākūteśvara. Bādāmī (Cave III 578, Malegitti Sivālaya, North Fort Temple) |
| *600* | Fall of Sāsānian Empire (637), Arab-Muslim Empire<br><br><br><br>Lindisfarne Gospel | Gandhāra Art: Fondūkistān, Ming-Oï. Late Gupta Art: Harshavardhana of Thanesar (606–647). Bhīnmāl, Brahmor, Jageśvar, Nālandā. Orissa: Paraśurāmesvara. Deccan: Pulakeśin I (610–42), Aihole, Bādāmī, Elūrā 5–9, Aurangābād, Ajantā 1–5, 21–27, Elephanta, Gop. South: Pallavas: Dalavānūr, Bhairavakonda, Undavalī, Sittanavāśal, Māmallapuram, Kānchī (Kailāsa). |
| *700* | Qusair 'Amra Sind conquered (712)<br><br>Baghdad (754) | Late Gupta Art: Yaśovarman of Kanauj (700–52) Gwālior (Telikā-Mandir), Bajaurā, Masrūr. Bengal: Pālas, Bodhgayā, Pahārpur, Nālandā. Orissa: Nalatigiri. Pratihāra Art: Osiān, Jagatsukh, Pathārī. Kashmīr: Lalitāditya (725–56), Pandrethān, Parihāsapura, Mārtānd, Malot, Wangāth, Būniyar & c. Deccan: Pattadakal (746/7). Elūrā (Dasāvatāra, Kailāsa). South: Kānchī (Vaikunthaperumāl, & c.) |

|  |  |  |
|---|---|---|
| **GREATER INDIA** | **CENTRAL- AND**<br>**EAST ASIA** | |
| | Buddhist cave-temples in Tun-Huang | *400* |
| Sigiriya (Murals) in Ceylon<br>Import of Gupta Sculptures & Bronzes | Lungmen Caves (Beginning) | |
| | Northern Wei Style (510—40)<br>Lungmen Caves. | *500* |
| Kambuja Kingdom in Cambodia (Sambor-Prei<br>Kuk). Champa (Mi-Son Ei). Art of **Dvāravatī** | Northern Ts'i Dynasty (550)<br>Tien-lung-shan.<br>Buddhism introduced in Japan (552).<br>Mānadeva Reliefs in Nepal. | |
| | Sui Dynasty (581).<br>Empress Suiko in Japan (593—628) | |
| śrīvijaya in Sumatra & Malaya. Prei-Khmeng &<br>Kompong Prah in Cambodia (Prasat Andet) | T'ang Dynasty (618): Tun-Huang,<br>Lung-Men, Tien-Lung-Shan, Ch'angan<br>**Pagodas**,. | *600* |
| | Early Nara Period in Papan (645—707):<br>Horyuji Yakushi — Trinity. | |
| Chandī Pawon, Mendut & Sari in Java | Buddhism introduced in Tibet (638),<br>First Buddhist temple at Lhasa (651) | |
| Style of Hoa-Lai in Champā | Ti'en-lung-shan, Tun-huang,<br>Wu-Tao-Tse (700—760).<br>Civil War (755—63). Sho-Soin 756. | *700* |
| Borobudur & Chandī Kalasan in Java | Tempyo Period in Japan (708—811):<br>Todaijī Heian Period (782—888):<br>Kobo Daishi, Shingon & Tendai Sects. | |
| | Dandan Oiliq in Eastern Turkistān | |

| | MEDITERRANEAN AND SOUTH WESTERN ASIA | INDIA |
|---|---|---|
| *800* | Charlemagne | Bengal & Orissa: Nālandā, Pahārpur, Vaitāl Deul. Kashmīr: Avantipur, Pātan, & c. Pratihāras: Osiān, Gwālior (875), Auwā, Sīrwa, Deogarh (862), Khajurāho (Chaunsat Joginī) & c. |
| | Sāmarrā (854 ff.) Ibn Tūlun (876—9) at Fostāt (Egypt) | Deccan: Elūrā (Lankeśvara), Mālkhed. Sind: Mansūra-Brāhmanābād. |
| *900* | | Bengal: Bahulārā (Siddheśvar), Begunia Temples. Orissa: Bhuvaneśvar, Lingarājā). Pratīhāra: Chamba, Jageśvar, Sikar, Modherā I. Chandella: Khajurāho (Lakshamana 954). Chāhamāna: Vīsalpur, Barolli, Menāl, Bijolia. Kashmīr: Diddā (958—1003). Deccan: Elūrā (Kailāsa), Mālkhed sacked (972). |
| | Cairo (970) Mahmūd of Ghazna (998—1030): Tower, Tomb | śrāvana Belgola (Gommateśvara). South: Chola Art, Erumbar (935), śrīnivāsanālūr (940), Kodumbālūr, Kalugamalai. |
| *1000* | | Bengal: Pāla Revival under Rāmapāla (1084—1126). Kashmīr: Last Renaissance, Marol, Tibet. Rājput States: Khajurāho, Mahobā, Chandrehe, Tewāri, Bilhāri Sohāgpur. Nāgdā, Ājmer, Gwālior (Sāsbahu), Anahīlavāda, Sidhpur, Modherā II, Dilwāra I, Udaypur (Nīlkanthesvar), Ūn, Nemāvar. Orissa: Purī (Jagannāth). Śilāhāra: Ambarnāth, Sinnār. Western Chālukya: Haveri (Siddheśvara 1087). |
| | Ghazna: Tower of Masūd (1098—1115) | South (Chola): Tanjūr (Brihadīśvara). Gangaikondasolapuram, Tirubhuvanam, Darāsuram & many others. |
| *1100* | | Bengal: Senas, Rāmpal, Lakshmanavatī, Destruction of Buddhist Monasteries (1196). Rājput States: Mahobā, Kumbharia, Jalor, Nāgdā, Chitorgarh, Tarangā, Girnār, Palitāna, Somnāth. Western Chālukyas: Ittagi (1112), Lakkundi (Kāśīvisvesvara, 1171), Kuruvatti, Gadag. Hoysalas: Belūr (1113), Halebīd (Hoysaleśvara 1141). Cholas: Additions to many temples. |

| GREATER INDIA | CENTRAL- AND EAST ASIA | |
|---|---|---|
| Polonnāruva Capital of Ceylon. Chandī Plaosan, Sewu & Parambanam in Java. Phnom Kulen, Ruluos, Prah Ko & Bakheng (Bakong, Lolei) in Cambodia. Dong-Du'ong Style (Mison A 10, Khuong-My) in Champā. Old Pagān in Burma | Kyoto Capital of Japan (794): Jingojī & c. Nepālese Era (880): Nepālese Art. | *800* |
| Angkor I & Koh Ker Capitals of Cambodia (Phnom Bakheng, P. Krom, P. Bok, Prasat Kravon. Baksei Chamkrong, Mebon, Banteay Srei). Destruction of Mi-Son (982) | Five Dynasties in China (907), Liao (907): Tun Huang<br><br>Northern Sung Dynasty (960—1125) | *900* |
| Eastern Java (Udayana & Airlanga). Lopburi & Laos under Cambodia. Kleang Style (Ta Keo, Phimeanakas) & Baphuon in Cambodia. Binh-Dinh Capital of Champā (Binh-Lam, Po-Nagar of Nha-Trang). Pagān in Burma (Kyanzitta, Suwezigon, Ānanda). | Saskya Monastery in Tibet (1071). Fujiwara Period in Japan (1069—1185). Emperor Hui-tsung (1082—1135). Li-Lung-Mien. | *1000* |
| Parākrāma Bāhu I (1158—86), Polonnāruva: Gal Vihara & Watadāge (Ceylon). Angkor Wat (1113—50), Baphuon, Phimai, Banteay Samre, Beng-Mealea in Cambodia, 1177 Sack of Angkor by Cham. Tour d'Argent, d'Ivoire, de Cuivre, d'Or at Binh-Dinh in Champā. Pagān in Burma (Thatbinnyu, Shwe-Gugyi). | Southern Sung Dynasty (Kao Tsung, 1127). Chin Dynasty (1114). Mu-Chi in China. Kamakura Period in Japan (1186—1335). Zen Buddhism. | *1100* |

| | |
|---|---|
| St. Trophime (Arles) <br> Mausoleum of Mumīna Khātūn (1186) <br> at Nakhshewān | Muslim Conquest of North India (1192—96). <br> Delhi: Quwwat-ul Islām (1193), Qutb-Minār <br> (1199). |
| *1200* <br><br> Nôtre Dame (Paris) <br><br> Cologne Cathedral <br> Niccola Pisano | Orissa: Konārak (1238—64). <br> Rājput States: Kirādu, Osiān, Jālor, Nādol, <br> Sādrī, Dilwāra II, Dabhoi, Modherā III. <br> Deccan: Deogiri, Warangal, Pālampet, <br> Somnāthpur (1268). <br> South: Pāndya Art. |
| Māristān of Sultan Qalewūn (1284/5) <br> at Cairo | Delhi: Quwwat-ul-Islām (expanded), Sultān <br> Gharī, Tombs of Iltutmish & Balban, Budāon <br> (Mosque), Ajmer (Arhai-di-ka Jhompra 1200), <br> Multān (Tombs of Bahā-ud-dīn & Shams Tabrizi. |
| *1300* <br> Giotto <br> Mausoleum of Uljaitū Khudābanda at <br> Sultānīya (1316) <br> Simone Martini (Siena) <br> Alhambra in Spain, Sultan Hasan at <br> Cairo <br> Bībi Khānūm Madrasa, Samarkand <br> (1399) | Vijayanagar founded (1336), Kānchī (Kāmākshi <br> 1395), Dilwāra III. <br><br> Muslim Conquest of Deccan & South (1306—26), <br> Delhi: Quwwat-ul-Islām (expanded), Sirī, <br> Tughlaqābād, Bijai-Mandal, Kotila-i Fīroz Shāh, <br> Hauz-i Khāss, Nizām-uddīn & Daulatābād. <br> Sack of Delhi by Tīmūr of Samarkand (1398). <br> Bengal: Gaur (1354), Adīna Masjid. Deccan: <br> Gulbarga (Mosque, Bahmanī Tombs). |
| *1400* Imām Rizā, Mashhad <br><br> Brunelleschi, Masaccio, Donatello, <br> Van Eyck, Ghiberti, Fra Angelico, <br> Van der Weyden <br> Alberti, Mantegna. <br> Botticelli. <br> Leonardo da Vinci <br><br> Madrasa of Ulugh Beg at Samarkand <br> (1447/9) <br> Mehmedīya, Stambul, Behzād <br> Gūr-i Mīr, Samarkand | Rājputāna: Art Renaissance, Rānā Kumbha <br> (1433—68). <br> Chitorgarh, Rānakpur (1440), Dilwāra & c. <br> Vijayanagar: śrīśailam (1404), & c. <br><br> Delhi: Mubārakpur, Mehrauli, Sirī, Lodi Mosque <br> (1494). Jaunpur. <br> Kashmir: Srinagar (Mosque of Sikandar, Zain-ul- <br> 'Ābidīn). <br> Mālwa: Dhār, Māndū (Hoshangs Tomb, Jāmi <br> Masjid, Palaces, & c.) <br> Gujarat: Ahmadābād (1419), Sarkhej (1451), <br> Champaner (1484). Bengal: Pāndua (1354—1442). <br> Bīdar (1428). Ahmadnagar (1490). |

*1200*

Singasāri in Java, Chandī Kidal, Jabung, Jago.
Angkor reconstructed, Bayon, Banteay Chmar in
Cambodia. U'Thong, Chieng-Sen & Sukhotai
Styles in Siam. Pagān in Burma (Mahābodhi,
Mingalazedi, Tilominlo), 1287 Sack by Kublai
Khan.

Yüan Dynasty (1271—1368)

*1300*

Majapahit in Java (Panataran). Foundation of
Ayuthiā (1350). Ava Capital of Burma

Ashikaga Period in Japan (1338—1565)

Ming Dynasty (1368), Peking Palaces,
Restoration of Great Wall, Porcelain.

Angkor taken by the Siamese.
Po Klaung Garai in Champa

Sesshū (1420—1506).
Tashilhunpo founded (1445).

*1400*

Japan:
Monotobu (1476—1559).

| | MEDITERRANEAN AND SOUTH WESTERN ASIA | INDIA |
|---|---|---|
| *1500* | Michelangelo, Raphael, Dürer, "Grünewald", Bosch, Holbein | Vijayanagar: Most buildings, Kānchī (Ekāmranatha 1509—30). Chidambaram (N. Gopuram 1520). |
| | | Delhi (Jamālī Mosque 1530, Purāna Killa, 1541—45), Sāsarām (1545). Gujarat: Ahmedābād, Mehmedābd (1538—54). Mālwa: Māndū (—1531). Bengal: Gaur (Sona Masjid 1546), Mālda (1533—38). |
| | Titian, Correggio | Deccan: Bījāpur Citadel (1510—34), Golkonda (1512—50). Bīdar (1528 ff.) Gwālior: Mān Mandir (1500—16). |
| *1550* | Palladio, Sulaimānīya at Stambul. Veronese. | Vijayanagar sacked (1565). South: Tadpatri (śrīrāma 1550/60), Vellūr (1560), Chidambaram (Hall 1595), śrīrangam (1590). |
| | Tintoretto, de la Porta. | |
| | Masjid-i Shāh, Chihīl Sūtun at Isfahän | Delhi: Khair-ul-Manāzil (1562). Humāyūn's Tomb (1568—80), Āgra (1565—73), Fathpur Sikrī (1573—80). Allahābād (1583—84), Lahore (1580— |
| | Caravaggio. Rizā 'Abbāsī in Persia. | 1618), Gwālior (Muh. Ghaus 1563). Bījāpur (Jāmi Masjid, Gagan Mahal, Chand Baori 1557—80). Nauraspur 1599. Haidarābād 1589 (Chār Minār 1591). Amber (1569 ff.), Bīkāner (1592). Early Rājput Paintings. |
| *1600* | Greco | Chandragiri (1639—40). South: Madurai (Tirumala Nāik 1623—59), Trichinopoly (Jambukeśvar), Rāmesvaram. |
| | Rubens, Frans Hals, Van Dyck | |
| | Poussin, **Bernini** | Delhi: Shāhjahānābād & Red Fort (1628—58), Mosque (1644—58). Āgra: Palace (1637). Tāj-Mahal (1630—48), Itimād-ud-Daula (1628), Mosque (1644). Lahore: Wazīr Khān's Mosque (1634), Palaces (1631—34), Asaf Khān's Tomb (1641), Shālimār Garden Kashmir (c. 1620). Daulatābād (1600—33, 1636). Bījāpur: Ibrāhīm-Rauza (1626—28), Gol-Gombaz (1626—56). Amber Palace (1627). Udaipur Palaces (1628). Rājasthānī Painting. |
| *1650* | Claude Lorrain Velazquez, Rembrandt, Vermeer. Versailles | Udaipur (Jagannāth, 1651), Kulū Temples. |

*1500*

End of Majapahit, Bali. Phnom-Penh Capital of
Cambodia. Style of Ayuthiā in Siam. Po Rome
in Champā.

Most present monuments in Nepāl     *1550*
(middle 16th—19th century).

Kandy Capital of Ceylon (1592)

Momoyama-period in Japan
(1576—1603)

Tokugawa Period in Japan     *1600*
(1603—1867): Edo (1613), Nikko.
Potala Palace at Lhasa (1643).

Ch'ing Dynasty (1644—1911)

*1650*

# INDIA

|  |  |  |
|---|---|---|
|  |  | Lahore: Bādshāhī Mosque (1673), Aurangābād: Palace (1670—82), Bibi-kā-Rauza (1678). Tanjūr under Marātha Rule (1677/8). Basohlī Painting. |
| *1700* |  | Delhi: Last Mughal Mosques. Murshīdābād (1720/5). |
|  | Watteau | Golkonda: Purāna Mahal (c. 1720). Jaipur founded (1728). |
|  | Hogarth | Guler School of Painting (since c. 1738). Udaipur Palaces. |
| *1750* | Tiepolo | Delhi: Qudsiā Bāgh (1750—53), Safdar Jang (1743). |
|  | Reynolds, Gainsborough | Faizābād (1753—76). Lakhnau (since 1775): Great Imāmbārā, Rūmī Darwāza. Murshīdābād: Chauk Mosque (1767). Seringapatam: Lāl Bāgh, Daryā Daulat Bāgh. Jodhpur Palaces. |
|  | Blake | Kāngrā Painting (Sansār Chand II 1775—1823). Sind Mausolea. |
| *1800* | Goya | Amritsar: Golden Temple |
|  | Constable | Lakhnau: Kaisar-Bāgh |
|  | Delacroix | Calcutta, Bombay: British Classical Architecture. |
|  | Turner |  |
| *1850* |  |  |
|  | Manet |  |
|  | Renoir, Monet, Whistler |  |
|  | Rodin, Pissaro, Degas, Cezanne, Van Gogh, Gauguin Munch, Toulouse-Lautrec |  |
| *1900* |  | Bengal School of Painting (A. N. Tagore, N. L. Bose). New Delhi (1913—31). |
|  | Barlach, Matisse, Picasso. Modern Architecture | Amrit Sher Gil (+ 1941). Modern Indian Painting. Independence (1947). |
| *1950* |  | Chandīgarh (Le Corbusier). |

| GREATER INDIA | CENTRAL- AND EAST ASIA | |
|---|---|---|
| | Korin (1658—1716). | |
| | | *1700* |
| Ayuthiä destroyed by Burmese (1757), Bangkok | Utamaro (1753—1806). | *1750* |
| Mingun in Burma | | |
| | | *1800* |
| Mandalay Capital of Burma, Amarapura | Meiji Period in Japan (1868—1912) | *1850* |
| | Chinese Republic (1912) | *1900* |
| | | *1950* |

# SELECT BIBLIOGRAPHY

*The literature on Indian art is so extensive today as to fill a bulky volume. Most material is dispersed, in specialized monographs, in a great number of reports and periodicals. Moreover, references to the equally numerous historical, epigraphical, archaeological and ethnological publications are constantly necessary. It seems therefore advisable here to offer merely a selection of key works, many of which contain comprehensive bibliographies which the reader may consult for further reference.*

## HISTORICAL AND CULTURAL BACKGROUND

*A. L. Basham,* The Wonder That Was India, London 1954.

The Cambridge History of India, Cambridge 1922 ff., 6 vols.

*Sir George Dunbar,* History of India, London 1936.

*G. T. Garratt* (ed.), The Legacy of India, London 1937.

*R. Grousset,* Les Civilisations de l'Orient, II: L'Inde, Paris 1929–30.

*H. G. Rawlinson,* India: A Short Cultural History, London 1937, 1952.

*L. Renou,* La Civilisation de l'Inde Ancienne, Paris 1950.

*K. M. Sarkar,* A Survey of Indian History, Bombay 1947.

*R. A. Nilakanta Sastri,* History of India, Madras 1950, 2 vols.

*R. A. Nilakanta Sastri,* History of Southern India, Madras 1955.

## GENERAL BOOKS

*Mulk Raj Anand,* The Hindu View of Art, London 1933, etc.

*J. Auboyer,* Arts et Styles de l'Inde, Paris 1951.

*K. de B. Codrington,* Ancient India, London 1926.

*A. K. Coomaraswamy,* Arts and Crafts of India and Ceylon, Edinburgh 1913.

*A. K. Coomaraswamy,* Bibliographies of Indian Art, Boston, Mass. 1925.

*A. K. Coomaraswamy,* History of Indian and Indonesian Art, London 1927.

*E. B. Havell,* Ideals of Indian Art, London 1911.

*E. B. Havell,* A Handbook of Indian Art, London 1921.

*Stella Kramrisch,* Grundzüge der Indischen Kunst, Dresden 1924.

*Stella Kramrisch,* The Art of India, London 1954.

*Leigh Ashton* (Ed.), The Art of India and Pakistan (Royal Academy Exhibition 1947–48), London 1950.

*B. Rowland,* Art and Architecture of India, Cambridge, Mass. 1933.

*V. A. Smith,* History of Fine Arts in India and Ceylon, Oxford 1911; ed. by K. de B. Codrington, Oxford 1930.

*Sir Richard Windstedt* (Ed.), Indian Art, London 1947.

*H. Zimmer,* The Art of Indian Asia, ed. by J. Campbell, New York 1955.

## ARCHAEOLOGY

Annual Reports of the Archaeological Survey of India, Calcutta–Delhi 1902–37.

*Sir John Cumming* (Ed.), Revealing India's Past, London 1939.

*A. Cunningham,* Archaeological Survey Reports, 1871–85.

## ARCHITECTURE (GENERAL)

*C. Batley,* The Design Development of Indian Architecture, London 1934, 1949 (2nd edition).

*Percy Brown,* Indian Architecture, 2 vols., Bombay 1943.

*J. Fergusson and J. Burgess,* A History of Indian and Eastern Architecture, London 1910.

*E. B. Havell,* Indian Architecture, London 1927 (2nd edition).

*H. Parmenties,* L'Art Architectural dans l'Inde et en Extrême Orient, Paris–Bruxelles 1934.

*S. K. Saraswati,* A Survey of Indian Architecture, Calcutta 1954.

*Sidney Toy,* The Strongholds of India, London 1957.

## SCULPTURE (GENERAL)

*W. Cohn,* Indische Plastik, Berlin 1923.
*Stella Kramrisch,* Indian Sculpture, Calcutta 1933.
*K. M. Munshi, A. Goswami and Others,* Indian Temple Sculpture. Introduction by Jawaharlal Nehru, Delhi 1956.
*S. K. Saraswati,* A Survey of Indian Sculpture, Calcutta 1954.

## PAINTING (GENERAL)

*Percy Brown,* Indian Painting, Calcutta—London 1927, etc.
*N. C. Mehta,* Studies in Painting, Bombay 1926.

## INDUSTRIAL ARTS

*G. P. Baker,* Calico Painting and Printing in the East Indies, 17th and 18th Centuries, London 1921.
*J. B. Bhushan,* Indian Jewellery, Bombay 1954.
*A. K. Coomaraswamy,* The Indian Craftsman, London 1909.
*H. Cousens,* Illustrations of Sind Tiles, London 1906.
*W. Egerton,* Illustrated Handbook of Indian Arts, London 1880.
*T. H. Hendly,* Asian Carpets, 16th and 17th Century: Designs from the Jaipur Palaces, London 1905.
*T. H. Hendly,* Indian Jewellery, London 1906—09.
*J. Irwin,* Indian Embroidery (Victoria and Albert Museum), London 1951.
*R. Pfister,* Les Toiles Imprimées de Fostat et l'Hindostan, Paris 1938.
*Ch. E. de Ujfalvy,* Les Cuivres Anciens du Cachemire, Paris 1883.
*Sir George Watt and Percy Brown,* Indian Art at Delhi 1903, Calcutta 1903.
*M. Wheeler, P. Jayakar and J. Irwin,* Textiles and Ornaments of India, New York 1955.

## BEGINNINGS OF INDIAN ART

*V. D. Krishnaswami,* Megalithic Types of South India, (Ancient India, no. 5, 35, 1949).
*E. Mackay,* Early Indus Civilizations, London 1948 (2nd ed.).
*J. Marshall,* Mohenjo-Daro and the Indus Civilization, London 1931, 3 vols.

*Stuart Piggot,* Prehistoric India, Harmondsworth-New York 1950.
*B. Subba Rao,* The Personality of India, Baroda 1958.
*Sir Mortimer Wheeler,* The Indus Civilization, Cambridge 1953.

## EARLY INDIAN ART

*L. Bachhofer,* Early Indian Sculpture, Paris 1929.
*D. Barrett,* Sculptures from Amarāvatī in the British Museum, London 1954.
*B. M. Barua,* Gaya and Bodh-Gaya, Calcutta 1934.
*B. M. Barua,* Barhut, Calcutta 1934—37, 3 parts.
*Jas. Burgess,* The Buddhist Stūpas of Amarāvatī and Jaggayyapetta, London 1887.
*Jas. Burgess and Jas. Fergusson,* Cave Temples of India, London 1880.
*Ramaprasad Chanda,* Dates of the Votive Inscriptions on the Stupas at Sanchi, Calcutta 1919.
*Ramaprasad Chanda,* The Beginnings of Art in Eastern India, Calcutta 1927.
*A. K. Coomaraswamy,* Yakshas, Washington 1927—28.
*A. K. Coomaraswamy,* Early Indian Iconography, (Eastern Art I, 1, 1928; I, 3, 1929; II, p. 240, 1930).
*A. K. Coomaraswamy,* La Sculpture de Bodhgaya, Paris 1935.
*A. Cunningham,* Mahabodhi or The Great Buddhist Temple at Buddha Gaya, London 1892.
*A. Cunningham,* The Stupa of Bharhut, London 1879.
*A. Foucher,* The Beginnings of Buddhist Art, London 1917 = Les Débuts de l'Art Bouddique, Paris 1911.
*A. Grünwedel & E. Waldschmidt,* Buddhistische Kunst in Indien, Berlin 1932.
*J. & Mme J. R. Hackin,* Recherches Archéologiques à Bégram 1937, Paris 1939.
*J. & Mme J. R. Hackin, J. Carl & P. Hamelin,* Nouvelles Recherches à Bégram, Paris 1954.
*R. Heine-Geldern,* Archaeological Traces of the Vedic Aryans, (Jisoa IV, p. 87, 1936).
*A. H. Longhurst,* Buddhist Antiquities of Nāgarjunikonda, Delhi 1938.
*Chintamoni Kar,* Classical Indian Sculpture, London 1950.

B. B. Lal, Sisupalgarh 1948, (Ancient India no. 5, p. 62, 1949).

Mireile Levi d'Ancona, An Indian Statuette from Pompeii, (Artibus Asiae 13, pt. 3, p. 16, 1950).

R. C. Majumdar and A. D. Pusalker (Ed.), The Vedic Age, London 1951.

R. C. Majumdar and A. D. Pusalker (Ed.), The Age of Imperial Unity, Bombay 1953, 2.

J. H. Marshall, Rājagriha and Its Remains, (A.R., A.S.I. 1905—06, p. 86 ff.).

J. H. Marshall, Taxila, London 1951, 3 vols.

J. H. Marshall & A. Foucher, The Monuments of Sānchī, Delhi 1938, 3 vols.

T. N. Ramachandran, Nāgārjunikonda, Delhi 1953.

Nihar Ranjan Ray, Maurya and śunga Art, Calcutta 1945.

H. D. Sankalia and M. G. Dikshit, Report on Excavations at Brahmapurī in Kolhapur, Poona 1950.

C. Sivaramamurti, Amarāvatī Sculptures in the Madras Government Museum, Madras 1942.

K. A. Nilakanta Sastri (Ed.), Age of the Nandas and Mauryas, Banaras 1952.

K. R. Subramanian, Buddhist Remains in Andhra between 225 and 610 A.D., Madras 1932.

R. E. M. Wheeler, A. Ghosh and Krishna Deva, Arikamedu: An Indo-Roman Trading Station on the East Coast of India, (Ancient India, no. 2, p. 17, 1946).

Paul Mus, Barabudur, Esquisse d'une Histoire du Bouddhisme fondée sur la Critique Archéologique des Textes, Hanoi 1935.

## CLASSIC ART

V. S. Agrawala, Gupta Art, Lucknow 1945.

V. S. Agrawala, The Terracottas of Ahichhattra, (Ancient India, no. 4, p. 104, 1947/8).

Franz Altheim, Alexander und Asien, Tübingen 1952.

L. Bachhofer, On Greeks and Sakas in India, (JAOS 61, p. 233 ff., 1941).

R. D. Banerji, The Temple of Siva at Bhumara, Calcutta 1924.

R. D. Banerji, Bas-reliefs of Badami, Calcutta 1928.

E. Barger and Ph. Wright, Excavations in Swat and Explorations in the Axus Territories of Afghanistan, Calcutta 1941.

J. Barthoux, Les Fouilles de Hadda, 3 vols., Paris 1930.

H. Cousens, The Chalukyan Architecture in the Kanarese Districts, Delhi 1926.

Bharata, Nātyaśāstra, translated by Manomohan Ghosh, Calcutta 1951.

H. Deydier, Contribution à l'Etude de l'Art du Gandhara: Essai de Bibliographie, Paris 1950.

B. B. Dutt, Town Planning in Ancient India, Calcutta 1925.

A. Foucher, L'Art Gréco-Bouddhique du Gandhara, 3 vols., Paris 1905 ff.

A. Foucher & Mme E. Bazin Foucher, La Vieille Route de l'Inde, de Bactres à Taxila, Paris 1947.

R. Ghirshman, Bégram, Recherches Archéologiques et Historiques sur les Kouchans, Le Caire 1946.

A. Godard & J. Hackin, Les Antiquités Bouddhiques de Bamiyan, Paris 1927.

P. K. Gode, The Role of the Courtesan in the Early History of Indian Painting, (Ann. Bhandarkar Or. Res. Inst. 22, p. 24, 1941).

H. Goetz, The Last Masterpiece of Gupta Art: The Great Temple of Yaśovarman at Gwalior, "Telika Mandir", (Art & Letters 29, p. 47, 1955).

H. Goetz, The Early Wooden Temples of Chamba, Leiden 1956.

A. Grünwedel, Altbuddhistische Kultstätten in de, 2 vols., Paris 1914.
Chinesisch-Turkistan, Berlin 1912.

A. Grünwedel, Alt-Kutscha, Berlin 1920.

J. Hackin & J. Carl, Nouvelles Recherches Archéologiques à Bâmiyân, Paris 1933.

J. Hackin & J. Carl, Recherches Archéologiques au Col de Khair Khâneh près de Kabul, Paris 1936.

Harald Ingholt, Gandharan Art in Pakistan, London—New York 1957.

G. Jouveau-Dubreuil, Archéologie du Sud de l'In-

G. Jouveau-Dubreuil, Pallava Antiquities, London 1916—18, 2 vols.

G. Jouveau-Dubreuil, Pallava Painting, Pondicherry 1920.

Stella Kramrisch, The Vishnudharmottaram, part III, Calcutta 1924.

*Stella Kramrisch*, Die Figurale Plastik der Gupta-Zeit, (WBKKA 5, pt. 15, 1931).

*Stella Kramrisch*, A Survey of Painting in the Deccan, Hyderabad 1937.

*Stella Kramrisch*, The Hindu Temple, Calcutta 1946.

*A. v. Le Coq*, Die Buddhistische Spätantike in Mittelasien, 7 vols, Berlin 1922—33.

*J. E. van Lohuizen—de Leeuw*, The "Scythian Period", Leiden 1949.

*A. H. Longhurst*, Pallava Architecture, Calcutta 1924, 1928, 1930, 3 pts.

*R. C. Majumdar and A. S. Altekar* (Ed.), The Vakataka-Gupta Age, Calcutta 1946.

*R. C. Majumdar* (Ed.), The Age of Imperial Unity, Bombay 1952 2.

*R. C. Majumdar and A. D. Pusalker* (Ed.), The Classical Age, Bombay—London 1954.

*Sir John Marshall*, Taxila, 3 vols., Cambridge 1951.

*J. Marshall, M. B. Garde and J. Ph. Vogel*, The Bāgh Caves in the Gwalior State, London 1927.

*C. Minakshi*, The Historical Sculptures of the Vaikunthaperumāl Temple at Kānchī, Delhi 1941.

*D. R. Patil*, The Monuments of Udaygiri Hill, Gwalior 1948.

*A. Rodin, A. Coomaraswamy, E. B. Havell and V. Goloubew*, Sculptures Çivaites de l'Inde, Paris—Bruxelles 1921.

*B. Rowland and A. Coomaraswamy*, The Wall Paintings of India, Central Asia and Ceylon, Boston—London 1938.

*Aurel Stein*, Zoroastrian Deities on Indo-Scythian Coins, (Ind. Antq., 17, p. 89, 1888).

*Aurel Stein*, Ancient Khotan, Oxford 1907.

*Aurel Stein*, Serindia, 5 vols., Oxford 1921.

*V. A. Smith*, The Jain Stupa and Other Antiquities of Mathurā, Allahabad 1907.

*M. A. Stein*, Innermost Asia, Oxford 1928.

*W. W. Tarn*, The Greeks in Bactria and India, Cambridge 1938, 1951 2.

*M. S. Vats*, The Gupta Temple of Deogarh, Delhi 1952.

*J. Ph. Vogel*, La Sculpture de Mathurā, Paris—Bruxelles 1930.

*E. Waldschmidt,* Gandhara-Kutscha-Turfan, Leipzig 1925.

*Gh. Yazdani,* Ajanta, 4 vols., Hyderabad—London 1930—55.

## MEDIAEVAL HINDU ART

*P. K. Acharya*, Indian Architecture according to Mānasāra, Oxford 1921.

*K. Ambrose and Ram Gopal*, Classical Dances and Costumes of India, London 1951.

*Mulk Raj Anand*, The Hindu View of Art, London 1933.

*T. G. Aravamuthan*, Portrait Sculpture in South India, London 1931.

*R. D. Banerji*, The Haihayas of Tripuri and their Monuments, Calcutta 1931.

*R. D. Banerji*, Eastern Indian School of Mediaeval Sculpture, Delhi 1933.

*Jitendranath Banerji*, The Development of Hindu Iconography, Calcutta 1941 (completely revised) 1956.

*Projesh Banerji*, Dance of India. Preface by Udai Shankar, Allahabad 1943.

*D. R. Bhandarkar*, Temples of Osia, (A.R., A.S.I. 1908—09, p. 100).

*N. K. Bhattasali*, Iconography of Buddhist and Brahmanical Sculptures in the Dacca Museum, Dacca 1929.

*B. C. Bhattacharya*, Indian Images, Calcutta—Simla 1921, Calcutta 1954.

*Benoytose Bhattacharyya*, The Indian Buddhist Iconography, London 1924, (revised and enlarged) Calcutta 1958.

*N. K. Bose*, Canons of Orissan Architecture, Calcutta 1932.

*Ph. N. Bose*, Principles of Indian śilpaśāstra, Lahore 1926.

*Jas. Burgess*, Report on the Elura Cave Temples, London 1883.

*Jas. Burgess and H. Cousens*, Architectural Remains of Northern Gujarat and Baroda State, London 1903.

*R. Burnier*, Hindu Mediaeval Sculpture, Paris 1950.

*V. R. Chitra and T. N. Srinivasan*, Cochin Murals, Cochin 1940.

*P. V. Jagadisa Ayyar*, South Indian Shrines.

*A. K. Coomaraswamy and Gopalakrishnayya*, The Mirror of Gesture, New York 1936.

H. *Cousens,* Architectural Antiquities of Western India, London 1926.

H. *Cousens,* Mediaeval Temples of the Dekkan, Calcutta 1931.

H. *Cousens,* Somanatha and Other Mediaeval Temples in Kathiawad, Calcutta 1931.

K. N. *Dikshit,* Excavations at Paharpur, Bengal, Delhi 1938.

O. C. *Gangoly,* South Indian Bronzes, Calcutta 1915.

M. *Ganguly,* Orissa and Her Remains, Calcutta 1912.

H. *Goetz,* The Kailāsa of Ellora and the Chronology of Rāshtrakūta Art, (Artibus Asiae 15, 1/2, p. 84, 1952).

H. *Goetz,* The Beginnings of Mediaeval Art in Kashmir, (J. Bombay Univ., n.s. 21, pt. 2 [Arts No. 27], p. 63, 1952).

H. *Goetz,* The Sun Temple of Mārtānd and the Art of Lalitāditya Muktāpīda, (Art & Letters, n.s. 27, pt. 1, p. 1, 1953).

A. *Goswami and O. C. Gangoly,* The Art of the Rashtrakutas, Calcutta—Bombay 1958.

F. H. *Gravely and T. N. Ramachandran,* Catalogue of the South Indian Hindu Images in the Madras Government Museum, Madras 1932.

E. B. *Havell,* The Ideals of Indian Art, London 1911.

G. *Jouveau—Dubreuil,* Iconography of Southern India, Paris 1937.

G. *Jouveau—Dubreuil,* Dravidian Architecture, Madras 1917.

R. C. *Kak,* Ancient Monuments of Kashmir, London 1933.

*Stella Kramrisch,* Pala and Sena Sculpture, (Rūpam 40, p. 107, 1929).

*Stella Kramrisch,* Dravida and Kerala in the Art of Travancore, Ascona 1953.

*Stella Kramrisch, J. H. Cousins and R. V. Poduval,* The Arts and Crafts of Travancore, London 1948.

*Stella Kramrisch,* The Hindu Temple, Calcutta 1946.

B. *Laufer,* Das Citralakshana, Leipzig 1913.

R. V. *Leyden,* The Crystal and the Fruit, (Mārg. V, no. 2, p. 6, 1951).

A. H. *Longhurst,* Hampi Ruins, Delhi 1933.

M. Th. de *Mallmann,* Introduction à l'Etude d'Avalokiteśvara, Paris 1948.

N. C. *Mehta,* Gujarati Painting in the Fifteenth Century, London 1931.

*Moti Chandra,* Jain Miniature Paintings from Western India, Ahmedabad 1949.

B. V. N. *Naidu, P. S. Naidu and O. V. R. Pantulu,* Tandava Lakshanam or the Fundamentals of Ancient Hindu Dancing, Madras 1936.

R. *Narasimhachar,* The Kesava Temple at Somanathapur, Bangalore 1917.

R. *Narasimhachar,* The Kesava Temple at Belur, Bangalore 1919.

R. *Narasimhachar,* The Lakshmidevi Temple at Dodda Gaddavalli, Bangalore 1919.

*Sarabhai Nawab,* Jain Tirthas in India and their Architecture, Ahmedabad 1944.

Ch. *Pandey,* Indian Aesthetics, Banaras 1950.

K. K. *Pillai,* The Sucindram Temple, Madras 1953.

P. H. *Pott,* Yoga en Yantra in hunne beteekenis voor de Indische Archaeologie, Leiden 1946.

T. N. *Ramachandran,* Tiruparuttikunram and Its Temples, Madras 1934.

T. A. *Gopinath Rao,* Talamana or Iconometry, Calcutta 1920.

T. A. *Gopinath Rao,* The Elements of Hindu Iconography, Madras 1928, 4 vols.

*Ram Gopal and S. Dadachanji,* Indian Dancing, London 1951.

*Ragini Devi,* Nitranjali, New York 1928.

*Leela Row,* Nritta Manjari, Calcutta 1946.

H. D. *Sankalia,* The University of Nalanda, Madras 1934.

H. D. *Sankalia,* Archaeology of Gujarat, Bombay 1941.

*Hirananda Sastri,* The Ruins of Dabhoi or Darbhavati, Baroda 1940.

C. *Sivaramurti,* Early Eastern Chalukyan Sculpture, Madras 1957.

H. K. *Sastri,* South Indian Images of Gods and Goddesses, Madras 1916.

J. M. *Somasundaram,* The Great Temple at Tanjore, Madras 1935.

M. A. *Stein* (transl.), Kalhana, Rājataranginī, 2 vols., Westminster 1900.

P. *Thomas,* Kama Kalpa or the Hindu Ritual of Love, Bombay 1957.

J. *Ph. Vogel*, Antiquities of Chamba State I, Calcutta 1911.

G. *Yazdani*, The Temples of Palampet, Calcutta 1922.

G. *Yazdani*, History of the Deccan, I, pt. 8: Fine Arts, London—Bombay 1952.

H. *Zimmer*, Kunstform und Yoga im Indischen Kultbild, Berlin 1926.

## INDIAN COLONIAL ART

E. *Aymonier*, Le Cambodge, Paris 1900—1904.

H. *C. P. Bell*, Annual Reports of the Archaeological Survey of Ceylon.

J. *Boisselier*, La Statuaire Khmère et son Evolution, Saigon 1955.

P. *N. Bose*, The Indian Colony of Champa, Madras 1925.

L. *P. Briggs*, The Ancient Khmer Empire, Philadelphia 1951.

G. *Coedès*, Pour Mieux Comprendre Angkor, Paris 1947.

G. *Coedès*, Les Etats Hindouisés d'Indochine et d'Indonésie, Paris 1948.

J. *Y. Claeys*, L'Archéologie du Siam, Hanoi 1931.

*Chas. Duroiselle*, The Ānanda Temple at Pagān, Delhi 1937.

L. *Fournereau*, Le Siam ancien, Paris 1908.

G. *Groslier*, La Sculpture Khmère, Paris 1908.

N. *J. Krom*, Inleiding tot de Hindoe-Javaansche Kunst, Den Haag 1923.

P. *N. Leuba*, Les Chams et leur Art, Paris—Bruxelles 1923.

S. *Lévi*, Le Népal, Paris 1905—08.

R. *Le May*, Buddhist Art in Siam, Cambridge 1938.

R. *Le May*, The Culture of South East Asia, London 1954.

*Th. B. van Lelyveld*. La Danse dans le Théâtre Javanais, Paris 1931.

C. *C. Mandis*, The Early History of Ceylon, London 1916, 1928 2.

H. *Marchal*, Archaeological Guide to Angkor, Saigon 1933 2.

G. *E. Mitton*, The Lost Cities of Ceylon, London 1916, 1928 2.

S. *Paranavitana*, Ceylon: Sigiriya Frescoes, New York.

H. *Parmentier*, L'Art Khmer Primitif, Paris 1927.

H. *Parker*, Ancient Ceylon, London 1909.

The Polonnaruva Period, Special Issue in Commemoration of the 800th Anniversary of the Accession of King Parakrama Bahu the Great 1153—1953, (Ceylon Historical Journal IV, 1954—44).

H. *G. Quaritch Wales*, Towards Ankor, London 1937.

H. *G. Quaritch Wales*, Culture Change in Greater India, (JRAS 1948).

H. *G. Quaritch Wales*, The Making of Greater India, London 1951.

N. *C. Ray*, Brahmanical Gods in Burma, Calcutta 1932.

H. *Schnitger*, The Archaeology of Hindu Sumatra, Leiden 1937.

*Ph. Stern*, L'Art du Champā et son Evolution, Paris 1948.

W. *F. Stutterheim*, Indian Influences in Old Balinese Art, London 1935.

*Th. H. Thomann*, Pagan, Heilbronn 1923.

K. *With*, Java, Hagen 1920.

## ART OF THE ISLAMIC PERIOD

W. *G. Archer*, Garhwal Painting, London 1954.

W. *G. Archer*, Indian Painting in the Punjab Hill States, London 1952.

A. *A. Bilgrami*, Landmarks of the Deccan, Hyderabad 1927.

L. *Binyon*, The Court Painters of the Grand Moguls, London 1921.

*Percy Brown*, Indian Painting under the Mughals, London 1923.

*Jas. Burgess*, Muhammedan Architecture of Bharoch, Cambay, Dholka, etc. in Gujarat, London 1896.

*Jas. Burgess*, The Muhammedan Architecture of Ahmedabad, London 1900.

A. *K. Coomaraswamy*, Rajput Painting, Oxford 1916.

H. *Cousens*, Bijapur and Its Architectural Remains, Bombay 1916.

H. *Cousens*, Antiquities of Sind, Calcutta 1929.

H. *Dattabaruva*, Chitrabhāgavata, Nalbadi (Assam) 1950.

J. *C. French*, Himalayan Art, London 1931.

A. *Führer*, Sharqi Architecture in Jaunpur, London 1889.

O. C. *Gangoly,* Ragas and Raginis, Calcutta 1935, Bombay 1948.

H. *Glück,* Die Indischen Miniaturen des Haemzae-Romans, Wien 1925.

H. *Goetz,* Art and Architecture of Bikaner, Oxford 1950.

*Th. H. Hendley,* The Razm-Namah, Jaypore 1893.

K. *Khandelavala,* Pahari Miniature Painting, Bombay 1958.

E. *Kühnel and H. Goetz,* Indian Book Painting from Jahangir's Album, London 1925.

*J. A. Page,* Historical Memoir on the Qutb Delhi, Calcutta 1926.

*J. A. Page,* A Memoir on Kotla Firoz Shah Delhi, Delhi 1937.

*J. H. Ravenshaw,* Gaur, London 1878.

O. *Reuther,* Indische Paläste und Wohnhäuser, Berlin 1925.

Sha Rocco, Golconda and the Qutb Shahis, Hyderabad 1929.

E. *W. Smith,* Moghul Architecture of Fathpur Sikri, Delhi 1938.

*J. Stchoukine,* La Peinture Indienne à l'Epoque des Grand Moghols, Paris 1929.

C. *M. Villiers Stuart,* Gardens of the Great Mughals, London.

*J. Ph. Vogel,* Tile Mosaics of the Lahore Fort, Calcutta 1920.

F. *Wetzel,* Islamische Grabbauten in Indien in der Zeit der Soldatenkaiser, Leipzig 1918.

G. *Yazdani,* Bīdar: Its History and Monuments, London 1947.

G. *Yazdani,* Mandu: City of Joy, Oxford 1929.

*Maulvi Zafar Hasan,* Guide to Nizam-ud-din, Calcutta 1922.

## MODERN ART

K. *Khandalavala,* Amrit Sher Gil, Bombay 1946.

*Ramachandra Rao,* Modern Indian Painters, Madras 1953.

## GUIDE BOOKS

Delhi, Agra, Fathpur Sikri, Lahore, Kashmir, Gwalior, Chanderi, Jaipur, Banaras, Sarnath, Bodhgaya, Nalanda, Calcutta, Sanchi, Dilwara, Kanheri, Karle, Elephanta, Ellora, Ajanta, Aurangabad, Bijapur, Golconda, Hyderabad, Pattada-kal, Mamallapura, Belur and Halebid, Sravana Belgola, etc.

## MUSEUM HANDBOOKS

National Museum New Delhi, Lahore, Chamba, Mathura, Lucknow, Allahabad, Banaras, Sarnath, Patna, Calcutta, Nagpur, Jaipur, Gwalior, Sanchi, Baroda, Bombay, Madras, Trivandrum, Madura.

## ANNUAL REPORTS AND PERIODICALS

*India:*

Archaeological Survey of India (central and circles), Indian Archaeology, Ancient India, Indian Antiquary, J. Baroda Oriental Institute, Deccan College Bulletin, Annals Bhandarkar Oriental Research Institute, J. Bombay Asiatic Society, J. Asiatic Society, J. Bombay University, Mārg, March of India, J. U.P. Historical Society, J. Indian Museums, J. Andhra Research Society, Qu. J. Mythic Society, Epigraphia Indica, Epigraphia Indo-Moslemica, Indian Culture, J. Indian History, Roopalekha, Lalit-Kalā, Rūpam, J. Ind. Soc. Or. Art.

*Ceylon:*

Spolia Zeylonica, Ceylon J. of Science, Ceylon Historical J., Annual Reports Archaeological Survey of Ceylon.

*Indochina:*

Bull. Ecole Franç. d'Extrême-Orient.

*Indonesia:*

Batav. Genootschap, Tijdschrift voor Indische Taal-, Land- en Volkenkunde.

*Great Britain:*

Art and Letters, J. R. As. Soc., Oriental Art.

*Holland:*

Acta Orientala, Annual Bibliography of Indian Archaeology.

*France:*

Arts Asiatiques, Revue des Arts Asiatiques, Gazette des Beaux-Arts, J. Asiatique.

*Italy:*

East and West.

*U.S.A.:*

Ars Orientalis, Ars Islamica, Eastern Art, Art Bulletin, J. American Society Oriental.

*Abbreviations: B. = Buddhist, H. = Hindu, J. = Jain, M. = Muslim, Islamic, N.I. = North Indian, S.I. = South Indian, D. = Deccan.*

*Aiwān,* M. (vaulted) hall.

*Āmalaka,* coping stone of Hindu temple.

*Amman,* S.I. temple of divine consort.

*Ānda,* main body of stūpa.

*Antarala,* room between sanctuary and cult hall of H. temple.

*Apsaras,* heavenly nymph.

*Ārāma,* garden, B. monastery.

*Archā,* H. cult image.

*Āryaka,* special B. column.

*Āsana,* seat, sitting posture, throne.

*Ashtādhātu,* 8 metal-alloy, "bronze".

*Avatāra,* epiphany of god Vishnu.

*Āyagapata,* Jain votive tablet.

*Āyudha,* weapons, symbols in hands of B. and H. deities.

*Bāgh,* M. garden.

*Bandhana,* hair style, architectural moulding.

*Bangaldār,* (roof) of Bengali vaulted type.

*Bārādārī,* low M. garden pavilion.

*Bhadramukha,* mask on H. temple pediment.

*Bhanga,* body posture.

*Bhārat Natya,* H. temple dance.

*Bhavan,* house, garden pavilion.

*Bhoga,* artistic enjoyment.

*Bodhisattva,* B. saviour.

*Bodhivriksha* (Bodhi tree), at **Bodhgayā,** where the Buddha found enlightenment.

*Buddha,* "the Enlightened", founder of Buddhism, also his spiritual predecessors and cosmic prototypes.

*Burj,* M. tower, palace.

*Chaitya,* B. (and H.) sanctuary, *stūpa,* temple.

*Chaityaśālā,* B. monastic assembly hall.

*Chaukī,* throne, late H. palace.

*Chhajja,* pent-roof, eaves.

*Chhattrāvalī,* set of honorary umbrellas on B. stūpa.

*Chhattrī,* H. funerary shrine.

*Chīnī,* porcelain.

*Chitra,* H. painting.

*Dāgaba (Dagoba, Pagoda) =* B. stūpa.

*Dargāh,* M. place of pilgrimage.

*Darwāza,* M. gate, gateway.

*Devadāsī,* H. temple dancing girl.

*Devatā,* B. H. godling.

*Devī,* the Great Mother goddess, consort of śiva, under many names (Kālī, Pārvatī, etc.).

*Dharmachakra,* "Wheel of the Law", symbol of B. dogma.

*Dikpāla,* B. H. world guardian.

*Dīpalakshmī,* H. temple-lamp in shape of a girl.

*Dīpamālā,* high lampstand in front of H. temple.

*Dīvān,* M. audience and consultation room.

*Drāvida,* S.I. peoples, languages, temple style.

*Durbār,* M. royal audience (hall).

*Durga,* fortress.

*Durgā,* form of Devī.

*Dvārapāla,* protective genius of H. temple entrance.

*Gandharva,* H. godlings (heavenly musicians).

*Ganeśa,* elephant-headed god, son of śiva and Devi, guardian of all entrances and beginnings.

*Gangā,* H. river goddess of Ganges.

*Ganikā,* H. hetaira, actress.

*Garbhagriha,* sanctuary of H. temple.

*Garh,* H. fort, temple.

*Gavāksha,* B. H. dormer window.

*Ghāt,* H. bathing stairs.

*Giraspati = Kīrtimukha.*

*Gopura,* S.I. H. temple gateway.

*Gumbad,* M. cupola, tomb.

*Gumpha,* cave (-monastery).

*Hamsa,* goose, swan (B. H. ornament).

*Harem = Zenāna.*

*Harmikā,* small building on top of stūpa.

*Hasta,* arm postures in H. dance.

*Hawā Mahal,* M. summer palace.

*Jal,* water, *Jal-Mahal,* etc., water palace.

*Jālī,* perforated stone screen.

*Jāmi 'Masjid,* M. great mosque, city mosque.

*Jātaka,* B. fables, devotional stories.

*Kalaśa,* water vessel, vase, top of H. temple.

*Kalpalatā, Kalpadruma,* wishing tree (of Paradise), B. H. ornament.

*Kalyāna Mandapa,* hall of divine marriage in S.I. H. temple.

*Khāna,* M. house.

*Killa,* M. fortress.

*Kinnārī,* B. H. heavenly musicians, half human, half bird.

*Kīrtimukha,* lion (demon) mask, H. temple ornament.

*Koil, Kovil,* S.I. H. temple.

*Kot,* N.I. fort, palace; *Kotila,* small palace.

*Krishna, avatāra* of H. god Vishnu.

*Kshetrapāla* (J.) = H. *Dikpāla.*

*Kudū,* S.I. = *Gavāksha.*

*Kumbha,* vase, cushion, cushion capital, moulding.

*Kund,* H. temple pond.

*Kūshk (Kiosk),* M. pavilion, palace.

*Lakshana,* "sign of beauty", of the Buddha, Tīrthankaras, etc.

*Lakshmī,* consort of Vishnu, goddess of beauty, wealth, happiness.

*Lena,* cave, cave temple.

*Linga,* phallus, herme, symbol of H. god śiva.

*Livān,* gallery of M. mosque *(masjid).*

*Lokapāla,* B. = *Dikpāla.*

*Mahal,* M. palace, mansion.

*Mandala,* B. magic circle.

*Mandapa,* H. temple cult hall.

*Mandir,* H. temple, (palace).

*Mangala,* J. auspicious symbols.

*Mantra,* B. H. magic or prayer formula.

*Maqbara,* M. tomb.

*Maqsūra,* central hall of mosque.

*Mardāna,* men's quarter in M. house.

*Māth,* H. cloister.

*Masjid,* mosque.

*Mātrikā,* H. mother goddess.

*Meru,* world mountain (B. H.).

*Mithuna,* erotic couple (Yakshas, Gandharvas), in H. sculpture.

*Mudrā,* B. H. symbolic hand position.

*Mukha,* face, *Mukhalinga, Linga* with a mask of god śiva.

*Mukuta,* crown.

*Mūrti,* H. epiphany of god, cult image, sculpture.

*Nāga,* snake, dragon, water spirit, *Nāginī* (f.), *Nāgarājā,* king of —.

*Nāgara* (urban), N.I. temple style, secular painting.

*Nāma,* Persian book.

*Narathara,* frieze with scenes from human life in N.I. H. temple.

*Natarājā,* Lord of Dance, most famous form of H. god Siva.

*Natya,* dance, *N. śāstra,* textbook of d., *N. mandapa,* hall of the H. temple dancing girls.

*Navagraha,* the Nine Planets, motif in H. sculpture.

*Navaranga,* principal cult hall of D. and S.I. H. temple.

*Nāyikā* (heroine), motif in H. art.

*Pāda,* step, foot position.

*Padma,* lotus.

*Pancharam,* miniature house on H. temple lintels, cornices, roofs.

*Parivāra-Devatā = Dikpālas.*

*Pinjrā = * Jālī.

*Pītha,* socle, plinth, śākta holy place.

*Pokuna = * pond (Ceylon).

*Prabhā (-vali -mandala),* halo.

*Prajnā,* cognition, B. female deity.

*Prāsāda,* B. H. temple, palace.

*Pratima = Archā.*

*Pūrnaghata (-kalaśa),* full water-vessel, auspicious symbol.

*Rāgmālā* (string of melodies), H. art motif.

*Rangīn Mahal,* H. M., representation room in a palace.

*Rasa,* aesthetic mood.

*Ratha,* chariot, small H. temple.

*Rauza,* M. mausoleum.

*Sādhanā,* meditation in order to evoke a B. H. deity.

*Sahn,* court of mosque.

*Śakti,* divine power, consort of H. god.

*Śalabhanjika,* girl touching a tree (= *Vrikshakā*), H. art motif.

*Sannidhi,* D. H. and J. temple shrine.

*Sarāi,* M. palace.

*Sardāb,* cellar of M. house, summer-rooms, grave chamber.

*Satikkal*, D. memorial stone for a Sati, a widow burned alive.

*Shikārkūshk*, M. hunting lodge.

*Shīsh Mahal*, M. mirror room.

*śikhara*, tower of H. temple.

*śilpaśāstra*, H. textbook on sculpture and painting, *śilpin* = mason, sculptor.

*Simha*, lion, ornament motif.

*Simhāsana*, throne supported by lion figures.

*Śiva*, the Great God (Mahādeva), under many names.

*Śrī*, (goddess of) good fortune.

*Śringa*, dome of S.I. and D. H. temple.

*Stambha*, B. H. column.

*Sthāna*, posture.

*Stūpa*, B. relic shrine.

*Sūchī*, part of a *Vedikā* (B. balustrade).

*Surasundarī*, H. heavenly nymph.

*Sūrya*, H. sun god.

*Sutradhara*, H. architect.

*Sūtūn*, M. pillar.

*Tārā*, B. Madonna.

*Tepe Kulam*, S.I. H. temple pond.

*Thaba*, post of a B. balustrade.

*Tīrthamkara*, J. world teacher.

*Tiru*, S.I. = holy.

*Tope* = *thūpa*, *stūpa*.

*Torana*, gate of honour, arch of a B. *stūpa* or H. temple.

*Triratna*, a symbol of the "Three Jewels", the Buddha, his doctrine and monastic order.

*Urddhvapatta*, B. memorial stela.

*Ūrnā*, the lock or jewel between the eyebrows of the Buddha.

*Ushnīsha*, the protruding crown on the Buddha's head, coping stone of *stūpa* balustrade.

*Vāhana*, animal accompanying a H. deity.

*Vajrāsana*, "diamond" throne of the Buddha.

*Varsha*, season, art and literary motif.

*Vastuśāstra*, text book on architecture.

*Vedi*, H. sacrificial altar.

*Vedikā*, balustrade around a B. *stūpa*.

*Vesara*, D. style of H. temple architecture.

*Vihāra*, B. monastery.

*Vimāna*, closed cult room or shrine of a H. temple (mainly D. and S.I.).

*Vishnu*, H. god of heaven and lord of universe.

*Vīrakkal*, memorial stone for Hindu warrior (D.).

*Vyāli*, a lion with elephant proboscis, H. art motif.

*Yajnaśālā (Yagaśālā)*, *room for sacrifices.*

*Yaksha, Yakshī*, B. H. local tutelary deities (see also Gandharvas, *Mithuna*).

*Yamunā*, H. river goddess of the Jumnā.

*Yashti*, central post of a tumulus or *stūpa*.

*Yoga*, system of mental self-control and meditation, and its philosophy.

*Yūpa*, H. sacrificial post.

*Zenāna*, ladies' quarter of a M. house (= harem).

*Ziārat*, tomb of a M. saint (Pīr).

## Date Due

| Date Due | | | |
|---|---|---|---|
| FEB 11 '66 | | | |
| MAR 3 '67 | | | |
| DEC 2 '71 | | | |
| AUG 23 2002 | | | |
| AUG 28 2002 | | | |
| | | | |
| | | | |
| | | | |
| | | | |
| | | | |
| | | | |
| | | | |
| | | | |
| | | | |
| | | | |
| | PRINTED | IN U. S. A. | |